Extending jQuery

Extending jQuery

KEITH WOOD

MANNING

SHELTER ISLAND

For online information and ordering of this and other Manning books, please visit
www.manning.com. The publisher offers discounts on this book when ordered in quantity.
For more information, please contact

> Special Sales Department
> Manning Publications Co.
> 20 Baldwin Road
> PO Box 261
> Shelter Island, NY 11964
> Email: orders@manning.com

Manning Publications Co.
20 Baldwin Road
PO Box 261
Shelter Island, NY 11964

Development editor:	Cynthia Kane
Copyeditor:	Benjamin Berg
Technical proofreaders:	Renso Hollhumer, Michiel Trimpe
Proofreader:	Andy Carroll
Typesetter:	Marija Tudor
Cover designer:	Marija Tudor

ISBN: 9781617291036
Printed in the United States of America
1 2 3 4 5 6 7 8 9 10 – MAL – 18 17 16 15 14 13

brief contents

contents

foreword

Since jQuery's debut in 2006, it has grown into the most popular JavaScript library for managing and enhancing HTML documents. jQuery's cross-browser design allows developers to focus on building websites instead of puzzling out browser peculiarities. In 2013, more than one-half of the top million websites (measured by visitor traffic) use jQuery. Similarly, the jQuery UI library, which builds on jQuery, is the most popular source of UI widgets.

With that popularity comes the temptation for the jQuery team to add features so that nearly any problem encountered by a developer can be solved with the incantation of a jQuery method. Yet every feature added to the core code of jQuery means more bytes of JavaScript for website visitors to download, whether or not a feature is used in that site's development. Such a large monolithic library would degrade performance just for the convenience of web development, which isn't a good trade-off.

To combat the scourge of code bloat, jQuery's philosophy is to put only the most common functionality in the library and provide a foundation developers can extend. An incredible ecosystem of jQuery plugins has grown over the years, driven by each developer's need to scratch a particular itch and their generosity in sharing code with the wider jQuery community. Much of jQuery's success can be attributed to this ethos and the team fosters it through sites like plugins.jquery.com.

Keith Wood is well suited to be your guide through *Extending jQuery*. He's been a regular fixture in the jQuery Forum and a top contributor for several years, providing high-quality answers to the real-life problems developers encounter. He's also earned his street cred by developing several popular jQuery plugins. As a result, Keith has a practitioner's understanding of jQuery extensions combined with an instructor's intuition about which jQuery topics deserve a deep explanation rather than a passing mention.

This book delves into just about every facet of extending jQuery's functionality, whether for personal needs or professional profit. The best-known type of extension is the basic jQuery plugin that extends jQuery Core methods, but the book gives equal time to jQuery UI widget-based plugins that are often a better foundation for visually oriented extensions. Detailed documentation on the jQuery UI widget factory is scarce, which makes these chapters all the more valuable.

I'm especially pleased that Keith dedicates some time to the topics of unit tests. Having a set of thorough unit tests seems like needless extra work, right up until the point a few months later where an innocuous change to a plugin causes the entire web team hours of debugging on a live site while user complaints flood in. Unit tests can't find all bugs, but they act as a sanity check and prevent obvious regressions that manual testing by an impatient developer tends to miss.

Whatever your reason for learning about jQuery extensions, please consider contributing your work back to the community as open source if it seems that others might benefit from it. This is a natural fit with jQuery's own philosophy. Sharing your knowledge with others not only helps them, but it comes back to you in professional recognition.

DAVE METHVIN
PRESIDENT, JQUERY FOUNDATION

preface

I first encountered jQuery in early 2007 and immediately found it intuitive and simple to use. I was quickly selecting elements and showing and hiding them. Next I tried to use some of the third-party plugins on offer, but found that they varied widely in usefulness and usability.

I was fortunate to start my plugin writing with what was to become a major plugin in the jQuery community. I came across Marc Grabanski's Clean Calendar plugin, which he had converted into a jQuery plugin, and liked the interface it provided for entering a date. I started playing with it to add more features as a way to explore jQuery's capabilities and eventually offered these back to Marc. So started a collaboration on this plugin over the next couple of years.

At that point the Calendar plugin had been renamed Datepicker and had been chosen by the jQuery UI team as the basis for its date-picker offering.

Since that start I've been developing other plugins as the need or interest arose. Some of my most popular ones are an alternative Datepicker that also allows for picking date ranges or multiple individual dates, a Calendars plugin that provides support for non-Gregorian calendars, a Countdown plugin to show the time remaining until a given date and time, and an SVG Integration plugin that allows you to interact with SVG elements on the web page. During this time I've learned a lot about JavaScript and jQuery and how to write plugins for the latter.

Creating plugins is an ideal way to capture functionality in a reusable format, making it simple to incorporate into other web pages. It lets you more thoroughly test the code and ensures consistent behavior wherever it is used.

jQuery has grown significantly in size and functionality over the intervening years, but it has remained true to its purpose of making the developer's life easier. The thriving plugin community is a testament to the foresight of the jQuery team in providing a platform that can be easily extended. I hope that the insights presented in this book allow you to make the most of jQuery in your own projects.

acknowledgments

I'll begin by thanking John Resig and the jQuery team for providing such a useful tool for web developers throughout the world.

Thanks also to Marc Grabanski for allowing me to contribute to the Calendar/Datepicker plugin and for launching me into plugin development.

Writing a book is always a group effort, and I would like to acknowledge the editorial team at Manning: Bert Bates, Frank Pohlmann, and Cynthia Kane; the technical proofreaders Renso Hollhumer and Michiel Trimpe; and the entire production team for their support and guidance. Special thanks to Christina Rudloff for the initial approach from Manning regarding a jQuery UI book.

My thanks to all the developers who have contacted me over the years with comments, suggestions, bugs, and localizations for my plugins, with special thanks to those who have contributed something to my efforts—I'm enjoying the music and dancing!

I am grateful to the reviewers of the early versions of the manuscript, for providing insights that improved the final product: Amandeep Jaswal, Anne Epstein, Brady Kelly, Bruno Figueiredo, Daniele Midi, David Walker, Ecil Teodoro, Geraint Williams, Giuseppe De Marco, PhD, Jorge Ezequiel Bo, Lisa Z. Morgan, Mike Ma, Pim Van Heuven, and Stephen Rice.

Special thanks to Dave Methvin, president of the jQuery Foundation, for contributing the foreword and for endorsing my book.

And last, but not least, sincere thanks to my partner, Trecialee, for accepting the time spent away from her on this project (even though she doesn't understand the subject matter).

about this book

jQuery is the most widely used JavaScript library on the web, offering many abilities that make web development much easier. But it concentrates on providing features that are widely applicable and widely used, and can't do everything that you might want. You could code your extra requirements inline for each web page, but if you find yourself repeating code across several pages it may be time to create a plugin for jQuery instead.

A plugin lets you package your code in a single reusable module that can then be easily applied to any number of web pages. You benefit by having a single code base, with reduced testing and maintenance costs, and a consistent appearance and behavior throughout your website.

jQuery has been designed to accommodate these plugins, allowing them to become first-class members of the jQuery environment and to be used alongside the built-in functionality. This book explains how you can use best practice principles to produce a jQuery plugin that integrates with jQuery without interfering with other plugins and that provides a flexible and robust solution.

Who should read this book?

This is a book about extending jQuery to create reusable plugins. Readers may be technical leads wanting to know what can be extended within jQuery to enable the production of reusable modules within their projects. Or they may be web developers with a desire to know the details behind writing robust code for jQuery. Or perhaps they're third-party plugin developers who want to build a best practice plugin for general release to the jQuery community.

Given the target audience, a certain familiarity with jQuery is assumed. You're expected to be able to use jQuery to select elements and then operate upon them to change properties, show or hide the elements, or attach event handlers. You should be comfortable with using existing third-party plugins to add functionality to your pages.

For an introduction to jQuery itself please see *jQuery in Action, Second Edition*, by Bear Bibeault and Yehuda Katz (Manning, 2010).

jQuery is a JavaScript library, so you should also be familiar with the JavaScript language. Most of the plugin code is straight JavaScript with a few jQuery calls or integration points thrown in. The code often uses constructs such as anonymous functions, ternary operators, and even closures. That's fine if these terms are known to you. Otherwise you might want to brush up on your JavaScript first.

For a deeper insight into the JavaScript language, please see *Secrets of the JavaScript Ninja*, by John Resig and Bear Bibeault (Manning 2012).

Roadmap

Extending jQuery is divided into 4 parts. Part 1 (chapters 1-3) covers simple extensions to enhance your jQuery experience. Part 2 (chapters 4-7) looks at how best to implement plugins and functions. Part 3 (chapters 8-10) focuses on extending the jQuery UI to enhance your web pages. Part 4 (chapters 11-14) covers the best of the rest: animation, Ajax, event handling, and the Validation plugin, which is not part of jQuery but plays an important role.

- Chapter 1 presents a short history of jQuery and discusses what you can extend to add to its abilities in an integrated fashion.
- Chapter 2 looks at the modules that make up jQuery and goes into more detail about how you'd extend these. It then develops a simple plugin to show the basics of plugin development.
- Chapter 3 shows how you can extend jQuery's selectors to find more targeted elements on your web page.
- Chapter 4 takes a step back and talks about the best-practice principles that should be applied to development to produce a robust and useful plugin.
- Chapter 5 develops a collection plugin based around a framework that implements the principles from the previous chapter. Collection plugins operate on a set of elements selected from the page.
- Chapter 6 looks at function plugins that provide additional abilities not related to particular elements, using localization and cookie processing as examples.
- Chapter 7 discusses testing and packaging your plugin to ensure it works correctly and can be easily obtained and used. It also describes how you should document and demonstrate your plugin so that potential users can get the most out of it.
- Chapter 8 shows how you can use the jQuery UI widget framework to also create collection plugins—ones that integrate with other jQuery UI components in appearance and behavior.

- Chapter 9 explains how to use the jQuery UI Mouse module to interact with mouse drag operations within your plugin, by producing a widget that captures a signature.
- Chapter 10 completes the jQuery UI part with a look at how you can create your own visual effects, and how to adjust the rate of change for animated properties.
- Chapter 11 looks at how you can provide for the animation of property values that aren't simple numeric values, using background position as an example.
- Chapter 12 delves into the Ajax processing capabilities of jQuery to show how you can enhance them through prefilters, transports, and convertors.
- Chapter 13 discusses the jQuery special event framework and how it can be used to create new events within jQuery, as well as how to enhance existing events.
- Chapter 14 shows how to extend the Validation plugin to add extra validation rules that may be applied to individual elements alongside the built-in rules.

Code conventions and downloads

This book contains many JavaScript code listings and the occasional HTML and CSS snippet. Source code in listings and in the text is shown in a `fixed width font` to separate it from ordinary text. References to variable and function names within the text are also shown in this format. **`Bold monospace font`** highlights key parts of the code, usually function or variable names. Some code listings have been reformatted to fit within the bounds of the printed page. Code annotations accompany most of the source code listings to highlight the important parts. In many cases, numbered callouts in the code link to explanations in the following text.

jQuery and jQuery UI are open source libraries that are released under the MIT license[1] and can be downloaded directly from the corresponding websites: http://jquery.com/ and http://jqueryui.com/ respectively.

The source code for all examples in this book is available from the book's page on the Manning's website: http://www.manning.com/ExtendingjQuery.

Author Online

The purchase of *Extending jQuery* includes free access to a private web forum run by Manning Publications where you can make comments about the book, ask technical questions, and receive help from the author and other users. To access the forum and subscribe to it, visit http://www.manning.com/ExtendingjQuery. This page provides information on how to get on the forum once you are registered, what kind of help is available, and the rules of conduct on the forum.

Manning's commitment to our readers is to provide a venue where a meaningful dialogue between individual readers and between readers and the author can take place. It is not a commitment to any specific amount of participation on the part of

---

[1] Massachusetts Institute of Technology license agreement, https://github.com/jquery/jquery/blob/master/MIT-LICENSE.txt.

the author, whose contribution to the forum remains voluntary (and unpaid). Let your voice be heard, and keep the author on his toes!

About the author

Keith Wood has been a developer for over 30 years and has worked with jQuery since early 2007. He has written over 20 plugins—including the original Datepicker, World Calendar and Datepicker, Countdown, and SVG—and has made them available to the jQuery community. He frequently answers questions in the jQuery forums and was a top five contributor for 2012.

In his day job he's a web developer using Java/J2EE for the back end and jQuery on the front end. He lives in Sydney, Australia, with his partner Trecialee and spends his spare time dancing.

about the cover illustration

The figure on the cover of *Extending jQuery* is captioned a "Dolenka," which means a woman from the village of Dolenci, on the border between Slovenia and Hungary. This illustration is taken from a recent reprint of Balthasar Hacquet's *Images and Descriptions of Southwestern and Eastern Wenda, Illyrians, and Slavs* published by the Ethnographic Museum in Split, Croatia, in 2008. Hacquet (1739–1815) was an Austrian physician and scientist who spent many years studying the botany, geology, and ethnography of many parts of the Austrian Empire, as well as the Veneto, the Julian Alps, and the western Balkans, inhabited in the past by people of many different tribes and nationalities. Hand-drawn illustrations accompany the many scientific papers and books that Hacquet published.

The rich diversity of the drawings in Hacquet's publications speaks vividly of the uniqueness and individuality of the Alpine and Balkan regions just 200 years ago. This was a time when the dress codes of two villages separated by a few miles identified people uniquely as belonging to one or the other, and when members of an ethnic tribe, social class, or trade could be easily distinguished by what they were wearing. Dress codes have changed since then and the diversity by region, so rich at the time, has faded away. It is now often hard to tell the inhabitant of one continent from another, and today's inhabitants of the picturesque towns and villages in the Italian Alps are not readily distinguishable from residents of other parts of Europe.

We at Manning celebrate the inventiveness, the initiative, and the fun of the computer business with book covers based on costumes from two centuries ago brought back to life by illustrations such as this one.

Part 1

Simple extensions

The most widely used JavaScript library on the web today, jQuery offers many functions to make life easy for front-end developers. You can make jQuery even better by extending it to provide additional functionality in a reusable format.

Chapter 1 contains a brief history of jQuery, then looks at what you can extend within jQuery. It finishes with a few examples of existing jQuery plugins, showing the breadth of possibilities.

In chapter 2 you'll find a description of the jQuery architecture and possible extension points, each of which is discussed in more detail. Then, to get you started, you'll see how to develop a simple plugin that you can use immediately.

The simplest extensions that you can create are enhanced selectors for jQuery—the building blocks behind finding the right element to operate upon. These are covered in chapter 3, with numerous examples of how to create your own.

jQuery extensions

This chapter covers

- jQuery's origins and purpose
- What you can extend in jQuery
- Examples of existing extensions

Today, jQuery is the most widely used JavaScript library on the web. It offers many functions to make life easier as a front-end developer, such as the ability to traverse the HTML Document Object Model (DOM) to find the elements you want to work with and apply animations to those elements. Moreover, the developers of jQuery have recognized that it can't (and shouldn't) do everything, and have provided extension points that allow additional functionality to be integrated into the normal jQuery processing. This foresight has contributed to its popularity.

In this book I explain how you can extend various aspects of jQuery to provide greater reuse and easier maintenance of your code. Alongside the standard plugin that operates on a collection of elements on a web page, you can create custom selectors, utility functions, custom animations, enhanced Ajax processors, custom events, and validation rules. I cover testing, packaging, and documenting your code to make sure that others can make maximum use of it as well.

1.1   jQuery background

The jQuery website defines jQuery as "a fast, small, and feature-rich JavaScript library. It makes things like HTML document traversal and manipulation, event handling, animation, and Ajax much simpler with an easy-to-use API that works across a multitude of browsers" (http://jquery.com).

It's a library of JavaScript functions that allows you to easily access the HTML DOM and inspect or update it, enabling you to provide more dynamic web pages and experiences in keeping with the Web 2.0 paradigm. Its main features are

- Element selection using a CSS-like syntax, with extensions
- Element traversal
- Element manipulation, including removal, content updates, and attribute changes
- Event handling, including custom events
- Effects and animations
- Ajax support
- A framework for extending its functionality (the subject of this book)
- Various utility functions
- Cross-browser support, including hiding differences between the browsers

jQuery is a freely available, open source library. It's currently licensed under the MIT License (http://jquery.org/license/). Previous versions were also licensed under the GNU General Public License, Version 2.

1.1.1   Origins

jQuery was initially developed by John Resig and was announced in January 2006, at BarCamp NYC.[1] He'd come across the Behaviour code written by Ben Nolan and saw the potential of its ideas—using pseudo-CSS style selectors to bind JavaScript functions to various elements in the DOM. But John wasn't happy with its verbosity and lack of hierarchical selectors.[2] His suggested syntax and subsequent implementation became the basis for jQuery.

Listing 1.1 shows Behaviour code to attach a click event handler to all `li` elements within an element with the ID `example`; the click event handler removes the clicked item. Listing 1.2 shows the now-familiar corresponding jQuery code.

Listing 1.1   Sample Behaviour code

```
Behaviour.register({
    '#example li': function(e){
        e.onclick = function(){
```

---

[1] John Resig, "BarCampNYC Wrap-up," http://ejohn.org/blog/barcampnyc-wrap-up/.
[2] John Resig, "Selectors in Javascript," http://ejohn.org/blog/selectors-in-javascript/.

```
        this.parentNode.removeChild(this);
    }
  }
});
```

Listing 1.2 Equivalent jQuery code

```
$('#example li').bind('click', function(){
    $(this).remove();
});
```

Why was it given the name jQuery? Originally, the library was called *jSelect* to reflect its ability to select elements within a web page. But when John checked for that name on the web, he found it was already taken, and changed the name to jQuery.[3]

1.1.2 Growth

Since its initial announcement, jQuery has been through numerous incremental releases, as shown in table 1.1 (not all versions are shown). Over the years, it's grown greatly in terms of functionality and size.

Table 1.1 jQuery versions (not all are shown)

Version	Code date	Size	Notes
1.0	August 26, 2006	44.3 KB	First stable release
1.0.4	December 12, 2006	52.2 KB	Last 1.0 bug fix
1.1	January 14, 2007	55.6 KB	Selector performance improvements
1.1.4	August 23, 2007	65.6 KB	jQuery may be renamed
1.2	September 10, 2007	77.4 KB	
1.2.6	May 26, 2008	97.8 KB	
1.3	January 13, 2009	114 KB	Sizzle selector engine introduced into core, live events, and events overhaul
1.3.2	February 19, 2009	117 KB	
1.4	January 13, 2010	154 KB	Performance improvements, Ajax enhancements
1.4.1	January 25, 2010	156 KB	`height()` and `width()` added, `parseJSON()` added
1.4.2	February 13, 2010	160 KB	`delegate()` added, performance improvements
1.4.3	October 14, 2010	176 KB	CSS module rewrite, metadata handling
1.4.4	November 11, 2010	178 KB	
1.5	January 31, 2011	207 KB	Deferred callback management, Ajax module rewrite, traversal performance
1.5.2	March 31, 2011	214 KB	

---

[3] Comments by John Resig, "BarCampNYC Wrap-up," http://ejohn.org/blog/barcampnyc-wrap-up/.

Table 1.1   jQuery versions (not all are shown) *(continued)*

Version	Code date	Size	Notes
1.6	May 2, 2011	227 KB	Significant performance improvements to the `attr()` and `val()` functions, `prop()` added
1.6.4	September 12, 2011	232 KB	
1.7	November 3, 2011	243 KB	New Event APIs: `on()` and `off()`, event delegation performance
1.7.2	March 21, 2012	246 KB	
1.8.0	August 9, 2012	253 KB	Sizzle rewritten, animations reimagined, more modularity
1.8.3	November 13, 2012	261 KB	
1.9.0	January 14, 2013	261 KB	Tidy up for jQuery 2.0
1.9.1	February 4, 2013	262 KB	Bug and regression fixes
2.0.0	April 18, 2013	234 KB	Drop support for IE 6-8
1.10.0	May 24, 2013	267 KB	Version/feature synchronization with 2.x line
1.10.2	July 3, 2013	266 KB	
2.0.3	July 3, 2013	236 KB	

Although the size of the jQuery library has grown substantially, when you minimize the code (stripping unnecessary comments and whitespace) it's reduced to about one-third of its source size (the latest version is only 91 KB). When that minified version is served from the web in a gzip format, it's further reduced to about a third again, resulting in a download cost of about 32 KB for the latest version. By using one of the CDNs (content delivery networks) available, that file may already be cached on the client, removing the need to download it at all.

Using CDNs

To download jQuery from one of the CDNs that hosts it, include one of the `script` tags shown in this sidebar. You may need to change the version of jQuery requested to suit your requirements.

Using jQuery's CDN provided by MediaTemple

```
<script src="http://code.jquery.com/jquery-1.9.1.min.js">
</script>
```

You can include the jQuery Migration plugin from this site too, to assist in the transition from older versions of jQuery to jQuery 1.9 and later.

```
<script src="http://code.jquery.com/
    jquery-migrate-1.1.1.min.js"></script>
```

(continued)

Using Google's CDN[a]

```
<script src="http://ajax.googleapis.com/ajax/libs/
  jquery/1.9.1/jquery.min.js"></script>
```

All jQuery releases are available on the Google CDN, but jQuery doesn't control this CDN and there may be a delay between a jQuery release and its availability there.

Using Microsoft's CDN[b]

```
<script src="http://ajax.aspnetcdn.com/ajax/jQuery/
  jquery-1.9.1.min.js"></script>
```

All jQuery releases are available on the Microsoft CDN, but jQuery doesn't control this CDN and there may be a delay between a jQuery release and its availability there.

a. Google Developers, "Google Hosted Libraries—Developer's Guide," https://developers.google.com/speed/libraries/devguide#jquery.
b. ASP.NET, "Microsoft Ajax Content Delivery Network," http://www.asp.net/ajaxlibrary/cdn.ashx.

jQuery now includes the *Sizzle* selector engine, which enables the fundamental ability to find the elements within the DOM upon which you wish to operate. Whenever possible, Sizzle delegates these selectors to the underlying browser implementation, but resorts to JavaScript when necessary to ensure a common experience across all the major browsers.

1.1.3 Today

jQuery has become the most popular JavaScript library on the internet and has been adopted by many organizations and individuals for use in their websites. It's formally supported by Microsoft and ships as part of the Visual Studio product suite. BuiltWith reports more than 60% of the top 10,000 websites use jQuery, along with more than 50% of the top million.[4] W3Techs reports jQuery usage at 55% of all websites and 90% of those using any JavaScript library.[5]

The plugin developer community is thriving, and most make their code freely available in the spirit of the underlying jQuery library. You can search the web for appropriate modules, or use the newly revamped "official" repository of jQuery plugins (http://plugins.jquery.com). Some plugins are great, with solid code, good documentation, and examples. Others aren't so good, being hard to use, buggy, and/or poorly documented. Once you've read this book and applied its principles, your plugins should fall into the former category.

---

[4] BuiltWith, "jQuery Usage Statistics," http://trends.builtwith.com/javascript/jQuery.
[5] W3Techs, "Usage of JavaScript libraries for websites," http://w3techs.com/technologies/overview/javascript_library/all.

You can also find a lot of activity on the jQuery forums (https://forum.jquery.com), with more than 250,000 responses to more than 110,000 questions. Within the forums you'll find special sections devoted to using and developing jQuery plugins.

The ongoing development of jQuery is now managed by the jQuery Foundation (http://jquery.org). It was formed in September 2009 to look after all the jQuery projects, including jQuery Core, jQuery UI, jQuery Mobile, Sizzle, and QUnit. Contributions and donations by the jQuery community provide the financial basis for this support.

1.2 Extending jQuery

If jQuery offers so much functionality, why would you want to extend it? To keep the size of the jQuery code manageable, only those functions that are generic and widely used are included in the core code (although there's debate over what's used and useful). Basic element accessing and modification, event handling, animation, and Ajax handling are provided as functionality that most users require, whereas more specialized abilities are left to others to add.

Fortunately, the jQuery team has recognized that core jQuery can't do everything, so they've provided numerous integration points where others can extend the functionality of jQuery while benefitting from its existing infrastructure and abilities.

As well as extending jQuery to provide additional functionality, packaging your extension as a plugin allows you to easily reuse those abilities on other web pages. As a result you have only one copy of the code to maintain, and any improvements are immediately applied wherever they're used. You can test your plugin code in isolation and under controlled circumstances to ensure that it works as expected.

1.2.1 What can you extend?

Just as the core library provides many abilities, you'll find numerous ways to extend jQuery. The ones I'll cover in this book are listed in the next sections.

SELECTORS AND FILTERS

jQuery selectors and filters allow you to identify and collect the elements from the web page that you wish to operate upon. Although standard selectors by node name, ID, and class are built into jQuery, there's scope for adding pseudo-class selectors (extending the CSS-defined pseudo-classes) that allow you to filter a previous selection consistently and succinctly. You can also add set filters that are aware of the entire collection of previously selected elements and each one's position within that list. Chapter 3 explains how to create these selectors.

By creating a custom selector, you can consolidate the selection process into one location, making it easier to reuse that code elsewhere, ensuring a consistent implementation across your projects. It's also easier to maintain the selector and immediately apply any bug fixes or enhancements to all instances.

COLLECTION PLUGINS

Collection plugins are functions that you can apply to collections of elements as retrieved by a selector. These functions are what most people think of when the term *jQuery plugin* is used, and they make up the largest portion of the available third-party plugins. The new abilities supplied by a collection plugin are only limited by your imagination and can range from making simple attribute changes, through behavioral changes from monitoring events on those elements, to completely replacing the original component with an alternate implementation.

Chapter 4 presents a series of guidelines to use when you create your plugin, and chapter 5 describes the plugin framework that I use for my plugins and how it implements those guidelines. The guidelines encapsulate best practice approaches to writing your plugin, helping it to integrate well with jQuery while reducing the possibility of external code interfering with it, or of it affecting other code.

A key component to writing your plugin is testing its functionality, and using a unit test tool enables you to easily and consistently run tests on your code, proving that it works as expected. Once your code is ready to release, it needs to be packaged for distribution so that others can obtain it easily and integrate it with their own project. You should also provide a web page that demonstrates your plugin's capabilities to allow prospective users to see how it works and what it can do. And you must supply documentation for every aspect of your plugin to let others get the most out of it. Chapter 7 covers these aspects of plugin development.

FUNCTION PLUGINS

Function plugins are utility functions that don't directly operate on collections of elements. They offer additional abilities within the jQuery framework and usually use jQuery's own functionality to perform their duties. Chapter 6 details how to add these utility functions.

Examples of these function plugins include support for sending debugging messages to a console for monitoring code execution, or for retrieving and setting cookie values for a web page. By making these abilities available as a jQuery plugin, you provide the user with a familiar way to invoke the code and reduce possible interference with external code. Several of the guidelines mentioned earlier still apply to these sorts of plugins, as do the steps of testing, packaging, demonstrating, and documenting the plugin.

JQUERY UI WIDGETS

jQuery UI "is a curated set of user interface interactions, effects, widgets, and themes built on top of the jQuery JavaScript Library" (http://jqueryui.com/). It defines a widget framework that allows you to create plugins that work in a consistent manner and that can take advantage of the numerous themes available for styling the UI. Chapter 8 looks at the widget framework and how you can use it to build your own component.

The jQuery UI widget framework also implements the plugin guidelines presented in chapter 4 and provides common functionality to all jQuery UI widgets in a consistent manner. By basing your plugin on this framework, you gain these built-in abilities automatically and can concentrate on delivering your widget's unique functionality. If you apply the classes defined in the ThemeRoller styling to your new widget, it'll immediately be visually integrated with other jQuery UI components and will change appearance if you apply a new theme.

Several of the jQuery UI widgets rely on mouse drag actions to implement their functionality, and the jQuery UI team has recognized the importance of this interaction. By having your widget extend the jQuery UI Mouse module instead of the basic Widget one, you gain support for drag operations, complete with customizable conditions for starting a drag, and can again focus on implementing the functionality of your own widget. Chapter 9 describes how to use the Mouse module to create a widget that depends on using the mouse.

JQUERY UI EFFECTS

jQuery UI also provides a set of effects that may be applied to elements within your page. You can use many of these to show or hide an element, such as `blind`, `clip`, `fold`, and `slide`. Some bring your attention to an element, such as `highlight` and `pulsate`. You can define your own effect and apply it to elements as you would the standard ones. Chapter 10 shows how to create new UI effects.

ANIMATING PROPERTIES

jQuery provides an animation framework that you can apply to any element style attribute that has a simple numeric value. It allows you to vary that attribute from one value to another, controlling the duration of the change and the incremental steps along the way. But if the value you want to animate isn't a simple numeric value, you need to implement the functionality yourself. For example, jQuery UI provides a module that allows you to animate from one color to another. In chapter 11 we'll create an animator for a complex attribute value.

AJAX PROCESSING

jQuery's Ajax functionality is one of its clear benefits, making it incredibly easy to load remote data and then process it. As part of the Ajax call, you can identify what type of data is expected by the success callback: plain text, HTML, XML, JSON. A conversion process happens behind the scenes to transform the byte stream received by the remote call into the appropriate format. You can add your own transformations to allow you to produce specialized formats directly by identifying what type you want returned. Chapter 12 details how to extend the Ajax processing to handle a common file format directly.

EVENT HANDLING

jQuery's event handling capabilities allow you to attach multiple event handlers to elements to respond to user interactions, system events, and custom triggers. jQuery provides several hooks to let you create your own event definitions and trigger points, resulting in code that's consistent with the existing functionality. Chapter 13 describes the implementation of a new event to simplify interactions with the mouse.

VALIDATION RULES

The Validation plugin written by Jörn Zaefferer is widely used to validate user entry on the client side before submitting completed values to the server. Although the plugin isn't part of the core jQuery functionality, it also provides extension points that allow you to create custom validation rules and have them applied as part of the existing processing. Chapter 14 illustrates how to create your own validation rules and integrate them with the built-in behavior.

1.3   Extension examples

Hundreds of jQuery plugins are available on the web to improve your web page experience. The numbers are a testament to the power and simplicity of jQuery itself, and the developers' foresight in providing the extensions points that allow it to be enhanced. I can't cover all of these plugins in this book, but the following sections offer a brief sampling to show the extent of the possibilities.

1.3.1   jQuery UI

The jQuery UI project (http://jqueryui.com/) is built on top of the core jQuery library as a collection of plugins. It encompasses several widgets, including Tabs, Datepicker, and Dialog (see figure 1.1), as well as various UI behaviors such as Draggable and Droppable. In addition, it provides several animations for use in showing or hiding elements, or in drawing your attention to them.

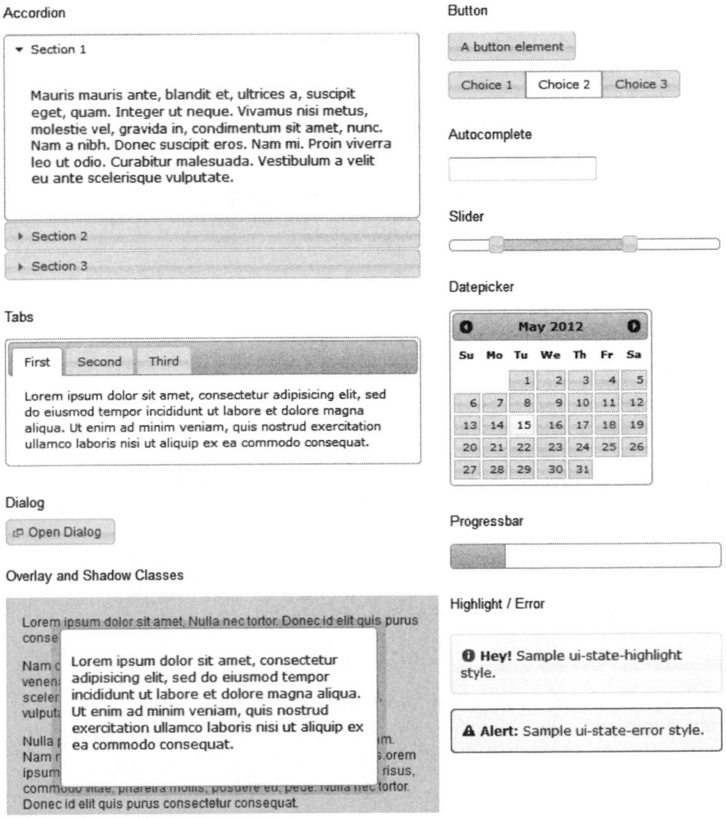

**Figure 1.1
Sampler of jQuery UI
widgets and styles**

jQuery UI uses its own widget framework to provide a consistent base for its UI components. The framework manages widget creation and destruction, maintenance of state, and interactions with the mouse. Chapters 8 and 9 examine the widget framework and describe how to create your own widgets based on it.

The project integrates its components and behaviors with the ThemeRoller tool (http://jqueryui.com/themeroller/) to simplify generating a consistent theme that defines the appearance of all of its widgets.

Numerous demonstrations and comprehensive documentation accompany jQuery UI, allowing you to make the most of its abilities. Through the package's modular design, you can create a custom download that only includes the parts you need. Alternatively, you can load the package from one of the CDNs on which it's hosted, along with the standard themes.

1.3.2 *Validation*

As mentioned earlier, Jörn Zaefferer's Validation plugin[6] is widely used to provide client-side validation (see figure 1.2). It simplifies the assignment of validation rules to elements and manages their state and associated error messages. It aims to be unobtrusive—only generating an error when the form is submitted or a field is changed.

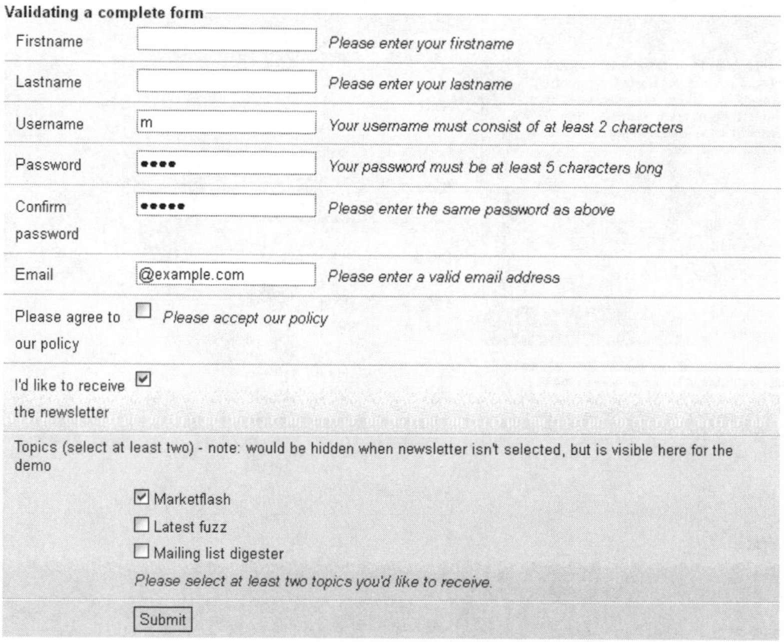

Figure 1.2   The Validation plugin in action, showing various error messages (in italics) resulting from validation issues, alongside the affected fields

---

[6] jQuery Validation Plugin, http://jqueryvalidation.org/.

Rules can be specified inline as attributes on each field, in code for named elements, or via a function chained to a jQuery selection. Numerous built-in validation rules are available, including `required`, `digits`, `date`, `email`, and `url`. Some validation rules can take additional parameters to modify their behavior, such as `minlength` and `maxlength`. Rules can be made dependent on the state of other elements on the page.

This plugin provides its own extension point, allowing you to define custom validation rules that you can then apply to the specified elements in the same manner as built-in ones. Chapter 14 describes how to write these rules.

Each rule has an associated error message for display to the user. These messages can be individually overridden, or can be translated into one of more than 30 other languages included in the package. You can control the positioning and grouping of error messages via options to the initialization call.

The plugin has extensive documentation and examples to assist you in its use. All told, it's a well-written and documented plugin, as well as a highly useful one.

1.3.3 Graphical slider

Plugins can enhance your web page by presenting content in a different and more appealing fashion. For example, the Nivo Slider plugin (http://nivo.dev7studios .com/) converts a simple list of images into a slideshow with various transitions between the pictures.

The eye-catching display shown in figure 1.3 is the result of applying the Nivo Slider to the HTML in listing 1.3. Although this is the default presentation, it's easy to generate and it looks good. As you'd expect, you'll find numerous options for customizing the plugin's appearance and behavior.

Figure 1.3   The Nivo Slider in action

Listing 1.3   Markup for a graphical slider

```
<div class="slider-wrapper">
    <div id="slider" class="nivoSlider">
        <img src="images/slide1.jpg" alt="" />
        <img src="images/slide2.jpg" alt=""
            title="You can add captions too..." />
        <img src="images/slide3.jpg" alt="" />
    </div>
</div>
```

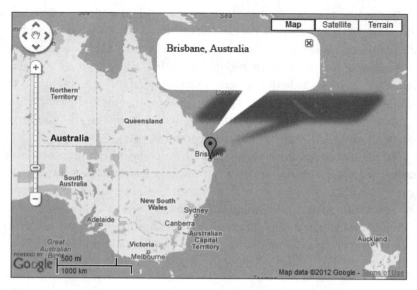

Figure 1.4   Google Map integration with the gMap plugin

1.3.4   *Google Maps integration*

Some plugins wrap existing APIs to make them easier to access or to hide any cross-browser differences. The gMap plugin (http://gmap.nurtext.de/) is one such example, allowing you to integrate a Google Map into your web page. Although you could use Google Maps' own JavaScript API, plugins like this one encapsulate that functionality to provide a simpler interface.

The map shown in figure 1.4 results from the code in the following listing, demonstrating how easy the plugin is to use.

Listing 1.4   Adding a Google Map

```
$('#map').gMap({zoom: 4,
    markers: [{address: 'Brisbane, Australia',
        html: 'Brisbane, Australia', popup: true}]
});
```

1.3.5   *Cookies*

The jQuery Cookie plugin (https://github.com/carhartl/jquery-cookie) makes it easy to interact with the cookies associated with a web page. This plugin differs from previous examples in that its functionality doesn't apply to specific elements on the web page. Instead it offers a utility function that lets you work with cookies for the entire page.

Creating a cookie is as simple as providing its name and value:

```
$.cookie('introShown', true);
```

You can provide additional parameters to customize the cookie—setting its expiry period (by default, cookies expire at the end of the current session), the domain and path to which it applies, whether the cookie requires secure transmission, and whether the cookie value is encoded.

```
$.cookie('introShown', true, {expires: 30, path: '/'});
```

Retrieving a cookie value is only a matter of providing its name. If there's no cookie with a given name, a `null` is returned.

```
var introShown = $.cookie('introShown');
```

Delete a cookie by setting its value to `null`.

```
$.cookie('introShown', null);
```

The Cookie plugin is covered in detail in chapter 6.

1.3.6 Color animation

Basic jQuery includes animation abilities for element attributes that consist of a simple numeric value. Any other format for an attribute requires a special handler to be able to animate it correctly. As part of the Effects module in the jQuery UI project (http://jqueryui.com), you can animate colors (http://jqueryui.com/animate/), which may be set to a hexadecimal value (`#DDFFE8` or `#DFE`), an RGB triplet [`rgb(221, 255, 232)` or `rgb(86%, 100%, 91%)`], or a named color (`lime`).

After converting the various color formats into a common format, each component of the color (red/green/blue) is separately animated from its starting value to its finishing value. By providing this ability as an animation plugin, you can then use the standard jQuery functionality to apply it:

```
$('#myDiv').animate({backgroundColor: '#DDFFE8'});
$('#myDiv').animate({width: 200, backgroundColor: '#DFE'});
```

Chapter 11 covers animation plugins.

What you need to know

jQuery is the most widely used JavaScript library on the web.

jQuery provides basic and commonly used functionality, but is designed to be extended in many different ways.

There is a thriving third-party plugin community built around jQuery.

The abilities of a plugin are only limited by your imagination.

1.4 Summary

jQuery has grown to be the most widely used JavaScript library on the web today. Although it has a lot of built-in functionality, it concentrates on providing the basic infrastructure and features used by many people across many websites. Recognizing that it can't provide everything for everyone, it includes numerous extension points where others can extend its behavior.

You can add functionality to nearly every part of jQuery, from defining custom selectors, through animating non-numeric attribute values and generating new events, to creating full-blown UI components. The only limit is your imagination.

Creating a plugin for your code lets you more easily reuse it in many of your web pages. It reduces your testing and maintenance burdens because you have only one copy of the script.

You'll see in the next chapter how easy it is to extend jQuery by creating a simple plugin, before delving deeper into the best-practice design of more complex plugins.

A first plugin

2

This chapter covers

- The jQuery architecture
- Creating a simple collection plugin

jQuery is a JavaScript library that makes it much simpler to interact with the elements on a web page. It's typically used by finding elements of interest, either by direct selection or by traversing the DOM, then applying some functionality to those elements. You can manipulate elements—adding or removing them, or changing their attributes and properties—and add event handlers to them to respond to actions from the user. You can animate elements by changing their properties over time. And jQuery lets you use Ajax to request extra information from the server easily, without disrupting the current page and its contents.

In the previous chapter, I mentioned that jQuery can't do everything, so it offers a number of extension or integration points, which has led to a thriving third-party plugin community.

This chapter looks at the jQuery architecture that allows plugins to operate alongside the built-in code, and then presents a simple collection plugin (one that operates on a set of selected elements) to show what can be done. The remaining chapters examine each extension point in detail, explain how to use them to

17

enhance jQuery's abilities, and present a set of guiding principles and best practices for developing your plugins.

2.1   jQuery architecture

Although the jQuery source code consists of multiple files for development purposes, during its build phase these are combined into a single JavaScript file, either mini-mized for production use or in full for debugging use. Each source file focuses on a particular aspect of the jQuery functionality, and several of these have extension points to enable other developers to enhance the built-in capabilities.

An *extension point* is an attribute or function within jQuery where you can register new functionality of a particular type (such as collection functions or Ajax enhance-ments), which is then treated exactly the same as the corresponding standard fea-tures. Calls are made back into your plugin code at times in processing that reference your extension.

Figure 2.1 shows the files or modules that make up jQuery, and the dependencies between them.

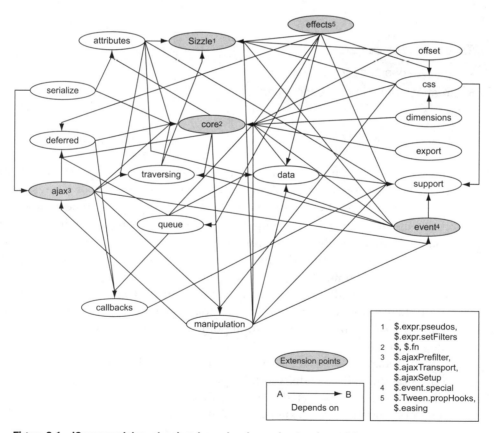

Figure 2.1   jQuery modules, showing dependencies and extension points

The main modules for extending jQuery (shaded in figure 2.1) are the *Sizzle* library, which provides the selection abilities within the DOM; the *core* module, which has the jQuery function itself; the *ajax* module for Ajax processing; the *event* module for event handling; and the *effects* module for animation capabilities.

2.1.1 *jQuery extension points*

The possible extension points for jQuery and jQuery UI are listed in table 2.1 and are described in the next sections. Recall that $ is an alias for the `jQuery` function (unless released via a `noConflict` call).

Table 2.1   jQuery extension points

Extension point	Purpose	Examples	See
`$`	Utility functions	`$.trim` `$.parseXML`	Ch 6
`$.ajaxPrefilter`	Ajax prefilters	`$.ajaxPrefilter('script',` `...)`	Ch 12

`$.ajaxSetup`	Ajax data type converters	`$.ajaxSetup({converters:`
		`{'text xml',`
		`$.parseXML}})`
			Ch 12

`$.ajaxTransport`	Ajax transport mechanisms	`$.ajaxTransport('script',` `...)`	Ch 12
`$.easing`	Animation easings	`$.easing.swing` `$.easing.easeOutBounce`	Ch 10
`$.effects`	jQuery UI visual effects (jQuery UI 1.8-)	`$.effects.clip` `$.effects.highlight`	Ch 10
`$.effects.effect`	jQuery UI visual effects (jQuery UI 1.9+)	`$.effects.effect.clip` `$.effects.effect.highlight`	Ch 10
`$.event.special`	Custom events	`$.event.special.mouseenter` `$.event.special.submit`	Ch 13

`$.expr.filters`
`$.expr[':']`
`$.expr.setFilters`
	Selectors
	(jQuery 1.7-)
		`$.expr.filters.hidden`
		`$.expr.setFilters.odd`
			Ch 3

`$.expr.pseudos`
`$.expr[':']`
`$.expr.setFilters`
	Selectors
	(jQuery 1.8+)
		`$.expr.pseudos.enabled`
		`$.expr.setFilters.first`
			Ch 3

`$.fn`	Collection plugins	`$.fn.show` `$.fn.append`	Ch 5
`$.fx.step`	Attribute animations (jQuery 1.7-)	`$.fx.step.opacity`	Ch 11

Table 2.1   jQuery extension points *(continued)*

Extension point	Purpose	Examples	See
`$.Tween.propHooks`	Attribute animations (jQuery 1.8+)	`$.Tween.propHooks.scrollTop`	Ch 11
`$.validator.addMethod`	Validation plugin rules	`$.validator.addMethod( 'USPhone', ..., ...)`	Ch 14
`$.widget`	jQuery UI widgets	`$.widget('ui.tabs', ...)`	Ch 8, 9

2.1.2   *Selectors*

jQuery includes the Sizzle selection engine as part of its code. This standalone library performs the selection processing, allowing you to locate elements of interest within the web page. Where possible, it delegates operations to native functions provided by the browser for increased performance. It implements the remainder in JavaScript directly. For example, to find all `label` elements that immediately follow an `input` field (checkbox labels, perhaps) within an element with the ID `preferences`, you'd use

```
$('#preferences input + label')...
```

Sizzle lets you select elements by node name, by ID, by class, by immediate child or any descendent, or by attribute values. You can also use various pseudo-class selectors, including those defined in the Cascading Style Sheets (CSS) specification and others added by Sizzle itself, such as `:checked`, `:even`, and `:not`. By combining multiple selectors in one selection string, you can find exactly the elements you want to work with.

Pseudo-class selectors

From the CSS specification: "Pseudo-classes classify elements on characteristics other than their name, attributes, or content; in principle characteristics that cannot be deduced from the document tree."[a] These selectors are identified by a colon (:) and include positional selection (such as `:nth-child(n)`), content selection (`:empty`), and negation (`:not(selector)`).

---

a. W3C, Cascading Style Sheets Level 2 Revision 1 (CSS 2.1) Specification, "5.10 Pseudo-elements and pseudo-classes," http://www.w3.org/TR/2011/REC-CSS2-20110607/selector.html#pseudo-elements.

You can add your own pseudo-class selectors and incorporate them into the selection process by extending `$.expr.pseudos` (or `$.expr.filters` in versions of jQuery prior to 1.8). Ultimately, a selector is just a function that accepts an element as its parameter and returns `true` if that element is accepted or `false` if it is rejected.

By extending `$.expr.setFilters`, you can filter elements based on their position within the current set of matching elements. You provide a function that returns the filtered set of elements (for jQuery 1.8 or later) or returns a Boolean flag indicating inclusion (for jQuery 1.7 and earlier).

See chapter 3 for more detail on adding custom selectors and filters to jQuery/ Sizzle.

2.1.3 Collection plugins

Collection plugins operate on the set of elements that result from a selection process or a subsequent DOM traversal. As such, they're the most common type of jQuery extension.

These plugins must extend $.fn with a function that implements their abilities so that they can be integrated into jQuery's built-in processing. If you look under the hood, you'll see that $.fn is just an alias for $.prototype. This means that any functions added to the former are available on any jQuery collection object, such as the result of calling jQuery with a selector or DOM element(s). As such, they can be invoked on that collection with the appropriate context.

All collection plugins should return the current set of elements, or a new set if they provide some sort of traversal function, so that they can be chained with other jQuery calls—a key paradigm of jQuery operations.

A set of principles encapsulating best practices is presented in chapter 4; chapter 5 then introduces a plugin framework that implements these practices when creating new collection plugins.

2.1.4 Utility functions

JavaScript functions that don't operate on collections of elements (such as the built-in trim and parseXML) can be included in the jQuery world by extending $ directly. Although there's no real need to do so (they could be defined as standalone functions in JavaScript), they often make use of other jQuery capabilities, and their inclusion offers a consistent approach to using jQuery. Adding them to jQuery also helps to reduce the clutter in the global namespace, reduces the chance of creating a name conflict, and keeps the related functions together.

Utility functions don't have a fixed parameter list but can accept whatever is appropriate for their operation.

Chapter 6 looks at adding new utility functions to jQuery.

2.1.5 jQuery UI widgets

jQuery UI is an official collection of UI components, behaviors, and effects built on top of the basic jQuery library. It provides a widget framework that implements the best-practice principles for creating new components or behaviors.

Widgets are created by a call to the $.widget function in jQuery UI. This function accepts the name of the new widget (including a namespace to help avoid name conflicts), an optional reference to a base "class" from which to inherit, and a collection of custom functions and overrides to enhance the basic abilities. The widget framework manages applying the widget to selected elements; setting, retrieving, and storing options that control the widget's appearance and behavior; and tidying up when the widget is no longer required. Behind the scenes, the $.widget.bridge function provides the mapping between the collection function invoked by the user and the abilities supplied when defining the widget.

See chapter 8 for further detail on jQuery UI widgets and the framework that they provide. Chapter 9 examines how to use the Mouse module of jQuery UI to implement a new component that revolves around mouse drag functionality.

2.1.6   *jQuery UI effects*

Another major part of jQuery UI is a series of effects for animating elements on a web page. Most of these animations work when hiding or showing an element, like `blind` and `drop`, but some serve to draw the user's attention to that element, such as `highlight` and `shake`.

New effects can be integrated with jQuery UI's effects processing by extending `$.effects.effect` (or `$.effects` in versions of jQuery UI prior to 1.9). These effects are then available (identified by name) for use within the `effect` or enhanced `show`, `hide`, or `toggle` functions provided by jQuery UI. Each effect is a function that adds a callback function to the current element's `fx` queue to implement its animation when earlier queued events have completed.

Easings define how an attribute value changes over time, and they may be applied to animations to control the acceleration and deceleration of the movements. Although easings are part of basic jQuery, only two instances are offered—`linear` and `swing`. jQuery UI provides an additional 30 easings. To add your own easing, you extend `$.easing` to define a function that returns the amount of change in an attribute value (normalized to be between 0 and 1) given the current elapsed time within the animation duration (also normalized to be between 0 and 1).

For more information on jQuery UI effects, and easings in general, see chapter 10.

2.1.7   *Animating properties*

jQuery's animation capabilities allow you to alter the values of various attributes on selected elements. These attributes typically affect an element's visual appearance, resulting in movement of that element, changes to its dimensions or border sizes, or adjustments to the fonts of its contents. But jQuery only knows how to animate simple numeric attributes (including a units specification). To be able to animate more complex attributes, you need to add custom animations.

You enable the animation of other attribute values by extending `$.Tween.propHooks` to provide two functions that retrieve and set that attribute value. In versions of jQuery prior to 1.8, you extended `$.fx.step` and supplied a function that performed one step in the animation.

Chapter 11 explains how to add new animation abilities to jQuery.

2.1.8   *Ajax processing*

Ajax processing is a key part of the capabilities provided by jQuery, making it simple to retrieve information from a server and integrate that into the current page without the need for a full refresh. Since the retrieved data may be in a variety of formats,

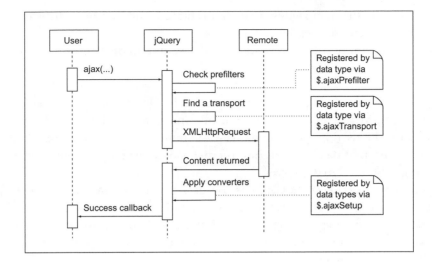

Figure 2.2
Ajax sequence
diagram showing
extension points

jQuery defines *prefilters* for controlling the retrieval process before it starts, *transports* for retrieving the fundamental data, and *converters* for processing that data into a usable format. Each of these mechanisms may be enhanced to meet special requirements. Figure 2.2 shows the sequence of processing for a successful standard Ajax call.

By calling the $.ajaxPrefilter function, you can define a function that's invoked when a particular format of data is requested, such as html, xml, or script. Since your function is provided a reference to the XMLHttpRequest object to be used for the retrieval, you have control over how each request proceeds, including the ability to cancel it altogether.

To handle the actual retrieval of the data, you can call the $.ajaxTransport function to define a function that's called for a given data format, which allows you to customize access to that data (such as loading image data directly into an Image element). By default, the XMLHttpRequest object is used.

Finally, the data returned is generally in a text format, but it may be more useful after some initial processing, such as parsing XML into a DOM. Through the $.ajax-Setup function, you can define new converters that transform the incoming content into another format and return the latter as the result of the Ajax request.

To enhance the Ajax abilities of jQuery by defining your own prefilters, transport protocols, and converters, see chapter 12.

2.1.9 *Events handling*

jQuery allows you to attach event handlers to selected elements to respond to user actions. These handlers are invoked for basic mouse, keyboard, and state change events. If necessary, you can define a custom event that enables additional situations to be dealt with.

You can add a custom event by extending $.event.special. Each event definition supplies the type of that event and also provides functions to set up processing for the event, to tear down that setup when no longer required, and to trigger the event when the appropriate circumstances arise.

See chapter 13 for details on creating custom events and dealing with them.

2.1.10   *Validation rules*

Although the Validation plugin isn't part of the basic jQuery library, it's a widely used plugin that also provides an extension point, allowing you to add new validation rules. These rules can be used in conjunction with the built-in ones, such as `required` and `number`, to ensure that data entered into the fields of a form are present and correct before being submitted to the server.

A call to `$.validator.addMethod` lets you define a custom validation rule by providing its name, a function that returns `true` if an element and its value are valid or `false` if not, and a message to display in the latter case. You can use the `$.validator.addClassRules` function to enable your new rule automatically via the `class` attribute on individual elements.

Chapter 14 looks at defining your own validation rules.

2.2   *A simple plugin*

jQuery plugins can do just about anything, as evidenced by the vast selection of available third-party offerings. They can range from simple plugins that affect a single element to ones that change the appearance and behavior of multiple elements, like the Validation plugin.

The most common type of plugin created for jQuery is a collection plugin that adds functionality to a set of elements retrieved via the jQuery selection process or a subsequent traversal of the DOM. As a simple example of this type, you could create a watermark plugin that provides an in-field label when necessary. This will give you a feel for how a plugin is constructed.

2.2.1   *Placeholder text*

To conserve space within a form, sometimes the label for a field is omitted and is replaced by a placeholder (a label value within the field itself that disappears when you start working with the field). If the field is left blank, the placeholder is redisplayed. For a better user experience, the placeholder text is usually grayed out to show that it's not the actual text for that field. This labeling functionality is often referred to as a *watermark*.

The placeholder text could be specified as part of the plugin initialization, but it's better to have that text specified against each field, thus allowing multiple fields to be set up at once, with each one retaining its own label. The `title` attribute of input fields is ideal for holding the placeholder text. It's intended to be a short description of the field and may be rendered by the browser as a tooltip when hovering the mouse over the field. For visually impaired viewers, it may be spoken to identify the field when it gains focus.

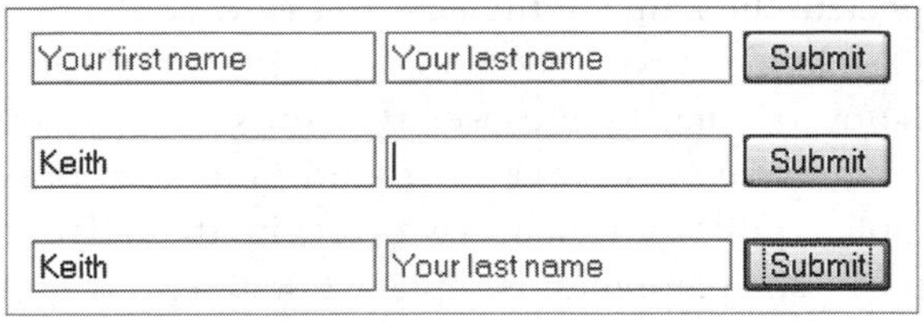

Figure 2.3 Watermark plugin in operation: before interaction, after entering first name, and ready to submit

When the field gains focus, you need to remove the placeholder text if it's present, and change the styling of the field to clear the grayed look. Similarly, when the field loses focus, you should restore the placeholder text and styling if the field value is still blank. Figure 2.3 shows the Watermark plugin in operation at various times when entering data.

For maximum flexibility, the styling of the fields when showing the placeholder text should be controlled via CSS. You can assign a class to the field when displaying the text and remove that class when it gains focus or a real value is entered. The actual appearance is then left to a CSS style and can be easily overridden by the user.

2.2.2 Watermark plugin code

Because this plugin applies to elements on the page, it's a collection plugin, which means it operates on a collection of elements found via a selection process or subsequent traversal through the DOM. As such, it needs to extend $.fn to integrate its abilities into the select and apply process.

This listing shows the complete code for the Watermark plugin.

Listing 2.1 Watermark plugin

```
$.fn.watermark = function(options) {                                    Declare
    options = $.extend({watermarkClass: 'watermark'}, options || {});    plugin
    return this.focus(function() {              When field               ❶ function
        var field = $(this);                    ❸ is focused...
        if (field.val() == field.attr('title')) {
            field.val('').
                removeClass(options.watermarkClass);        ...remove
        }                                                   ❺ placeholder
    }).blur(function() {            When field
        var field = $(this);       ❻ loses focus...
        if (field.val() == '') {
            field.val(field.attr('title')).
                addClass(options.watermarkClass);           ...restore
        }                                                   ❽ placeholder
    }).blur();
};                              Initialize field
                                ❾
```

Set options ❷ ...if showing placeholder... ❹ ...if blank... ❼

The plugin extends $.fn by declaring $.fn.watermark ❶ to allow it to be incorporated into the jQuery select and operate processing. The new attribute is named for the ability it provides and will be accessed by that name. The attribute's value is a function that accepts one parameter (options) and adds the new abilities to the targeted fields. Only one option is expected: the name of the class to use when styling the field to indicate that it contains placeholder text. You should provide a default value for that option but allow it to be overridden by the user ❷. You start by defining the default as an object with the attribute `watermarkClass` and value `watermark`. That object is extended by any supplied options, which may overwrite the default. The `||` `{}` construct ensures that the `options` parameter is replaced by an empty object (one with no changes) if it wasn't supplied in the initialization call.

To allow this plugin to be chained to other plugin calls, a key part of the jQuery philosophy, the function must return the set of elements that it's operating upon ❸. Because most of the built-in jQuery functions also return that same set, you can return the result of your application of the standard jQuery functionality.

You add a `focus` handler to each selected field ❸, and within that handler you save a reference to the current field as a jQuery object, because it'll be used several times. Next, you check whether the current field value is equal to the `title` attribute of the field ❹. If so, you remove the placeholder text by setting the field value to blank ❺, and remove the marker class specified in the options.

As you're working with the same fields and performing the same actions upon them all, you can chain the addition of a `blur` handler ❻. Once again, save a reference to the current field for repeated use. This time you compare the current field value with blank ❼, and restore the placeholder text (from the `title` attribute) and marker class if it's empty ❽.

Finally, you should trigger the `blur` processing just defined ❾ to initialize the field depending on its current value.

2.2.3   *Clearing the watermarks*

Because the placeholder text is set as the value of each field, that value would be submitted and subsequently used unless some additional processing is done. The use of the placeholder is purely a user interface artifact, so clearing those values before submission should also be performed on the client.

A simple way to clear any placeholder values is to define a second collection plugin that performs the task. The following listing shows this additional function.

Listing 2.2   Clearing a watermark

```
$.fn.clearWatermark = function() {                          Declare plugin
    return this.each(function() {                       ❶  function
        var field = $(this);
        if (field.val() == field.attr('title')) {                   ❸  ...if showing
            field.val('');                                              placeholder...
        }
    });                                                 ❹  ...remove it
};
```

For each field... ❷

Once again, you define the plugin function by extending `$.fn` with `$.fn.clear-Watermark` because you're still working with a collection of elements from the page ❶, and allow the plugin to be chained by returning a reference to the current set of matched elements via the each function ❷. For each selected element, you compare the current value with that field's title ❸ and reset the field value if they're the same ❹.

You should call this function just before you submit the field values to the server or otherwise use them for further processing. You can easily restore the placeholder text if necessary by triggering the blur handler on each field.

2.2.4 *Using the Watermark plugin*

To use the Watermark plugin, place the preceding code directly into the web page where it's required, or move the code into a separate JavaScript file (jquery.watermark.js) and load that into your page instead. Similarly, the styling for the plugin can be included in the page itself, or it can be loaded from a separate CSS file (jquery.watermark.css). Using separate files for the plugin code and its styling makes it easier to add the same functionality to other pages.

Figure 2.4 shows a web page that uses the Watermark plugin; the next listing shows the markup behind that page.

Figure 2.4 The Watermark plugin sample page

Listing 2.3 Using the Watermark plugin

```
<!DOCTYPE HTML PUBLIC "-//W3C//DTD HTML 4.01//EN"
    "http://www.w3.org/TR/html4/strict.dtd">
<html>
<head>
<title>jQuery Watermark</title>
<link type="text/css" href="jquery.watermark.css" rel="stylesheet">     ❶ Load Watermark styling
<script type="text/javascript"                                          ❷ Load jQuery
    src="http://ajax.googleapis.com/ajax/libs/jquery/1.8.3/jquery.min.js">
</script>
<script type="text/javascript" src="jquery.watermark.js"></script>      ❸ Load Watermark plugin
<script> type="text/javascript"
$(function() { // Shorthand for $(document).ready(function() {          ❹ When the DOM has loaded...
    $('input.wmark').watermark();                                       ❺ ...apply Watermark plugin
    $('#submit').click(function() {                                     ❻ When submit is clicked...
        $('input.wmark').clearWatermark();                              ❼ ...clear watermarks
        alert('Welcome ' + $('#first').val() + ' ' + $('#last').val());
        $('input.wmark').blur();                                        ❽ ...restore watermarks after use
    });
});
</script>
</head>
<body>
<h1>jQuery Watermark</h1>
<p>                                                                     ❾ The affected fields
    <input type="text" id="first" class="wmark" title="Your first name">
```

```
      <input type="text" id="last" class="wmark" title="Your last name">
      <input type="button" id="submit" value="Submit">
</p>
</body>
</html>
```

You start by loading the CSS file containing the styling for the Watermark plugin **❶**. The style causes the placeholder text to be shown grayed out (assuming that the default marker class is used):

```
.watermark { color: #888; }
```

The jQuery library must be loaded first **❷** to ensure that it's available for use by the subsequent plugin code **❸**. When the rest of the DOM has been loaded and is ready for use **❹**, you can use the new plugin.

You add the plugin abilities to the selected fields (those input fields with the wmark class) by invoking the plugin function **❺**. Recall that the plugin returns the original set of selected elements, so further processing on those elements could be chained to this call here. Because the fields are initially blank, the plugin automatically applies itself to them and fills them with the placeholder text extracted from each field's title attribute.

When the fields are submitted for further processing **❻**, you should first clear out any placeholder values from the fields **❼** before using the field values themselves. Following that processing, you can restore the placeholder text by triggering the blur handler on the affected fields **❽**.

The actual fields that the Watermark plugin applies to are found within the body of the document **❾** and are tagged with the wmark class for ease of selection.

When you open this page in your browser, you'll see the placeholder text in both input fields with a grayed out appearance at first. As you move the focus to a field, the placeholder text disappears and you can enter an appropriate value. If you exit the field without entering any value, the placeholder text is restored and the field is grayed again. When the Submit button is clicked, any placeholder text is removed, the field values are shown in an alert box, and the placeholder text is restored if necessary.

This simple collection plugin gives you a taste of what a jQuery plugin can achieve with only a few lines of code. By placing the code in a separate file, you can easily reuse it on other pages requiring the same functionality. Subsequent chapters will describe the best-practice principles that you should strive to apply to your plugins to make them robust and functional. You'll also see two plugin frameworks that provide the infrastructure for common plugin requirements and learn how to test, package, and document your plugin so that others can make the most use of it.

What you need to know

jQuery is designed to be extended.

jQuery has many extension points that allow you to add different types of functionality to it.

Creating a simple plugin is easy.

Extend `$.fn` to add a collection plugin that operates on a set of selected elements.

Place your plugin code in a separate file to allow for reuse on other pages.

Try it yourself

Amend the Watermark plugin to get its placeholder text from the `data-label` attribute instead of from the `title`. This allows you to use the latter for a longer tooltip, while still providing a label for the field when it's empty.

2.3 Summary

With much foresight, the jQuery developers concentrated on providing the most widely used infrastructure and functions in the jQuery library, while including extension points so that extra abilities could be added later. These enhancements integrate into the built-in jQuery offerings and are treated no differently.

There are numerous extension points within jQuery, each allowing you to enhance one aspect of the library. From custom selectors, to the collection and utility plugins, through jQuery UI widgets and effects, to custom Ajax processing and events, you have the ability to make jQuery work the way you want. Each of these extension points is discussed in detail in the chapters of this book.

A simple collection plugin illustrates how a basic plugin is constructed, providing useful functionality in only a few lines of code. Packaging that code in a separate file allows you to easily reuse its capabilities in other web pages.

In the next chapter, you'll see how you can extend jQuery by adding custom selectors to its built-in offerings—one of the simplest extensions you can make.

Selectors and filters 3

This chapter covers

- Existing types of jQuery selectors
- Adding your own pseudo-class selectors
- Adding set filters

One of the principles behind jQuery is the select-and-act mode of operation—you select one or more elements of interest and then do something with them. jQuery includes an embedded copy of the Sizzle selector engine ("a pure JavaScript CSS selector engine designed to be easily dropped into a host library"; http:// sizzlejs.com/) to perform your selections. Internally, Sizzle delegates to built-in browser functionality when available, and it applies the selectors itself in JavaScript if necessary.

Although numerous built-in selectors are available, sometimes it's cleaner and clearer to create a custom selector that you can integrate with jQuery's other abilities. Fortunately, adding a new selector is one of the easiest enhancements you can make to jQuery.

> **NOTE** Although initially developed as part of jQuery, the Sizzle selector engine has been released as a separate project for use with any JavaScript

library. To enable development by a wider community, the Sizzle code has been turned over to the Dojo Foundation (http://dojofoundation.org/; not to be confused with the Dojo Toolkit). Interest has come from other Java-Script communities, with the aim of enhancing the engine for everyone's benefit.

3.1 What are selectors and filters?

jQuery *selectors* are based on the selectors defined in the CSS specifications. They're string values that identify elements of interest within the HTML DOM. Within jQuery, *filter* is another term for selector. Both narrow down the set of matching elements from an existing collection, which starts with all the nodes in the current context.

3.1.1 Why add new selectors?

jQuery has a vast array of built-in selectors, so why would you want to add new ones? If you have a multistep selection process to find particular elements on a page, and that same process is used many times, either on that one page or across several pages, then you should consider creating a custom selector to implement it.

Although you could obtain a collection of elements using a combination of jQuery selectors and functions, creating a custom selector means that your particular selection process is more legible, concise, and consistent across the multiple web pages that use it. By choosing an appropriate name, your selector directly indicates what's desired, rather than having to work through multiple steps that may obscure the intent. Similarly, your invocation code is briefer and there's less chance of forgetting a step, because there's only one definition of the underlying selection process. The selector code is also easier to test, and any bug fixes or enhancements are immediately applied to all instances where it's used.

For example, to pick items other than the first or last in a list, you could use the following combination of built-in selectors:

```
$('li:not(:first, :last)', list)...
```

Or you could define your own selector and use that instead:

```
$('li:middle', list)...
```

If you want to find all paragraphs with some form of emphasized text in them, you could write this:

```
$('p:has(b | i | em | strong)')...
```

Or you could ensure you don't omit or mistype an element by defining your own selector:

```
$('p:has(:emphasis)')...
```

The next two subsections briefly review the selectors built into jQuery. After that you'll see how to define your own selectors.

3.1.2   Basic selectors

There are many basic selectors in jQuery, allowing selection by element name, ID, class, and/or attribute and value (as shown in table 3.1). Most of these are implemented by native functions provided by the browser, so they'll perform better than other selectors.

The selectors can be combined to create specific selections. For example, to find all the `label` elements that immediately follow an `input` element (perhaps these are checkbox labels), and that are located within the element with the ID of `content`, you would use this:

```
$('#content input + label')...
```

Table 3.1   Basic jQuery selectors

Name	Selector pattern	Functionality
All selector	*	Selects all elements regardless of their name
Element selector	element	Selects all elements with a matching name; for example, input
ID selector	#identifier	Selects one element with the matching ID; for example, #field1
Class selector	.class	Selects all elements with a matching class; for example, div.tabs
Descendant selector	parent child	Selects all *child* elements that are contained anywhere within *parent* elements; for example, #list1 li
Child selector	parent > child	Selects all *child* elements that are the direct children of parent elements; for example, #tabs > div
Next adjacent selector	prev + next	Selects all *next* elements that are immediately preceded by a sibling *prev* element; for example, input + label
Next siblings selector	prev ~ siblings	Selects all *siblings* elements that follow after *prev* elements and have the same parent; for example, h2 ~ p
Has attribute selector	[name]	Selects all elements that have the named attribute, regardless of its value; for example, input[readonly]
Attribute equals selector	[name="value"]	Selects all elements that have the named attribute with the exact given value; for example, label[for="field1"]

Table 3.1 Basic jQuery selectors *(continued)*

Name	Selector pattern	Functionality
Attribute not equal selector	`[name!="value"]`	Selects all elements that either don't have the named attribute or that do have the named attribute but not with the exact given value; for example, `a[target!="_blank"]`
Attribute starts with selector	`[name^="value"]`	Selects all elements that have the named attribute with a value that starts with the given value; for example, `a[href^="http:"]`
Attribute ends with selector	`[name$="value"]`	Selects all elements that have the named attribute with a value that ends with the given value; for example, `a[href$=".pdf"]`
Attribute contains selector	`[name*="value"]`	Selects all elements that have the named attribute with a value that contains the given value; for example, `a[href*="google"]`
Attribute contains word selector	`[name~="value"]`	Selects all elements that have the named attribute with a value that contains the given word, delimited by spaces; for example, `a[title~="Google"]`
Attribute contains prefix selector	`[name|="value"]`	Selects all elements that have the named attribute with a value that's either equal to the given value or starts with that value followed by a hyphen (-); for example, `a[class|="ui-state"]`
Multiple attribute selector	`[name1="value1"]` `[name2="value2"]`	Selects all elements that match all of the supplied attribute selectors; for example, `input[type="checkbox"][disabled]`
Multiple selector	`selector1,selector2`	Combines all elements selected by each of the individual selectors; for example, `input, select, textarea`

3.1.3 Pseudo-class selectors

In addition, jQuery provides numerous pseudo-class selectors that implement and extend the CSS-defined pseudo-class offerings. Pseudo-classes are defined in the CSS specification as classifying elements based on characteristics other than their name, attributes, or content-criteria that can't be deduced from the document tree. These selectors are identified by a colon (:) followed by the selector name and an optional parameter.

For example, to find all checkbox controls that have been checked, you could combine two pseudo-class selectors:

```
$('input:checkbox:checked')...
```

Note that most of these selectors are implemented in JavaScript and can't be delegated to the built-in browser functionality, and so will run a little slower than the basic selectors.

Pseudo-class selectors come in a number of different types. Normal pseudo-class selectors only inspect the element itself—its attributes or content—before deciding to include or exclude it. Some pseudo-class selectors (*set filters*) take into account the entire list of elements resulting from a previous selection and filter those based on their position within that collection. Another type (*child filters*) looks at the relationship of an element to its siblings, regardless of whether those siblings form part of the current collection. In normal usage these types make no difference, but they're important when writing your own selectors.

The jQuery built-in pseudo-class selectors are shown in table 3.2.

Table 3.2 jQuery pseudo-class selectors

Name	Selector pattern	Type	Functionality
Animated selector	`:animated`		Selects all elements currently being animated; for example, `div.content:animated`
Button selector	`:button`		Selects all button elements and inputs of type button; for example, `form :button`
Checkbox selector	`:checkbox`		Selects all inputs of type checkbox; for example, `input:checkbox`
Checked selector	`:checked`		Selects all elements (checkboxes and radio buttons) that are checked; for example, `input[name="gender"]:checked`
Contains selector	`:contains(value)`		Selects all elements that contain text equal to a given value; for example, `h1:contains(Chapter)`
Disabled selector	`:disabled`		Selects all disabled elements; for example, `input:disabled`
Empty selector	`:empty`		Selects all elements that have no children, including text nodes; for example, `span:empty`
Enabled selector	`:enabled`		Selects all enabled elements; for example, `input:enabled`
Equals index selector	`:eq(index)`	Set	Selects the element at the given index (zero-based) within the previous selection; for example, `li:eq(1)`
Even selector	`:even`	Set	Selects all even-numbered elements (zero-based) within the previous selection; for example, `tr:even`

Table 3.2   jQuery pseudo-class selectors *(continued)*

Name	Selector pattern	Type	Functionality
File selector	`:file`		Selects all inputs of type file; for example, `input:file`
First selector	`:first`	Set	Selects the first element within the previous selection; for example, `select option:first`
First child selector	`:first-child`	Child	Selects all elements that are the first child of their parent; for example, `table td:first-child`
First of type selector	`:first-of-type`	Child	Selects all elements that are the first among siblings of the same element name (new in jQuery 1.9); for example, `p:first-of-type`
Focus selector	`:focus`		Selects the element that is currently focused; for example, `input:focus`
Greater than index selector	`:gt(index)`	Set	Selects all elements within the previous selection with an index greater than the given value; for example, `li:gt(1)`
Has selector	`:has(selector)`		Selects all elements that contain at least one element that matches the given selector; for example, `form:has(input.error)`
Header selector	`:header`		Selects all header elements: h1, h2, etc.; for example, `:header`
Hidden selector	`:hidden`		Selects all elements that are hidden; for example, `form input:hidden`
Image selector	`:image`		Selects all inputs of type image; for example, `input:image`
Input selector	`:input`		Selects all input, select, textarea, and button elements; for example, `form :input`
Language selector	`:lang(language)`		Selects all elements of the given language (new in jQuery 1.9); for example, `p:lang(fr)`
Last selector	`:last`	Set	Selects the last element within the previous selection; for example, `#mylist li:last`
Last child selector	`:last-child`	Child	Selects all elements that are the last child of their parent; for example, `table td:last-child`

Table 3.2   jQuery pseudo-class selectors *(continued)*

Name	Selector pattern	Type	Functionality
Last of type selector	`:last-of-type`	Child	Selects all elements that are the last among siblings of the same element name (new in jQuery 1.9); for example, `p:last-of-type`
Less than index selector	`:lt(index)`	Set	Selects all elements within the previous selection with an index less than the given value; for example, `option:lt(2)`
Not selector	`:not(selector)`		Selects all elements that don't match the given selector; for example, `div:not(.ignore)`
Nth child selector	`:nth-child(index)`	Child	Selects all elements that are the nth child of their parent; for example, `table td:nth-child(3)`
Nth last child selector	`:nth-last-child|(index)`	Child	Selects all elements that are the nth child of their parent counting from the last element to the first (new in jQuery 1.9); for example, `table td:nth-last-child(3)`
Nth last of type selector	`:nth-last-of-type|(index)`	Child	Selects all elements that are the nth last among siblings of the same element name (new in jQuery 1.9); for example, `p:nth-last-of-type(2)`
Nth of type selector	`:nth-of-type(index)`	Child	Selects all elements that are the nth among siblings of the same element name (new in jQuery 1.9), for example, `p:nth-of-type(2)`
Odd selector	`:odd`	Set	Selects all odd numbered elements (zero-based) within the previous selection; for example, `tr:odd`
Only child selector	`:only-child`	Child	Selects all elements that are the only child of their parent; for example, `li a:only-child`
Only of type selector	`:only-of-type`	Child	Selects all elements that have no siblings of the same element name (new in jQuery 1.9); for example, `p:only-of-type`
Parent selector	`:parent`		Selects all elements that are the parent of another node, including text nodes; for example, `li:parent`
Password selector	`:password`		Selects all inputs of type password; for example, `input:password`

Table 3.2   jQuery pseudo-class selectors *(continued)*

Name	Selector pattern	Type	Functionality
Radio selector	`:radio`		Selects all inputs of type radio; for example, `input:radio`
Reset selector	`:reset`		Selects all elements of type reset; for example, `form input:reset`
Root selector	`:root`		Selects the element that is the root of the document (new in jQuery 1.9); for example, `:root`
Selected selector	`:selected`		Selects all elements (select options) that are selected; for example, `#mylist :selected`
Submit selector	`:submit`		Selects all elements of type submit; for example, `input:submit`
Target selector	`:target`		Selects the element indicated by the fragment identifier of the document's URI (new in jQuery 1.9); for example, `:target`
Text selector	`:text`		Selects all inputs of type text and text areas; for example, `form :text`
Visible selector	`:visible`		Selects all elements that are visible; for example, `span:visible`

3.2   Adding a pseudo-class selector

It's easy to add your own pseudo-class selectors—you extend `$.expr.pseudos` (or `$.expr.filters` in versions of jQuery before 1.8.0) by defining the name of your selector and providing the function that evaluates it. Conversely, it's difficult to add other types of selectors, as the underlying Sizzle selection engine isn't designed to be extended in those ways.

3.2.1   The structure of a pseudo-class selector

An example of a pseudo-class selector from the jQuery code is the `:has` selector that returns elements containing at least one element that matches the provided subselector. For example, the following selector finds all `fieldset` elements that contain an `input` element with the class `error`:

```
$('fieldset:has(input.error)')...
```

> **NOTE**   There were substantial changes in the Sizzle selector engine and consequently jQuery's use of it in release 1.8.0 and later. For completeness, both pre- and post-1.8.0 versions of the custom selectors are included in this chapter.

The :has selector as defined in jQuery 1.8.0 is shown in the following listing (listing 3.2 contains the jQuery 1.7.2 version).

Listing 3.1   The :has selector definition (jQuery 1.8.0)

```
var Expr = Sizzle.selectors = {
    ...
    pseudos: {                                              ❶ Mark a selector
        ...                                                   that requires
        "has": markFunction(function( selector ) {            a parameter
            return function( elem ) {
                return Sizzle( selector, elem ).length > 0;  Accept or reject
            };                                             ❸ current element
        }),
        ...
    },
    ...
};
```

Define selector function ❷

The jQuery 1.8.0 and later pseudo-class selectors are designed to be more streamlined than those used in previous jQuery versions, and are ultimately functions that receive only the current element (elem) as their parameter and return true if the selector accepts that element or false if it doesn't. If the selector needs a parameter to complete its selection, that parameter is captured by a *closure* (a local scope that retains data values) surrounding the final function. To identify that a parameter is required, the closure function is marked as such. You don't need to worry about marking the function, nor wrapping it in a closure if the selector doesn't use a parameter.

    The :has selector does need a parameter value—the subselector for the contained elements to test for—so it needs to wrap the selector function in a closure that supplies the parameter value specified by the user (selector) ❶, and mark the function (via markFunction or its alias createPseudo) to indicate how it should be called. This wrapper function extends Expr.pseudos, which is later aliased by $.expr.pseudos. The selector function ❷ then searches for elements matching the given subselector. It invokes the Sizzle function directly to locate corresponding elements using the current element as the context ❸. Based on the number of elements located, it returns true if any were found or false if there were none.

> **NOTE** For backward compatibility, jQuery 1.8 and later maps the previously used filters attribute onto the new pseudos attribute. Plugins can use the older form at the moment, so that they work with all jQuery versions.

The following listing shows the :has selector as defined in jQuery 1.7.2.

Listing 3.2   The :has selector definition (jQuery 1.7.2)

```
var Expr = Sizzle.selectors = {
    ...
    filters: {
        ...                                    ❶ Define selector
        has: function( elem, i, match ) {         function
```

```
            return !!Sizzle( match[3], elem ).length;
        },
    ...
};
```
                                                                    ← Accept or reject
                                                                    ❷ current element

The jQuery 1.7.2 `:has` selector function ❶ receives as parameters the current element (`elem`), its index within the current collection (`i`), and the array of text fragments (`match`) that match the pseudo-class regular expression used by Sizzle to extract these selectors. The array contains the entire selector string at index 0 (`match[0]`), the name of the selector at index 1, any quotes (double or single) around the value within parentheses at index 2, and any selector parameter at index 3 (`match[3]`).

The selector function extends `Expr.filters`—which is also referenced by its alias `$.expr.filters`—and returns `true` if this selector accepts the supplied element or `false` if it doesn't. It does this by searching for a matching subelement within the context of the current element ❷.

> **NOTE** The `!!` construct in JavaScript forces any value to be a strict Boolean one. JavaScript has several *falsy* values and considers all the following as false: `false`, `NaN` (not a number), `''` (empty string), `0` (number), `null`, and `unde-fined`. Applying the `!` operator evaluates the value as `true` or `false` and then negates it, whereas the second `!` operator restores that Boolean value to its original sense.

Now that you've seen how pseudo-class selectors are implemented, you can create some for yourself, including an exact content match selector, a pattern matching selector, a selector for list or emphasized elements, and a selector for elements marked as containing foreign language content.

3.2.2 Adding an exact content selector

There's a built-in `:contains` selector that accepts elements that have the text supplied as the selector parameter somewhere within that element's body. But what if you only want elements with an exact string match of the whole content? You can add a `:con-tent` pseudo-class that does just that.

You'd call this selector as follows to find only those list items with exactly "One" as their content:

```
$('li:content(One)')...
```

In this case, the selector retrieves all the text content from the element body and compares that exactly with the given text, as shown in the next listing for jQuery 1.8.0 and in listing 3.4 for jQuery 1.7.2.

> **Listing 3.3 An exact content selector (jQuery 1.8.0)**

```
/* Retrieve all text content of an element.                          ❶ Normalize
   @param  element  (element) the DOM element to get the text from      text
   @return  (string) the element's text content */                      content
function allText(element) {                                         ←   retrieval
```

```
        return element.textContent || element.innerText ||
            $.text([element]) || '';
    }
    /* Exact match of content. */
    $.expr.pseudos.content = $.expr.createPseudo(function(text) {
        return function(element) {
            return allText(element) == text;
        };
    });
```

2 Define :content selector

3 Accept or reject current element

Because this selector uses a parameter value to specify what should be matched, in jQuery 1.8.0 and later you need to create a closure to capture that parameter value (`text`) and mark the final function as requiring that value (by calling `createPseudo`) **2**. The wrapper function extends `$.expr.pseudos` and is identified by the name of the selector. The selector implementation is the innermost function **3**. It retrieves all the text content from the element body (hiding any browser differences on the way by calling `allText` **1**) and compares that exactly with the given text, returning `true` to accept the current element or `false` to reject it.

Listing 3.4   An exact content selector (jQuery 1.7.2)

```
/* Retrieve all text content of an element.
   @param  element  (element) the DOM element to get the text from
   @return  (string) the element's text content */
function allText(element) {
    return element.textContent || element.innerText ||
        $.text([element]) || '';
}


/* Exact match of content. */
$.expr.filters.content = function(element, i, match) {
    return allText(element) == match[3];
};
```

1 Normalize text content retrieval

2 Define :content selector

The jQuery 1.7.2 code is quite similar, but different parameters are received by the selector function, and it must extend `$.expr.filters` **2**. Once more, calling `allText` retrieves all the text content from the element body **1** and an exact comparison with the given text (`match[3]`) accepts or rejects the current element by returning `true` or `false`.

> **NOTE**   At the moment you'll only add this code inline, before the normal `document.ready` callback that contains your jQuery initialization code. In the next chapters, you'll see how to structure your code as a standalone plugin that can be easily reused in other pages.

Selectors for different jQuery versions

To cater for all jQuery versions, you can test for the presence of the new functionality (the `createPseudo` function) and create the filter accordingly, as shown here. (The `!!` operator was explained in section 3.2.1.)

```
(continued)
var usesCreatePseudo = !!$.expr.createPseudo; // jQuery 1.8+

if (usesCreatePseudo) {
    $.expr.pseudos.xxx = $.expr.createPseudo(function(param) {
        ...
    });
}
else {
    $.expr.filters.xxx = function(element, i, match) {
        ...
    };
}
```

3.2.3 Adding a pattern matching content selector

In the previous section, you saw how to create an exact match selector. Now you can go one step further and provide a regular expression selector for element content: :matches. You could call this selector as shown in table 3.3.

Table 3.3 Pattern matching selectors

Selector	Matches
$('p:matches(One)')...	All paragraphs containing the text "One"
$('p:matches(One|Two)')...	All paragraphs containing the text "One" or "Two"
$('p:matches(~chapter \\d+)')...	All paragraphs containing the (case-insensitive) text "chapter" followed by a space and one or more digits
$('p:matches("\\.\\.\\.\\.$")')...	All paragraphs ending with the text "..." (each "." must be escaped because they normally have a special meaning)

As before, the selector function collates all the text content before applying the given regular expression, as you'll see in the next listing for jQuery 1.8.0 and in listing 3.6 for jQuery 1.7.2. Note that you must provide the expression as a string, so any embedded backslashes need to be escaped.

Listing 3.5   A pattern matching selector (jQuery 1.8.0)

```
/* Regular expression match of content. */
$.expr.pseudos.matches = $.expr.createPseudo(function(text) {    ◁┐  Define :matches
    return function(element) {                                        ❶ selector
        var flags = (text[0] || '') == '~' ? 'i' : '';
        return new RegExp(text.substring(flags ? 1 : 0), flags).
            test(allText(element));
    };                                                             ◁── 
});
```

Real selector function ❷ (pointing to `return function(element) {`)

Accept or reject the current element ❸ (pointing to the `return new RegExp...test(allText(element));` block)

This selector also requires a parameter to specify what pattern to match, so in jQuery 1.8.0 and later, you wrap it in a marked function (via `createPseudo`) to capture that pattern (`text`) and assign that wrapper to extend `$.expr.pseudos` ❶. The selector function ❷ then creates a regular expression based on the pattern provided and tests the text content of the current element against it ❸, returning `true` if it matches or `false` if it doesn't to accept or reject that element.

Unfortunately, pseudo-class selectors may only take one argument to modify their behavior. If you want to be able to specify case-insensitive pattern matches, you need some way of indicating that within that one parameter. As shown earlier, you could look for an initial tilde (~) character in the expression and interpret that as requesting a case-insensitive match. If you need a tilde as the first character, you can escape it with a backslash (or two).

Listing 3.6 A pattern matching selector (jQuery 1.7.2)

```
/* Regular expression match of content. */
$.expr.filters.matches = function(element, i, match) {     ← Define :matches
    var flags = (match[3][0] || '') == '~' ? 'i' : '';      ❶ selector
    return new RegExp(match[3].substring(flags ? 1 : 0), flags).   ←
        test(allText(element));                             Accept or reject
};                                                          current element ❷
```

In jQuery 1.7.2 you define the selector function to extend `$.expr.filters` and to receive several parameters identifying the current element (`element`) and the pattern to match (`match[3]`) ❶. As with the newer version, you generate a regular expression from the given pattern and test that against the text content of the current element ❷, returning `true` to accept the element or `false` to reject it.

JavaScript regular expressions

The use of regular expressions in JavaScript is an important part of using the language effectively. Regular expressions appear in many of the plugins in this book to test values or to break strings up into their component parts. You should be familiar with their syntax and usage patterns. See the appendix for a summary of regular expression usage, or see some of the many references and tutorials available on the web on this subject:

- JavaScript RegExp Object—www.w3schools.com/jsref/jsref_obj_regexp .asp
- Regular Expressions—https://developer.mozilla.org/en/JavaScript/Guide/Regular_Expressions
- Using Regular Expressions—www.regular-expressions.info/javascript.html
- Regular Expression Tutorial—www.learn-javascript-tutorial.com/Regular Expressions.cfm

3.2.4 *Adding element type selectors*

You can also use pseudo-class selectors to make it easier to refer to multiple element types, just as the built-in `:input` selector matches `input`, `select`, `textarea`, and button elements.

For example, you could collect both ordered and unordered lists under a `:list` selector, or all the emphasizing elements under a `:emphasis` selector. These selectors could then be used as follows:

- `$('#main :list')`... for all ordered and unordered lists in the `#main` element,
- `$('p:has(:emphasis)')`... for all paragraphs that contain an emphasized element.

Both selectors use simple regular expressions to match the node name of the element, as shown in the following listing. Because these selectors don't accept any parameters, they don't require any special handling in jQuery 1.8.0, and the code is identical for all versions.

Listing 3.7   Selectors for lists and emphasized markup

```
/* All lists. */
$.expr.filters.list = function(element) {            Define :list
    return /^(ol|ul)$/i.test(element.nodeName);   ❶  selector
};

/* Emphasized text. */
$.expr.filters.emphasis = function(element) {        Define :emphasis
    return /^(b|em|i|strong)$/i.test(element.nodeName);  ❷  selector
};
```

Because `$.expr.filters` is defined in jQuery 1.8.x as an alias for `$.expr.pseudos`, you can use the former for all versions of jQuery. You add the function for the list selector to that extension point and test whether the element name is either `ol` or `ul` by using a regular expression ❶. That expression matches from the start of the text (^) through to the end ($) looking for either of the given strings (|). Similarly, the function for the emphasis selector tests for the element name being one of `b`, `em`, `i`, or `strong` ❷, again via a regular expression.

3.2.5 *Adding a foreign language selector*

You're not restricted to the element name or content; you can check anything related to the element. For example, you could create a pseudo-class selector that finds all foreign language elements within the document.

Use the selector as follows:

- `$('p:foreign')`... for all paragraphs with a language specified other than the user's default language
- `$('p:foreign(fr)')`... for all paragraphs marked as being in French

The selector looks for the lang attribute on an element and operates in one of two modes. When no parameter is provided, it matches all elements with a lang value set, but not those that match the browser's current language. If a particular language is specified, it returns only those elements marked with that language. Listing 3.8 shows the code for this selector in jQuery 1.8.0, and listing 3.9 shows the selector in jQuery 1.7.2.

NOTE A :lang selector added in jQuery 1.9.0 provides similar functionality.

Listing 3.8   A foreign language selector (jQuery 1.8.0)

```
/* Browser's default language. */                           ❶ Create test for default
var defaultLanguage = new RegExp('^' +                         browser language
    (navigator.language || navigator.userLanguage).substring(0, 2), 'i');


/* Foreign language elements. */
$.expr.pseudos.foreign = $.expr.createPseudo(function(language) {
    return function(element) {                              Define :foreign
        var lang = $(element).attr('lang');                 selector ❷
        return !!lang && (!language ? !defaultLanguage.test(lang) :
            new RegExp('^' + language.substring(0, 2), 'i').
                test(lang));                                And compare ❹
    };
});
```
Extract element language ❸

First you create a regular expression that will test for the default language specified for the browser ❶. This selector may have a parameter provided, so in jQuery 1.8.0 and later it needs to use the marked function wrapper (createPseudo) to capture that value (language) ❷, and have that extend $.expr.pseudos. The selector function then looks for the lang attribute on the current element ❸ and operates in one of two modes based on the presence or absence of any parameter value. When no parameter is provided, it matches all elements with a lang value set, but not those that match the browser's current language ❹. If a particular language is specified, it only returns true for those elements marked with that language.

NOTE See section 3.2.1 for an explanation of the !! construct.

Listing 3.9   A foreign language selector (jQuery 1.7.2)

```
/* Browser's default language. */
var defaultLanguage = new RegExp('^' +
    (navigator.language || navigator.userLanguage).substring(0, 2), 'i');

/* Foreign language elements. */                            ❶ Define :foreign
$.expr.filters.foreign = function(element, i, match) {         selector
    var lang = $(element).attr('lang');
    return !!lang && (!match[3] ? !defaultLanguage.test(lang) :
        new RegExp('^' + match[3].substring(0, 2), 'i').test(lang));
};
```
Extract language and compare ❷

The jQuery 1.7.2 code is basically the same as the newer version, except that the selector function accepts all the parameters directly and extends $.expr.filters ❶. As before, it retrieves any lang attribute for the current element and compares that with the parameter value supplied (match[3]) ❷.

3.2.6 Selectors from the Validation plugin

The following selectors are defined in Jörn Zaefferer's Validation plugin.[1] These selectors, shown in listing 3.10, allow you to easily find all fields with no value, all fields with some value, or all unchecked fields. Because they don't require any parameters, the selectors are implemented identically in all jQuery versions.

Listing 3.10 Validation selectors

```
// Custom selectors
$.extend($.expr[":"], {                                    ❶ Add pseudo-class
    // http://docs.jquery.com/Plugins/Validation/blank          selectors
    blank: function(a) {return !$.trim("" + a.value);},
    // http://docs.jquery.com/Plugins/Validation/filled     ❸ Match
    filled: function(a) {return !!$.trim("" + a.value);},      non-blank
    // http://docs.jquery.com/Plugins/Validation/unchecked     fields
    unchecked: function(a) {return !a.checked;}            ❹ Match unchecked fields
});
```

Match blank fields ❷

Instead of extending $.expr.filters, Jörn extends $.expr[":"] ❶, which is an alias for the former. The blank selector function returns true if there is no value (including all spaces) in field a ❷. (Recall that JavaScript evaluates a blank string as false.) Conversely, the filled selector function returns true if there is some field value for a ❸ (negating the result of the previous blank function). The unchecked selector function returns true if the checked attribute of the field a is null or false ❹.

Note that these selectors return many elements that you wouldn't normally expect, so they should probably be combined with other form element selectors, such as :checkbox:unchecked.

3.3 Adding a set filter

Another type of pseudo-class selector that can be created is the *set filter*. Whereas previous selectors have looked at a single node, set filters take into account the entire collection of elements in the current selection. Typical examples are the :first, :last, :odd, and :even pseudo-class selectors.

NOTE The Sizzle selector engine contained substantial changes in the version embedded in jQuery 1.8.0 and later. For completeness, both pre- and post-1.8.0 versions of the custom selectors are included in this chapter.

---

[1] jQuery Validation Plugin, http://jqueryvalidation.org/.

3.3.1   *The structure of a set selector*

The :last selector is a built-in set selector that returns the final item in the previously matched collection of elements. Using it as an example, let's look at how a set selector works. It's defined in jQuery 1.8.0 as shown in the next listing; listing 3.12 contains the jQuery 1.7.2 version.

Listing 3.11   The :last selector definition (jQuery 1.8.0)

```
var Expr = Sizzle.selectors = {
    ...
    setFilters: {
        ...
        "last": function( elements, argument, not ) {      ① Define :last
            var elem = elements.pop();                         set selector
            return not ? elements : [ elem ];              ② Return filtered
        },                                                    element set
        ...
    }
};
```

In jQuery 1.8.0 and later, a new set filter extends Expr.setFilters (or its alias $.expr.setFilters) by providing the name of the new filter and assigning it a function to process the current set of elements ①. The parameters to this function are the current array of elements (elements), any parameter value supplied to the selector (argument), and a Boolean flag indicating whether the filter should be reversed (not). The function must return the filtered set of elements as an array ②. jQuery 1.8.0 makes only a single call to a set filter function, which processes the entire list in one go and returns either the requested elements or their inverse, depending on the value of the not flag.

> **NOTE**   In jQuery 1.8.2 there were further changes to the setFilters implementation. Internally jQuery now calls the createPositionalPseudo function for these filters. But that function isn't visible externally and new setFilters can still be created using the techniques described here.

Listing 3.12   The :last selector definition (jQuery 1.7.2)

```
var Expr = Sizzle.selectors = {
    ...
    setFilters: {
        ...
        last: function( elem, i, match, array ) {          ① Define :last
            return i === array.length - 1;                    set selector
        },                                                 ② Accept or reject
        ...                                                   current element
    },
    ...
};
```

Prior to jQuery 1.8.0, the selector function still extends Expr.setFilters (or its alias $.expr.setFilters) and is called for each element in the set in turn ①. As such, the parameters for the function are the current element (`elem`), its position within the list (`i`), the match components from the selector expression (`match`), and the collection of elements that make up the list (`array`). The function returns `true` if the current element is accepted or `false` if it's not ❷.

Identifying set filters prior to jQuery 1.8.2

Because set filters are treated differently from other pseudo-class selectors prior to jQuery 1.8.2, they must be identified somehow so that they can be invoked correctly. jQuery does this by explicitly matching their names in the regular expression within the Sizzle selection engine that extracts them from the selection string: `$.expr.match.POS`, for positional selectors.

```
var pos = ":(nth|eq|gt|lt|first|last|even|odd)(?:\\((\\d*)\\)|)(?=[^-]|$)";
$.expr.match.POS = new RegExp( pos, "ig" );
```

To add a new set filter into earlier jQuery versions, you also need to add its name into that list. If you don't, you'll receive an error: "Syntax error, unrecognized expression: unsupported pseudo: xxxxxx." You'll see how to add the name when creating a new selector in the next section.

jQuery 1.8.2 identifies set filters automatically, and there's no longer a need to update the `$.expr.match.POS` regular expression.

Using the templates shown previously, you can create your own set selectors, such as a middle elements selector and an updated position selector that handles indexing from the end of the list.

3.3.2 Adding a middle elements set selector

You can define a `:middle` selector that discards the first and last elements of a set, which may be useful in list item processing. It's used as follows:

```
$('li:middle')...
```

The selector function is shown in the following listing for jQuery 1.8.0, and in listing 3.14 for jQuery 1.7.2.

Listing 3.13 A middle elements selector (jQuery 1.8.0)

```
$.expr.match.POS = new RegExp(                          ❶ Recognize a new set selector
    $.expr.match.POS.source.replace(/odd/, 'odd|middle'), 'ig');

/* Middle elements. */                                  ❷ Define
$.expr.setFilters.middle = function(elements, argument, not) {    :middle set
    var firstLast = [elements.shift(), elements.pop()];           selector
    return not ? firstLast : elements;                  ❸ Return filtered
};                                                         element set
```

For jQuery versions 1.8.0 and 1.8.1, you need to add the selector's name into the regular expression that extracts them from the full selection string, so you redefine the

`$.expr.match.POS` regular expression, as defined in the previous section, to place your new selector name after the last one in the existing list ❶. The definition of the existing regular expression is retrieved via its `source` attribute, before replacing the text `odd` with `odd|middle`, and recompiling the new version of the expression back into the original variable. Don't forget to include the `ig` flags that indicate case-insensitive matches and multiple (global) matches. You can omit this change from jQuery 1.8.2.

From jQuery 1.8.0 on, you must deal with the entire set of elements as a whole and return the filtered list from the function, which extends `$.expr.setFilters` ❷. In this case, you extract the first and last items from the list (using the standard `Array` functions `shift` and `pop`) and save them in a new array ❸. Based on the value of the `not` parameter, you then return either those two items (`not` is `true`) or the remaining middle items of the list (`not` is `false`) directly.

Listing 3.14   A middle elements selector (jQuery 1.7.2)

```
$.expr.match.POS = new RegExp(
    $.expr.match.POS.source.replace(/odd/, 'odd|middle'));       ❶ Recognize a new
$.expr.leftMatch.POS = new RegExp(                                  set selector
    $.expr.leftMatch.POS.source.replace(/odd/, 'odd|middle'));

/* Middle elements. */                                           ❷ Define
$.expr.setFilters.middle = function(element, i, match, list) {      :middle set
    return i > 0 && i < list.length - 1;                            selector
};
                                                                 ❸ Accept or reject
                                                                   current element
```

In the earlier versions of jQuery, you also need to add the name for a new set filter into the regular expression that distinguishes them and extracts them from the selection string. Again, you update the `$.expr.match.POS` regular expression to include the new name ❶, although the earlier jQuery versions didn't add any flags to the regular expression. But prior to jQuery 1.8.0, you also need to add the new name to a second regular expression that is derived from the first (in jQuery 1.8.0 this happens automatically). If you are using one of these earlier versions of jQuery, you update `$.expr.leftMatch.POS` in the same manner as the previous expression.

The selector function here handles each element from the set separately ❷. You compare the position of the element within the set and reject the first and last by returning `false` for them ❸.

3.3.3 *Enhancing the equals selector*

One thing that's missing from jQuery is the ability to use a negative index in the `:eq` selector to specify positioning from the end of the collection, even though this functionality is available in the corresponding `eq()` function.

You could add it fairly easily to bring the two into line. Then you could use the selector as follows:

- `$('li:eq(1)')`... to find the second list item
- `$('li:eq(-2)')`... to find the second last list item

NOTE From jQuery 1.8.1 on, this functionality is now standard and doesn't need to be added as an enhancement.

Currently, though, entering a minus sign into an `:eq` selector results in the expression being ignored and the selector returning nothing or throwing an error. You first have to allow the use of a minus sign for this selector before you can implement the new functionality.

This listing shows the code for jQuery 1.8.0; listing 3.16 shows the same for jQuery 1.7.2.

Listing 3.15 Enhancing the equals selector (jQuery 1.8.0)

```
$.expr.match.POS = new RegExp(
    $.expr.match.POS.source.replace(/\\d\*/, '-?\\d*'), 'ig');    ◄─── ❶ Allow negative parameter values

/* Allow index from end of list. */
$.expr.setFilters.eq = function(elements, argument, not) {    ❷ Redefine :eq set selector
    argument = parseInt(argument, 10);
    argument = (argument < 0 ? elements.length + argument : argument);    ◄─── ❸ Calculate position
    var element = elements.splice(argument, 1);    ◄─── ❹ Return filtered element set
    return not ? elements : element;
};
```

You allow the entry of a minus sign by adjusting the expression used for set filters: the `$.expr.match.POS` pattern from the Sizzle selection engine. You redefine the expression to allow an optional minus sign before the numbers within the selector ❶. Within the existing POS regular expression, retrieved via its `source` attribute, you look for the occurrence of `\d*`, indicating any number of numeric digits, and replace that with `-?\d*`, to add the optional minus sign. Note that the backslashes must be escaped so that they can be used as literal values.

Then you can redefine the eq function itself to take a negative value into account ❷. If such a number is found, you add it to the length of the list of elements (remembering that it's negative and will be subtracted) and use the result as the index to compare against ❸. A positive value is passed through unchanged, retaining the existing functionality. With the required index computed, you remove the identified element and return that or the remainder of the list, depending on the value of the not parameter ❹.

Listing 3.16 Enhancing the equals selector (jQuery 1.7.2)

```
$.expr.match.POS = new RegExp(
    $.expr.match.POS.source.replace(/\\d\*/, '-?\\d*'));    ◄─── ❶ Allow negative parameter values
$.expr.leftMatch.POS = new RegExp(
    $.expr.leftMatch.POS.source.replace(/\\d\*/, '-?\\d*'));

/* Allow index from end of list. */
$.expr.setFilters.eq = function(element, i, match, list) {    ◄─── ❷ Redefine :eq set selector
    var index = parseInt(match[3], 10);    ◄─── ❸ Calculate position
```

```
    index = (index < 0 ? list.length + index : index);
    return index === i;                    ⟵┐   Accept or reject
};                                        ❹  current element
```

The jQuery 1.7.2 code is similar to the 1.8.0 code. As well as adjusting the normal set filter pattern (`$.expr.match.POS`), you must also change the corresponding
`$.expr.leftMatch.POS` pattern in the same way ❶, as for the previous middle selector.
Then redefine the `eq` function ❷, extract the parameter value from the component
matches (`match[3]`), and compute the required index based on its sign ❸. Return
`true` to accept the current element based on its position or `false` to reject it ❹.

What you need to know

Create a pseudo-class selector to standardize or clarify a selection process.

Extend `$.expr.pseudos` to add a pseudo-class selector (`$.expr.filters` before
jQuery 1.8).

Use `$.expr.createPseudo` to capture a parameter value.

Extend `$.expr.setFilters` to take into account the entire set of matched elements.

JavaScript regular expressions can help in matching patterns of characters.

Try it yourself

Create a replacement selector for the standard `:header` selector that includes the
new HTML5 `header` element in addition to the existing `h1` to `h6` elements.

3.4   Summary

jQuery works by allowing you to select a collection of elements upon which you perform some operation. It offers multiple ways of accessing the elements—by element
name, by ID or class, by attribute value, and by pseudo-class selectors—and can combine these for more specific queries. Although numerous options are available, sometimes it's more concise, legible, and consistent to define a custom selector to find what
you're after.

You've seen how to create new simple pseudo-class selectors, such as `:matches` and
`:emphasis`, which look at one node in isolation. Then you learned how to define set
filters, such as `:middle`, which take into consideration the current collection of elements. Using these techniques you can create your own custom selectors to ease your
development process.

In the next chapters, you'll see several design principles for jQuery plugins and a
framework that implements these principles. You'll also learn how to package your
plugin into a standalone module that can be reused on many pages.

Part 2

Plugins and functions

The most common third-party extension is a plugin that operates on a collection of elements selected from the document. This part of the book looks at how to implement such extensions using best practice techniques.

Before launching into the plugin itself, chapter 4 discusses a number of best practice principles that you should apply to your own development efforts. These guidelines will help to ensure you produce a robust and useful plugin.

Chapter 5 goes through the process of developing a collection plugin—one that operates on a collection of elements on the page. The use of a plugin framework helps apply the principles described in the previous chapter, while allowing you to concentrate on the actual functionality of your plugin.

A function plugin doesn't work with selected elements, but provides additional functionality for the page as a whole in a consistent manner. Chapter 6 examines two examples of this sort of extension to help deal with localization issues and with cookies for your pages.

To ensure the widest audience for your plugin you should test it, package it for distribution, document its abilities, and provide a showcase of what it can do. Chapter 7 covers all of these aspects of the development process.

Plugin principles 4

This chapter covers
- Plugin design
- Guiding principles for development

The scope for a jQuery plugin is wide open—from basic class changes and event handlers, through selectors and animations, to full-blown graphical widgets with remote access. The only limit is your imagination.

In the previous chapter you saw how to create custom selectors for use in jQuery, giving you some simple examples of one way to enhance its abilities. Now we'll take a step back and consider the plugin design and creation process as a whole. Whatever type of plugin you choose to create, you should follow best practice principles so that your plugin will survive and prosper within the wider jQuery and JavaScript environments.

This chapter discusses those principles and explains why they should be applied to your plugins. It also looks at the benefits of creating a plugin rather than just coding inline, and presents some questions to consider when designing your own plugin.

53

4.1   Plugin design

Deciding what to implement as a plugin is the first challenge. Generally candidates arise from a specific need in one of your projects. If you find yourself applying the same functionality to elements across different web pages, consider creating a plugin that can be reused as needed. For example, maybe you have several drop-down controls that operate together to allow the user to select a date, and you want to ensure that the number of days available matches the number of days in the selected month, to prevent the user from picking an invalid date.

4.1.1   Plugin benefits

The benefits of creating a plugin include the following:

- Ease of reuse
- Consistency
- Reduced maintenance

Maximize your code reuse by creating a plugin for common functionality. Then just load the plugin code into your page and apply it to your selected elements with a couple of lines of script, as shown in the following listing. Use your code in similar situations by providing options to customize the plugin for each instance.

Listing 4.1   Loading and invoking a plugin

```
<script type="text/javascript" src="js/jquery.js"></script>
<script type="text/javascript" src="js/jquery.myplugin.js"></script>
<script type="text/javascript">
$(function() {
    $('.myelements').myplugin({option1: true, option2: 'XYZ'});
});
</script>
```

By reusing the plugin code and styling, you ensure that the same functionality is applied whenever that plugin is used, and you gain a consistency of look and feel across your projects.

  If any bugs are found in the code, you only need to make the corrections in one place to have it apply to all instances in your projects. In-depth testing also only needs to be done once, as the code base doesn't change between implementations. Testing should be simpler and more repeatable, because you have more control over the environment for those tests. Similarly, any improvements made to the code are also immediately available throughout the application.

4.1.2   Planning the design

Once you have an idea for a plugin, lay out its basic design and consider these questions:

- What will it look like on the page (assuming it has a UI component)?
- How will it interact with the user—via keyboard, mouse, programmatically?

- What state does it need to manage for each instance? Or across all instances?
- How might the user want to customize the plugin's appearance or behavior?
- Which internal events would a user be interested in?

Don't be too ambitious. Keep your plugin focused on the problem it's designed to solve. You may be tempted to continually add new functionality to the plugin as new ideas and circumstances arise. In each case, ask these questions:

- Are the new abilities closely related to the plugin's main goal?
- Are they applicable across a number of instances, or are they just overhead for most use cases?
- Could or should the new abilities be implemented in a more generic manner to apply to a wider audience?

For example, an earlier incarnation of my Datepicker plugin had the built-in ability to pop up a dialog box to ask for a particular date. At the time, this seemed like useful and consistent functionality, because it involved obtaining a date from the user. But this introduced more complexity into the code while reducing its flexibility. It became obvious that the placement of the Datepicker within a dialog box could be done just as easily and with much more control over the other contents of the dialog box by using a separate Dialog plugin. Now the dialog box has additional functionality, such as being draggable and resizable, without having to duplicate existing code, and the Datepicker is less complex to boot. Figure 4.1 compares the two versions.

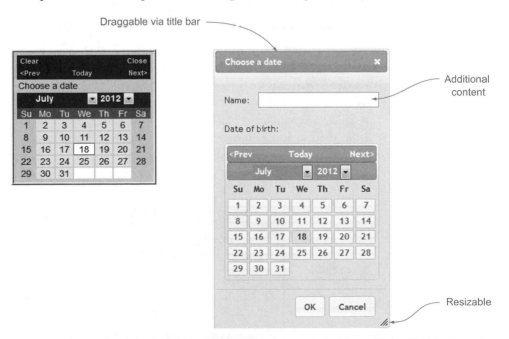

Figure 4.1 Previous built-in Datepicker dialog box (left), compared with new jQuery UI dialog box with embedded Datepicker (right)

4.1.3 Modularize the plugin

If the new functionality is complex enough that you want to avoid repeating the code numerous times, but it may not be applicable in many circumstances, you can extract the code into a separate module that can be optionally loaded by those users who want that specific ability. This way you retain the benefits of the plugin format, allow basic users to load just the basic functionality, and still have the additional code available for those who need it.

For example, a graphing plugin may have one or more separate modules for the less widely used chart types, such as scatter charts, radar charts, and map charts. Most users benefit from the reduced size of the main code, but those who want these extra charts can include them with a single line to import the extra script.

4.2 Guiding principles

I collected the following principles during the development of my plugins. They represent what I believe to be best practices for plugin design. They help to minimize your plugin's interference with the wider jQuery and JavaScript environments, while protecting your code from outside interference.

> **NOTE** Most of these principles are embodied in the plugin framework described in chapter 5, and in the jQuery UI widget framework presented in chapter 8, or are covered in chapter 7. The implementation and more detailed discussion of these principles is left until then.

4.2.1 Provide progressive enhancements

Ideally, plugins should provide progressive enhancements to your web pages. This means that the pages still function even if the user doesn't have JavaScript enabled, but users receive a richer experience if they do have it active.

The Datepicker is a good example of this principle. Without JavaScript, you still have a text input field into which the user can type a date, hopefully in the correct date format. With JavaScript, you gain the possibility of a popup calendar that the user can move through to choose their desired date, as shown in figure 4.2. The calendar

Figure 4.2   The Datepicker plugin progressively enhances a standard input field.

lets you see the dates in context and may impose restrictions on what can be chosen or offer additional feedback on the significance of certain days. A selected date populates the input field, just as if it had been entered manually, but ensures that it's in the correct format.

4.2.2 Only claim a single name and use that for everything

You should only claim a single name within the jQuery namespace and use that throughout to refer to your plugin. The purpose of this principle is to minimize the possibility that your plugin will clash with another.

Your name should be long enough to convey the purpose of the plugin and to reduce the possibility of interference, without being excessive. Good examples are `datepicker` and `validate`. Unfortunately, `slider` isn't such a good name. It's used within jQuery UI to identify a control to select a value within a range, but also by many other plugins for a control that manages a series of images or content with transitions between them.

Some plugins use one name for applying new functionality to collections of DOM elements, and then another, or several more, to provide additional features not directly related to such collections. For example, the Validation plugin uses `validate` as its main function, but it also defines `valid`, `rules`, and `removeAttrs` functions for use with jQuery collections. Every time you use another name, you increase the possibility that one of them will conflict with some other plugin, rendering one or both of them inoperable.

If you can choose one name within the jQuery namespace and only use that to interact with your plugin, then you greatly reduce the likelihood that you'll interfere with another plugin.

Allowing only one name for all your exchanges with the plugin may seem like a major hurdle to overcome, because you may want to provide additional interactions with the elements managed by your plugin. One way to provide these extra features, at least on collections of elements, is the method pattern described in section 4.2.6.

4.2.3 Place everything under the jQuery object

Placing your plugin within the jQuery namespace, either directly or via one of its extension points, removes the possibility that it'll interfere with code from other libraries. In many cases, you need to extend a certain jQuery attribute anyway to have the plugin integrate with jQuery's other abilities. Also, because you're developing a jQuery plugin, users expect to refer to it via jQuery itself.

For example, the Debug plugin (http://jquery.glyphix.com/), which allows you to write logging messages to the browser's console for debugging purposes, isn't tied to any particular elements on the page and could be implemented as a standalone package. But it uses jQuery's capabilities to make its own code simpler, so it qualifies as a jQuery plugin. Its main function is named `log` and is attached directly to the jQuery object to be invoked, as follows:

```
$.log('Debugging message');
```

Unfortunately, from the viewpoint of these principles, it then adds a collection function named debug to jQuery, as well as a global DEBUG flag. It'd be better to see this new function named the same as the main function and to have the global flag as $.log.debug to avoid potential interference from other libraries.

There's still a potential for conflicts between plugins within the jQuery namespace, but using a single named access point reduces that risk. Also, if you do encounter another plugin with the same name, it's likely to be implementing very similar (if not the same) functionality as your own, so it's probable that both wouldn't appear within one page.

4.2.4   *Don't rely on $ being the same as jQuery*

jQuery is a JavaScript library, along with various others such as Prototype, MooTools, and script.aculo.us. At times, users want to incorporate features from several of these in one page, and because JavaScript doesn't have a well-defined package or module structure, there can be conflicts between the libraries. In particular, all these libraries use $ as a shorthand for their main library function.

The designers of jQuery recognize this problem and have included mechanisms within jQuery to overcome it. Although you could always use jQuery when referring to the library, developers are often lazy typists and prefer to use fewer characters where possible, especially when this term is one of the most widely used.

In order to allow a shorter reference to jQuery and to avoid the use of $ altogether, you can use the noConflict function to return $ to whatever was using it previously, while defining a new variable to be used instead. The following listing shows what this looks like in practice, creating a new variable (jq) that's a synonym for jQuery.

Listing 4.2   Avoiding library conflicts

```
var jq = jQuery.noConflict();              ❶ Restore $ variable
jq(document).ready(function() {            ❷ Use replacement
    jq('p.main')...                            variable
});
```

In chapter 5, you'll see another mechanism for ensuring that $ does mean jQuery without the need for the noConflict call, which allows you to use the former throughout your own code.

4.2.5   *Hide the implementation details by using scope*

As mentioned earlier, JavaScript doesn't have a well-defined package or module structure. Unless otherwise specified, variables are declared within a global namespace beneath the window object, which may lead to conflicts between different plugins as they end up altering each other's variables. This type of interference can be difficult to track down, and it's better to avoid it in the first place.

You need some way to hide the internal workings of your plugin from others on the page to ensure that you don't interfere with their operation and, more importantly, that they don't interfere with yours. In object-oriented programming (OOP) this is called *encapsulation*. Fortunately JavaScript provides a mechanism for doing this in the form of *scope*.

When you define a function in JavaScript, you create a new scope: a new section of the code that has its own set of variable and function names. Within that function you can still see items that were declared in surrounding scopes, but code external to the function can't access the internally declared items. The following listing demonstrates this.

Listing 4.3 An example of different variable scopes

```
var i = 0;                          Global variable
                              ❶      declaration

function one() {
    i = 1;                                   Reference
    alert(i);                          ❷     global variable
}

function two(i) {                    Parameter hides
    i = 2;                        ❸   global variable
    alert(i);
}

function three() {                   Local declaration
    var i = 3;                    ❹   hides global variable
    alert(i);
}

alert(i);  // 0 - global variable
one();     // 1 - global variable
two(i);    // 2 - parameter variable
three();   // 3 - local variable      ❺   Unchanged
alert(i);  // 1 - global variable         global variable
```

A global variable `i` is declared and assigned the value 0 ❶. When function `one` is called, it also references that global variable, updates it, and displays the result ❷. But the call to function `two` copies the value of the global `i` into a separate parameter of the same name and only updates and displays the local copy ❸. Similarly, function `three` defines a local variable `i` that's separate from the global one, assigns it a value, and displays that ❹. When the final alert is executed, it refers back to the global variable `i` that's unchanged since the call to `one` and displays that earlier value ❺. The code results in this sequence of alerts: 0, 1, 2, 3, 1.

To protect your own code, you can wrap it in a function call to create a new scope around it. See section 5.3.2 for how this technique is used when writing your plugin.

4.2.6 *Invoke methods for additional functionality*

Having claimed only one name within the jQuery namespace, you then need some way of providing additional functionality through that name. jQuery UI uses a pattern in which you call your one function and pass in the name of a method you wish to invoke, optionally providing additional parameters to modify its action.

You initialize the main functionality of the plugin by calling its function directly on a collection of DOM elements, such as for the jQuery UI Tabs plugin:

```
$('#tabs').tabs(); // With optional initial settings
```

You can then interact with these elements by specifying which method you want and providing any required parameters:

```
$('#tabs').tabs('disable'); // Disable the tabs
$('#tabs').tabs('option', {active: 2}); // Open the third tab
```

The plugin framework described in chapter 5 and the jQuery UI widget framework in chapter 8 both provide this capability in an easy-to-use manner.

4.2.7 *Return the jQuery object for chaining whenever possible*

One of the mainstays of jQuery is its ability to chain function calls that apply to the same collection of DOM elements. This construct allows for compact code, and users expect new functions to behave in the same manner.

```
$('#myElement').myplugin({field: value}).show();
```

This capability is easily provided by returning the `this` variable, or its equivalent (such as the result of the `each` function), from your collection plugin's main function. Both the plugin framework described in chapter 5 and the jQuery UI widget framework in chapter 8 provide this functionality.

There are times when you want to return specific values from an instance of the plugin, such as the current value of the wrapped element. Of course you can do this, breaking the ability to chain further calls. Such deviations should be clearly documented so that users know what to expect from your plugin.

4.2.8 *Use the data function to store instance details*

Generally you'll need to store some state information about each plugin instance, such as its option values, its current disabled status, or references to other elements that it manages. Such details must be easily accessible for each targeted element.

The recommended mechanism is to use the jQuery `data()` function and add the details as a single object attached to the element targeted by the plugin. Using your single plugin name to identify the information once again reduces the likelihood of a clash with another plugin. As well as being able to access the details within your plugin, there's the possibility for external access. This may prove useful with tools such as FireQuery (a FireBug extension for Firefox) for debugging purposes.

For example, you can store information against an element by calling `data` and providing its name and value. The value can be a simple number or string, or even an object with its own attributes:

```
$('#myElement').data('simple', 123);
$('#myElement').data('complex',
    {url: 'www.example.com', timeout: 1000, cache: true});
```

You'd then retrieve the stored information by again calling data, but only providing the name of the required detail:

```
var simple = $('#myElement').data('simple'); // = 123
var complex = $('#myElement').data('complex');
    // = {url: 'www.example.com', timeout: 1000, cache: true}
```

You can obtain all information against an element by calling data without any name:

```
var all = $('#myElement').data();
    // = {complex: {url: 'www.example.com', timeout: 1000, cache: true},
    //    simple: 123}
```

In addition, if the targeted element is removed from the DOM, the associated details are also cleanly removed, preventing any memory leaks.

4.2.9 *Anticipate customizations*

Although your plugin provides certain functionality, there are usually aspects that may change between invocations. Users will always want to customize the way a plugin works or its appearance to fit their own requirements. If you can predict what users might want to change and provide options to cater for that, they're more likely to use your plugin.

For example, my Datepicker plugin provides many options for changing its behavior, some of which are shown in figure 4.3.

Obvious candidates for customization are any text values displayed by the plugin. These definitely need to be changed if you want to target other languages (see section 4.2.11). *Magic numbers* (literal values with special meaning) are also candidates for inclusion as options. These values may apply in the situations you envisage, but some-

Figure 4.3 Datepicker customizations: (top row) default configuration, with buttons instead of links, with year navigation as well as month traversal; (bottom row) without the direct selection of month and year, and showing two months.

one will come along and try to apply your plugin in a new way and will want to modify that setting.

The plugin framework in chapter 5 and the jQuery UI widget framework in chapter 8 show how options are maintained against an element and how they're used to alter a plugin's appearance or behavior.

Listen to the feedback from your plugin's users. They provide valuable information about how they use it and what sorts of things they want to alter. Try to incorporate their suggestions as options for the next person to use, so that you can happily point to a particular option to solve someone else's problem.

Don't use options to style your plugin. Instead, provide appropriate markup that's annotated with classes that can be styled via external CSS files. Such a separation of content and style is a best practice and makes it much easier for the user to change your plugin's appearance. See section 4.2.12 for an example.

4.2.10 *Use sensible defaults*

Allowing users to configure the plugin to behave the way they want is desirable, and many options may be available to customize all aspects of the plugin. But you don't want to overwhelm the user with choices and force them to provide lots of configuration just to use the plugin in a straightforward application.

All your options should have default values set—values that make sense in the majority of cases. This allows the user to apply the plugin with no options (they're all really optional) and still have it function in a standard manner. They can then enhance the plugin's behavior by overriding options on setup, or at a later stage by changing an option value.

For example, my Datepicker plugin has more than 40 options (not counting localization ones), but none of them have to be changed from their default values for the plugin to function in its basic configuration. Some of the options are shown in the following listing.

Listing 4.4 Options for the Datepicker plugin

```
this._defaults = {
    pickerClass: '', // CSS class to add to this instance of the datepicker
    showOnFocus: true, // True for popup on focus, false for not
    showTrigger: null, // Element to be cloned for a trigger, null for none
    showAnim: 'show', // Name of jQuery animation for popup,
        // '' for no animation
    showOptions: {}, // Options for enhanced animations
    showSpeed: 'normal', // Duration of display/closure
    popupContainer: null, // The element to which a popup calendar
        // is added, null for body
    alignment: 'bottom', // Alignment of popup -
        // with nominated corner of input:
        // 'top' or 'bottom' aligns depending on language direction,
        // 'topLeft', 'topRight', 'bottomLeft', 'bottomRight'
    fixedWeeks: false, // True to always show 6 weeks,
        // false to only show as many as are needed
    firstDay: 0, // First day of the week, 0 = Sunday, 1 = Monday, ...
```

```
...
onDate: null, // Callback as a date is added to the datepicker
onShow: null, // Callback just before a datepicker is shown
onChangeMonthYear: null, // Callback when a new month/year is selected
onSelect: null, // Callback when a date is selected
onClose: null, // Callback when a datepicker is closed
altField: null, // Alternate field to update in synch
    // with the datepicker
altFormat: null, // Date format for alternate field,
    // defaults to dateFormat
constrainInput: true, // True to constrain typed input to
    // dateFormat allowed characters
commandsAsDateFormat: false, // True to apply formatDate
    // to the command texts
commands: this.commands // Command actions that may be added
    // to a layout by name
};
```

Specifying all the possible options and providing default values for them also serves to document the ways in which the plugin can be configured.

Not every plugin can be reduced to requiring no options on initialization. For example, my Countdown plugin isn't particularly useful without a target time to count down to, but there's no one default value that would apply in most cases.

In a similar vein, you should provide default styling for the plugin as an external CSS file, based on the markup and classes you use. These default styles can then be overridden by users, either inline or via their own CSS files.

4.2.11 Allow for localisation/localization

To reach the widest audience for your plugin, you need to consider those parts of the world that don't speak English, or use a different variant of English. Any text values used by the plugin should be grouped together so that they can be easily translated into another language and then applied to your plugin to override its default values.

Localizing content doesn't just apply to text. Don't forget that date, number, and currency formats differ between regions. Such options should also be placed alongside the text options for translation. In addition, several languages read from right to left, and your plugin should cater to this as well. Figure 4.4 shows some localizations for my Datepicker plugin.

Figure 4.4 Datepicker localization: French, Japanese, and Arabic

Some of the differences between these versions, other than the obvious textual changes, are as follows:

- The drop-downs for selecting month and year appear in different orders.
- Each calendar starts on a different day of the week: Monday for French, Sunday for Japanese, and Saturday for Arabic.
- Arabic reads from right to left, but the other two read left to right.

The plugin framework presented in chapter 5 provides mechanisms for localizing your plugin to make it simple for others to provide translations. By following this approach, the Datepicker now has over 70 localizations available, all contributed by members of the jQuery community.

4.2.12   *Style your plugin with CSS*

Provide a CSS file with your plugin to style its appearance, as shown in figure 4.5. As well as being a best practice (separating styling from content), this allows the user to override or customize the plugin's display with minimal effort.

Figure 4.5   Styling the Datepicker plugin with CSS: default, Redmond, and Humanity styles

Add classes to the elements created and maintained by your plugin to enable them to be uniquely identified and styled appropriately. Try to use a common prefix (related to the plugin name) to help distinguish your classes from others that may be on the elements and to reduce the possibility of clashing with existing styles.

For example, the Datepicker has the basic structure and associated classes shown in the next listing. This markup is used in conjunction with the CSS styling from listing 4.6 to achieve the displays shown previously.

Listing 4.5   Datepicker markup structure

```
<div class="datepick" style="width: 218px;">          Overall Datepicker
    <div class="datepick-nav">                        container
        <a class="datepick-cmd datepick-cmd-prev">&lt;Prev</a>
        <a class="datepick-cmd datepick-cmd-today">Today</a>
        <a class="datepick-cmd datepick-cmd-next">Next&gt;</a>
```

Navigation container

Navigation links

```
        </div>
        <div class="datepick-month-row">         ⟵┐  A row of months
            <div class="datepick-month">           ⟵┐  An individual
                ...                                     month
            </div>
        </div>
        ...
</div>
```

Listing 4.6 Datepicker styling

```
.datepick {                        ⟵┐  The Datepicker container
    background-color: #fff;
    color: #000;
    border: 1px solid #444;
    border-radius: 0.25em;
    font-family: Arial,Helvetica,Sans-serif;
    font-size: 90%;
}
.datepick a {
    color: #fff;
    text-decoration: none;
}
.datepick-nav {                    ⟵┐  The navigation container
    float: left;
    width: 100%;
    background-color: #000;
    color: #fff;
    font-size: 90%;
    font-weight: bold;
}
.datepick-cmd {                    ⟵┐  Each navigation link
    width: 30%;
}
.datepick-month-row {              ⟵┐  A row of months
    clear: left;
}
.datepick-month {                  ⟵┐  An individual month
    float: left;
    width: 15em;
    border: 1px solid #444;
    text-align: center;
}
...
```

If you use options for styling purposes and apply them directly to the elements within your plugin, you run the risk of the user being unable to change the look of the components managed by the plugin. Inline CSS styles can only be overridden by external styles if you add the !important imperative, but you should avoid the use of this marker when possible.

Also, many properties are available to style each element, so how do you choose which ones to provide as plugin options? What if the user wants to change some other aspect of the style? They would have to mix plugin options with CSS rules, making it harder to see where the effects originate.

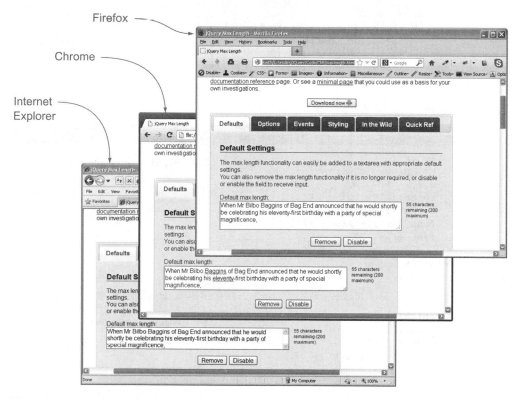

Figure 4.6 Test your plugin in the major browsers to ensure the same appearance and behavior.

4.2.13 *Test on the major browsers*

Once again, to maximize the use of your plugin, it needs to work on all the major browsers, as shown in figure 4.6. The plugin should behave the same way on all platforms and should look much the same as well.

I typically develop in Firefox, and the code then generally works in Chrome and Safari too. Internet Explorer often requires special attention, especially if you want to support its older versions.

4.2.14 *Create a repeatable test case suite*

Use an automated testing tool, such as QUnit, to produce a repeatable set of tests that can be run quickly and easily when making changes. The tests should cover all the options, methods, and functions available within the plugin. But QUnit doesn't test various visual aspects of the plugin, so you still have to fire up a sample page in each of the browsers.

I find that creating a demonstration page for your plugin serves two purposes. First, it shows a prospective user what the plugin can do, and possibly shows them the code that allows them to do it. Second, it provides a visual test bed that lets you see all aspects of the plugin and check its appearance in all the browsers.

Chapter 7 looks at testing plugins in more detail using QUnit.

4.2.15 *Provide demonstrations and documentation*

No matter how great your plugin is, if users don't understand how to apply it or configure it, it's not going to be widely used.

Each plugin should have a demonstration page that shows off most, if not all, of the plugin's abilities, as shown in figure 4.7 for the MaxLength plugin. As an added bonus, you should include the code that you use to achieve the various behaviors so that users can find what they're after and immediately copy the code to apply it in their own pages.

You should also document all of your plugin's abilities. Although there are likely to be comments within the code (at least, there should be), not everyone wants to plow through the script to find out how to use it. Provide a reference page for the plugin that

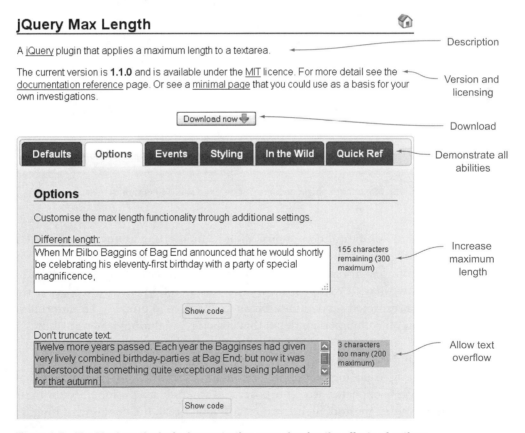

Figure 4.7   The MaxLength plugin demonstration page showing the effects of options

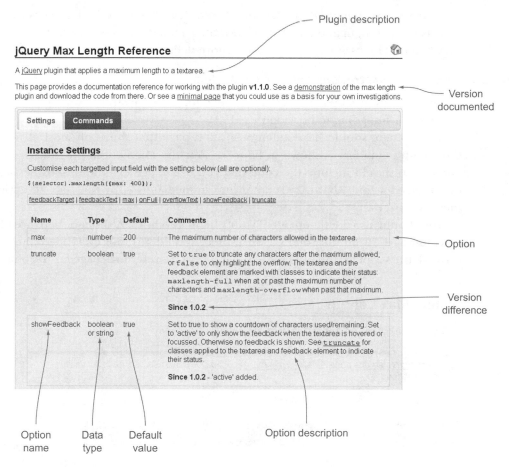

Figure 4.8   The MaxLength plugin documentation page showing option details

lists all of its configuration options, all of its methods, and any other functions that it provides. Figure 4.8 shows some of the documentation for the MaxLength plugin.

Each option should show its name, its expected type or types, its default value so users know what to expect from it, and a description of its purpose. If the option requires a restricted set of values, list and explain each one. If it has internal structure, such as an object map, then detail that structure, including inner attributes and their types and purposes. Provide sample code when the option is more than a simple string, number, or Boolean flag.

Similarly, each method should show its name and any parameters that it uses, along with its expected type, purpose, and whether it's optional. Identify the return value from the method, highlighting those that break the chaining of plugins.

What you need to know

Plan your plugin and its interactions before you start developing.

Where possible, use a plugin to enhance basic functionality.

Prevent name clashes and protect your code through scoping.

Anticipate customizations in your plugin to make it flexible, and then provide sensible default values.

Unit test your plugin to validate its functionality.

Document and demonstrate your plugin to assist in its adoption.

4.3   *Summary*

A jQuery plugin can do just about anything, from making basic class changes and adding event handlers, through defining selectors and providing animations, to generating full-blown graphical widgets with remote access. Choosing what to implement can be a challenge.

Plan your plugin in terms of its appearance and behavior. Look at how it interacts with jQuery, the user, and other elements on the page. Consider how it might be customized by the user. Don't get carried away with making a plugin that loses its focus and saddles the user with code that's rarely used.

To allow your plugin to interact correctly with jQuery and any other JavaScript libraries that may appear on the page, you should follow the established patterns of use and best practices. The principles described here lay out a set of guidelines that encompass best practices, regardless of the type of plugin being created.

In the next chapter and in chapter 8, you'll see how these principles are implemented by using two frameworks for plugin development: my own plugin framework, and the jQuery UI widget framework.

Collection plugins

Now that you've read the theory behind designing and implementing a plugin, you'll see how it's implemented in practice. To make things more concrete, you'll create a relatively simple plugin that provides a useful service, while still being complex enough to show most of the techniques involved in any plugin.

The plugin you'll build complements existing functionality provided by the browser. Normal text input fields have a `maxlength` attribute that allows you to limit how much text may be entered into a field. Such a restriction helps enforce limits that may be imposed by databases and other storage mechanisms. But the multiline `textarea` field has no such attribute and allows unlimited text entry. To address this situation, you can create a collection plugin to control the amount of acceptable text, and provide valuable feedback along the way.

5.1   What are collection plugins?

As you may recall from chapter 3, jQuery usually operates under a select and act pattern. You find the elements of interest, either directly by using selectors and filters, or by traversing the DOM from an existing selection, and then apply some functionality to them. For example, to hide all paragraphs with a class of note, you'd use the following code:

```
$('p.note').hide();
```

These actions are what I call *collection plugins*—they operate on a collection of DOM elements that are wrapped in a jQuery object. The majority of third-party jQuery plugins are of this type.

Collection plugins are defined by extending $.fn with the name of the new plugin and assigning that a function that implements the plugin's purpose. Behind the scenes, $.fn is an alias for $.prototype, the standard JavaScript mechanism for adding properties and methods to all instances of a type of object. Adding a new function to $.fn automatically makes it available to all jQuery objects, such as to the collections of elements found through the jQuery selection processing or a subsequent traversal of the DOM. These functions are invoked within the context of the current jQuery instance and therefore have access to the set of elements that it manages.

5.2   A plugin framework

Although you could develop each plugin on its own, as they each provide specific functionality, it makes sense to reuse code as much as possible, because it interacts with jQuery in much the same way. To this end, I've developed a plugin framework that has served me well in my own plugins. It provides common capabilities on all collection plugins and makes it easy to add extra options and methods. You'll see how the framework implements the guiding principles described in the previous chapter.

5.2.1   The MaxLength plugin

The sample plugin you'll develop provides a maximum length restriction for textarea fields, similar to the built-in maxlength attribute for input fields. It's called as follows, with default settings:

```
$('#text1').maxlength();
```

To customize the plugin, you can provide options to the initialization call:

```
$('#text1').maxlength({max: 400});
```

In addition to limiting the text that can be entered, the plugin provides feedback on how many characters have been used or remain available for input (figure 5.1).

Figure 5.1   The MaxLength plugin in operation

The plugin also allows you to warn users only when they reach the maximum number of characters, without preventing them from entering more. In this way, users know that they have to reduce the text, but they aren't cut off in the middle of a train of thought. Instead they can go back and edit the text themselves to bring it back into line. Different feedback appears when the length is more than the imposed maximum.

Feedback may be suppressed altogether, although it's a better user experience when it's provided, or it can be set to show only when the textarea is active—when hovering over it or when it has focus. And the user may be informed of a textarea reaching (or exceeding) its maximum via a callback event.

The MaxLength plugin follows the principle of *providing progressive enhancements*. It enriches the user experience with regard to entering limited text into a textarea field. Without JavaScript, you can still enter text, and the length restriction will be imposed on the server when the value is submitted (as it should be anyway).

5.2.2   *MaxLength plugin operation*

The plugin consists of an object containing several functions that interact to provide the required functionality, allowing the user to initialize and manage the provided features. The following listing shows the plugin's overall structure and the way that these functions are called during the plugin's lifecycle.

Listing 5.1   Plugin function outline

```
function MaxLength() {
    this._defaults = {...};                              Plugin default options
}

$.extend(MaxLength.prototype, {
    setDefaults: function(options) {...},                Plugin default overrides
    _attachPlugin: function(target, options) {...},      Set/retrieve
    _optionPlugin: function(target, options, value) {...}, options
    _curLengthPlugin: function(target) {...},
    _checkLength: function(target) {...},                Enforce length restrictions
    _enablePlugin: function(target) {...},               Enable element
    _disablePlugin: function(target) {...},              Disable element
    _destroyPlugin: function(target) {...}
});                                                      Remove the
                                                         functionality

$.fn.maxlength = function(options) {...};                jQuery bridge

var plugin = $.maxlength = new MaxLength();              Singleton instance
```

Initialization

Retrieve
current
length

A singleton instance of the plugin object (plugin) is created when you load the plugin code. The user interacts with this object directly via a reference attached to the jQuery object ($.maxlength) or through the bridging function ($.fn.maxlength) that allows the plugin's features to be applied to a collection of elements retrieved by the jQuery selection processing.

A set of plugin-wide default option values appears as the _defaults attribute of the singleton object. You can override these when you call the setDefaults function and supply the new values. The resulting defaults apply to all subsequent applications of the plugin.

You attach the plugin to one or more elements by calling the bridging function on your selection. That function transfers the call through to the _attachPlugin function, which initializes the targeted element(s) before calling _optionPlugin to process the current options (either from the defaults or from overrides in the initialization call) for that instance:

```
$('#text1').maxlength({max: 400});
```

The _optionPlugin function is also called in response to an option method call to update the affected element(s) to reflect the new option values. The current option values and other internal settings are stored against the associated element(s) as data.

```
$('#text1').maxlength('option', 'onFull', alertMe);
```

Ultimately, all paths lead to the _checkLength function (upon initialization or option changes, or when a key is released when the field has focus), which implements the length restriction of this plugin, and can notify the user if the field is full or overflowing.

To prevent access to the field, you can call the disable method, which results in the _disablePlugin function being called. Similarly, the enable method calls the _enablePlugin function to restore field access:

```
$('#text1').maxlength('disable');
```

At any time, you can retrieve the number of currently used and remaining characters by calling the curLength method. The calculated values are returned by the corresponding _curLengthPlugin function:

```
var lengths = $('#text1').maxlength('curLength');
```

If the plugin functionality is no longer required, you can remove it by invoking the destroy method, which in turn calls the _destroyPlugin function. This function undoes all of the setup performed by the initialization and option calls, returning the affected element(s) to their original state:

```
$('#text1').maxlength('destroy');
```

The following sections describe in more detail the operations of these functions and how they interact to provide the MaxLength abilities.

5.3 *Defining your plugin*

You have a few basic steps to take before you can start developing your plugin's specific functionality:

- Claim a name for the plugin.
- Protect your code from the wider JavaScript environment, and vice versa.
- Define a singleton-like object to provide access to common settings and behavior.

5.3.1 *Claiming a namespace*

Every plugin needs a name to identify it and to separate it from other plugins. You should pick a name that reflects the plugin's purpose and that you can use throughout, in keeping with the principle of *only claiming a single name and using that for everything* within jQuery. You might use a slightly different name within your documentation for the plugin, but the two should be closely related.

Note that this name is the access point to your plugin. If you choose the same name as another plugin, the two won't be able to operate together on the same page. Presumably, though, if they have the same name, they're providing similar, if not the same, functionality, so there's less likelihood that they'd both be required together.

For this plugin, you'll use the name `maxlength`, because this is exactly what the plugin provides. It's not too long, and not so short that it loses its meaning. In the documentation, you could refer to the plugin as MaxLength.

In keeping with general jQuery guidelines, the name should be in all lowercase characters. Also, your plugin code should appear within a file named jquery.<plugin-name>.js, with related files being named in the same pattern. For this plugin, the code appears in jquery.maxlength.js, and the associated CSS appears in jquery.maxlength .css.

5.3.2 *Encapsulation*

Two of the guiding principles—*hide the implementation details by using scope,* and *don't rely on $ being the same as jQuery*—can be solved by using some boilerplate code, shown in the following listing. This code serves to protect your plugin's implementation from the rest of the JavaScript environment—known as *encapsulation* in OOP.

Listing 5.2 Encapsulating the plugin code

```
(function($) { // Hide scope, no $ conflict          ◁──❶ Declare anonymous function
    ... the rest of the code appears here
})(jQuery);                                          ◁──❷ Immediately invoke it
```

First, you declare an anonymous function that serves as a new scope ❶—variables and functions defined within this function aren't visible externally. This means you can apply whatever naming convention you wish to your own plugin's internal code without worrying that it'll conflict with external code or another plugin. Anything that you want to be accessible from outside your plugin is made available via the `jQuery` object itself.

Having declared this wrapper function, you surround it with parentheses to ensure that it's available for use, and then immediately call it ❷. The parameter to the function call is the jQuery object. Referring to the function declaration, you see that it takes one parameter, which it calls $. The jQuery object is therefore mapped directly onto the $ parameter, and the latter may be used within the body of the function knowing that it'll always refer to jQuery and not be usurped by some other JavaScript library.

> **NOTE** You've probably seen that most jQuery code is wrapped in a $(document).ready(function() {...}) callback, or its shorthand form $(function() {...}). This is to ensure that the code isn't executed until the DOM is available for use. You do *not* wrap your plugin code in the same structure. This is because you want it to execute immediately when it's loaded and to be subsequently available when you run a normal jQuery initialization. If you do need to set up something within the DOM as part of your plugin, it should be deferred until it's needed—usually when your plugin is applied to a set of elements—or it can be wrapped in its own document.ready callback from within the plugin.

5.3.3 Using a singleton

To simplify interactions with the plugin, and to act as a central repository of information and behavior, I use aspects of the singleton pattern, where a single instance of an object has a global access point. In addition to defining the abilities of the object, via its internal functions, it contains constants and values that apply across all applications of the plugin to elements on the page. The following listing shows the definition of this singleton object.

Listing 5.3 Defining a singleton manager for the plugin

```
/* Max length manager. */
function MaxLength() {                                        ⟵ Declare
    this.regional = []; // Available regional settings,       ❶ JavaScript class
        // indexed by language code
    this.regional[''] = { // Default regional settings
        feedbackText: '{r} characters remaining ({m} maximum)',
        ... Other regional settings
    };
    this._defaults = {                          ⟵ Declare options and
        max: 200, // Maximum length             ❸ their default values
        ... Other default settings
    };
    $.extend(this._defaults, this.regional['']);   ⟵ Combine default region
}                                                  ❹ with default values

$.extend(MaxLength.prototype, {      ⟵ Define other constants
    ...                              ❺ and functions
});

/* Initialise the max length functionality. */
var plugin = $.maxlength = new MaxLength(); // Singleton instance
```

Create localizations array ❷ (pointing to `this.regional = [];`)

Create a singleton instance ❻ (pointing to the last line)

A class-like definition is declared in JavaScript as a function ❶. The name of this function isn't visible externally due to your use of the new scope from the previous section, so it doesn't have to be the single name you picked for the plugin. In fact, it may be more clear for your code if the name is different.

That function may have its own set of internal fields and subfunctions declared to define its state and behavior. The `this` variable refers to the current instance of that "class." Most importantly, the plugin defines a set of default options that control its behavior ❸. Ideally, these options provide the entire configuration necessary to allow the plugin to be applied to an element and have it work in a default manner. Your users may override any of these options when they initialize the plugin on their own elements.

To allow the options to be easily localized for other languages and cultures, an array of localizations is defined ❷ and is initialized with the default (English) settings. These are added to the other default settings once the latter have been defined ❹. As other localizations are provided, they can be applied as follows:

```
$('#text1').maxlength($.maxlength.regional['fr']);
```

You'll see more about localizing the plugin in section 5.5.2.

Additional constants and internal functions are defined by extending the function `prototype` ❺. These functions implement the abilities of the plugin. Several are common across all plugins, and the rest are specific to the current functionality.

Finally, to make the singleton available to external code, you create the one instance of it and assign it to an attribute of the `jQuery` object (as aliased by $) ❻, following the *place everything under the jQuery object* principle. Note that you use the single name selected for your plugin for this purpose. You also create a local variable, `plugin`, to reference the plugin for use within this module, making it easier to reuse the framework code in other plugins.

Using this technique makes it easy to reference plugin constants, variables, and functions even in callback functions that may have a different context. You'll see how to use this in later sections.

5.4   *Attaching to an element*

To apply the plugin functionality to elements on the page, you need to define the function that allows jQuery to invoke your code. All plugins that operate on collections of elements must extend `$.fn` in a fairly straightforward manner. But the situation becomes more complex when you also need to process methods and getter functions.

To this end, you'll see how to

- Attach the plugin to one or more elements in its simplest form
- Initialize the plugin as part of the attachment process
- Handle method names passed to the plugin for additional functionality
- Return requested values from the plugin

We'll start with the basics.

5.4.1 Basic attachment

jQuery provides an extension point for collection plugins, allowing them to be easily applied to groups of elements resulting from a selection and/or traversal process. Use this extension point to integrate your own plugin into the procedure, as follows.

Listing 5.4   Applying the plugin to an element

```
/* Attach the max length functionality to a jQuery selection.
   @param  options  (object) the new settings to use for these
                    instances (optional)
   @return (jQuery) for chaining further calls */          ❶ Declare main
$.fn.maxlength = function(options) {                           plugin function
   return this.each(function() {
      plugin._attachPlugin(this, options || {});                ❸ Initialize each
   });                                                              element
};
```

Chain jQuery calls ❷

Extend `$.fn` to define the function named for your plugin ❶. The function accepts one parameter, which contains any overrides to the default option values that control the behavior of the plugin. If omitted, all the default option values apply. Because the jQuery object (aliased by `$`) is globally available, you're able to access your plugin through it following this definition. Because you're extending `$.fn`, jQuery knows that your plugin applies to collections of elements and will pass that collection to your function when it's invoked as the contents of the `this` variable.

> **NOTE**   The `this` variable refers to the collection of elements resulting from the selection/traversal process. It's a jQuery object already and should *not* be wrapped in another jQuery call before accessing it.

To retain one of the key features of jQuery, and to follow another of the principles— *return the jQuery object for chaining whenever possible*—you should always return the `this` variable from your function ❷. Following this pattern allows chained calls on the selected objects and is expected by the users of your plugin. Here's an example:

```
$('#text1').maxlength().change(function() {...});
```

Because you generally want to process every element within the collection, the standard pattern is to invoke the `each` function and handle the elements individually. The result of the `each` call is the original collection, so it can be returned directly as the result of your own plugin function for chaining purposes.

Finally, you call a function within the plugin singleton object (`plugin`) to apply the functionality specific to your plugin—the `_attachPlugin` function ❸. You pass as parameters the current element under consideration (`this`) and the `options` provided to customize the plugin behavior. Because the `options` aren't required, they may be undefined. To simplify subsequent code, you ensure that the value is set to an empty object if currently undefined using the `options || {}` construct. Effectively this code evaluates the first expression (`options`) and returns that if it's "true" (not `undefined`, blank, zero, or `false`). Otherwise it evaluates the second half of the expression and returns a new empty object.

5.4.2 *Plugin initialization*

The _attachPlugin function initializes your plugin for a particular element on the page, as seen in listing 5.5. That element is passed as the first parameter to the function, and any options for configuring the plugin arrive as the second parameter. Here you add one-off functionality that manages the state of the plugin for this element and performs processing that doesn't depend on option values.

> **Listing 5.5   Initializing the plugin for an element**

```
/* Attach the max length functionality to a textarea.
   @param  target   (element) the control to affect
   @param  options  (object) the custom options for this instance */
_attachPlugin: function(target, options) {
    target = $(target);
    if (target.hasClass(this.markerClassName)) {          ❶ Don't reinitialize plugin
        return;
    }
    var inst = {options: $.extend({}, this._defaults),    ❷ Create instance settings
        feedbackTarget: $([])};
    target.addClass(this.markerClassName).               ❸ Add marker class
        data(this.propertyName, inst).
        bind('keypress.maxlength', function(event) {      ❺ Bind any event handlers
            if (!inst.options.truncate) {
                return true;
            }
            var ch = String.fromCharCode(
                event.charCode == undefined ?
                    event.keyCode : event.charCode);
            return (event.ctrlKey || event.metaKey || ch == '\u0000' ||
                $(this).val().length < inst.options.max);
        }).
        bind('keyup.maxlength', function() {
            plugin._checkLength($(this));
        });
    this._optionPlugin(target, options);                 ❻ Update the element with new options
},
```

(Attach instance settings to element ❹)

First, you test whether the given element has already been initialized under this plugin ❶ and perform no further actions if it has. Elements should only be initialized once, as you don't want multiple event handlers tied to them or other one-off processing applied more than once. You check for a particular class on the element to determine its current status with regard to this plugin. That class is assigned as one of the first steps in the initialization process ❸.

To keep track of the state of the plugin for this element, you create an instance object ❷ that stores values specific to that element, including any options or settings supplied by the user. The settings are created from an empty object, {}, which is extended by the default settings. If you were to use the _defaults object directly, any changes would be applied to that object and would then interfere with subsequent use of the plugin. User settings are applied in the _optionPlugin function ❻ that processes changes to options.

The instance data is stored against the element using the data function ❹ (in keeping with the principle of *using the data function to store instance details*). A constant name defined within this module—once more with a value of maxlength—allows easy and consistent access to data throughout the plugin. Therefore, the state of the plugin can be retrieved for any particular element and used within other functions in the plugin. The instance data is automatically cleared if the element is removed from the DOM.

Other functionality that doesn't depend on option values is also applied as part of the attachment process. In this case, you add event handlers that monitor the keypress and keyup events of the targeted textarea ❺ so that you can check the number of characters as soon as it changes. When creating event handlers within your plugin, you should always add a namespace to the event name (maxlength in this case). By doing so, you can easily remove the handlers added by your plugin without affecting any other event handlers that may have been added externally.

Finally, you invoke the _optionPlugin function to apply any option customizations to the plugin ❻. This function is covered in section 5.5.3.

5.4.3 Invoking methods

In section 5.4.1 you saw how to initialize the plugin for a collection of DOM elements. But in keeping with the principles of *claiming a single name* for the plugin and consequently *invoking methods for additional functionality*, you need to cater for these other situations. A string value may be passed to the plugin function to indicate what extra abilities are required from the plugin. Common examples include enabling or disabling the controls, or changing or retrieving option values. In the latter case you need to send extra values along with the call to identify which option is changing and its new value.

Most of this code, seen in the following listing, is boilerplate and is applicable to all collection plugins.

Listing 5.6 Invoking methods from the plugin

```
/* Attach the max length functionality to a jQuery selection.
   @param  options  (object) the new settings to use for these
                     instances (optional) or
                     (string) the method to run (optional)
   @return  (jQuery) for chaining further */
$.fn.maxlength = function(options) {                          ❶ Extract secondary parameters
    var otherArgs = Array.prototype.slice.call(arguments, 1);
    return this.each(function() {
        if (typeof options == 'string') {       ❷ Is this a method call?
            if (!plugin['_' + options + 'Plugin']) {    ❸ Check that method exists
                throw 'Unknown method: ' + options;     ❹ Throw an error if not
            }
            plugin['_' + options + 'Plugin'].           ❺ Invoke the method
                apply(plugin, [this].concat(otherArgs));
        }
        else {
            plugin._attachPlugin(this, options || {});
        }
    });
};
```

Because the number of parameters to the plugin function is unknown and depends on the particular method being invoked, you use the standard JavaScript `arguments` variable to access any after the first one. The `slice` function of the `Array` class extracts items from an array, which is what `arguments` is, and copies them to another variable ❶. `otherArgs` ends up being an array of all the parameters to `maxlength` after the first one, which is assumed to be a method name.

As before, you step through each element in the collection and process them individually. You now check the type of `options` to determine whether it's a method ❷. For a normal initialization call, `options` would be undefined or an object containing option overrides. If the type is a string, you're handling a method.

To avoid unpredictable errors, you check whether the given method can be executed. The convention for mapping methods to functions is to prefix the method name with an underscore (_) and suffix it with a standard name (`Plugin`) ❸. If such a function doesn't exist, an exception is thrown ❹. For example, the `option` method maps onto the `_optionPlugin` function.

> **NOTE** My convention is to use a leading underscore (_) to indicate functions that are supposed to be private to the singleton object, although JavaScript doesn't enforce this. Functions that are designed to be invoked directly don't have this underscore in their name. To further distinguish internal functions that act as method implementations from those that are purely for internal use, I append a standard name to the former. So, the function `setDefaults` is intended to be called directly, whereas `_curLengthPlugin` is intended to be invoked as method `curLength` and `_checkLength` is only used internally.

Otherwise the method function is invoked using the standard JavaScript `apply` function to ensure that the context for the call is the singleton object (first parameter) ❺. Any additional parameters sent to the plugin function, and now held in the `otherArgs` variable, are concatenated with the current element being processed to become the full set of parameters for that method.

You'll see the implementation of the methods themselves in later sections. Now that you can handle executing methods passed to the plugin, you also need to deal with those that return values from the plugin, as shown in the next section.

5.4.4   *Getter methods*

Although most methods invoke some extra activity on the specified elements, some are designed to return values, such as the current character count and number of characters remaining for this plugin. By necessity, these methods break the chaining pattern of jQuery—the ability to apply multiple actions to the same selection—because they return values other than the current collection of elements.

The following listing shows the getter invocation code, most of which is reusable in all collection plugins.

Listing 5.7 Applying the plugin to an element

```
// The list of methods that return values and don't permit chaining
var getters = ['curLength'];                                          ❶ List getter methods

/* Determine whether a method is a getter and doesn't permit chaining.
   @param  method     (string, optional) the method to run
   @param  otherArgs  ([], optional) any other arguments for the method
   @return  true if the method is a getter, false if not */
function isNotChained(method, otherArgs) {
    if (method == 'option' && (otherArgs.length ==0 ||            ❷ Test for getter methods
            (otherArgs.length == 1 && typeof otherArgs[0] == 'string'))) {
        return true;
    }
    return $.inArray(method, getters) > -1;
}


/* Attach the max length functionality to a jQuery selection.
   @param  options  (object) the new settings to use for these
                    instances (optional) or
                    (string) the method to run (optional)
   @return  (jQuery) for chaining further calls or
            (any) getter value */
$.fn.maxlength = function(options) {
    var otherArgs = Array.prototype.slice.call(arguments, 1);     ❸ If this method
    if (isNotChained(options, otherArgs)) {                          is a getter...
        return plugin['_' + options + 'Plugin'].
            apply(plugin, [this[0]].concat(otherArgs));          ❹ ...return the method's
    }                                                               value directly
    return this.each(function() {
        if (typeof options == 'string') {
            if (!plugin['_' + options + 'Plugin']) {
                throw 'Unknown method: ' + options;
            }
            plugin['_' + options + 'Plugin'].
                apply(plugin, [this].concat(otherArgs));
        }
        else {
            plugin._attachPlugin(this, options || {});
        }
    });
};
```

You need to provide a list of the methods that are getters ❶ because they can't otherwise be identified. These methods are treated differently from other ones to return their value.

Because the `option` method has multiple functionality—for either setting or retrieving an option value—it must be identified as a special case. The `isNotChained` function ❷ caters for this special method (based on the number of parameters supplied) and then checks in the list of getters defined previously, returning `true` for a getter method.

Any method identified as being a getter ❸ is then invoked immediately, with its value being returned directly as the result of the plugin function ❹. As with other methods, you use the `apply` function to call the method function with the singleton object as the context and pass along the first element in the collection and any additional parameters (from `otherArgs`). You send only the first element because you can return only one value; this pattern follows the standard practice of the jQuery getters, such as `attr`, `css`, and `val`.

You'd call this method as follows:

```
var counts = $('#text1').maxlength('curLength');
```

You'll see the code for the `_curLengthPlugin` function in section 5.7.1.

5.5   Setting options

Options allow you to configure the plugin to change its behavior. Among the guiding principles are *anticipating customizations* and *using sensible defaults.* Users will always want to customize the way a plugin works or appears, in order to fit it in with their own requirements. If you can predict what they might want to change and provide options to cater for that, they're more likely to use your plugin. But you want the plugin to be easy to use with a minimum of configuration, so all options should have default values that allow it to be used in the most common way.

To achieve these goals,

- Define defaults values for all options.
- Allow the plugin to be easily localized by separating out the applicable options.
- Handle retrieving and setting option values.
- Apply any option changes immediately.
- Allow the plugin to be enabled or disabled.

We'll look at each of these in turn.

5.5.1   Plugin defaults

You've already seen the placement of the default option values in the singleton object. These values may be overridden by the user when they initialize the plugin on their own elements. The `regional` settings are for localization purposes and are described in greater detail in the next section. The following listing shows all the options for the MaxLength plugin.

Listing 5.8   Default options for the plugin

```
/* Max length manager. */
function MaxLength() {
    this.regional = []; // Available regional settings,
        // indexed by language code
    this.regional[''] = { // Default regional settings
        feedbackText: '{r} characters remaining ({m} maximum)',
            // Display text for feedback message,
```

```
            // use {r} for remaining characters,
            // {c} for characters entered, {m} for maximum
        overflowText: '{o} characters too many ({m} maximum)'
            // Display text when past maximum,
            // use substitutions above and {o} for characters past maximum
    };
    this._defaults = {
        max: 200, // Maximum length
        truncate: true, // True to disallow further input,
            // false to highlight only
        showFeedback: true, // True to always show user feedback,
            // 'active' for hover/focus only
        feedbackTarget: null, // jQuery selector or function for
            // element to fill with feedback
        onFull: null // Callback when full or overflowing,
            // receives one parameter: true if overflowing, false if not
    };
    $.extend(this._defaults, this.regional['']);
}
```

To allow global changes to be made to the settings for all instances of your plugin, you define a `setDefaults` function on the singleton object, as shown in listing 5.9. The options provided to this function as a parameter extend the list of default options and are then applied to any new instantiations of the plugin, as seen in section 5.4.2. The function returns a reference to the singleton object, which is somewhat useless because other global functions aren't available on it, but it follows the chaining principle of jQuery and it doesn't hurt.

Listing 5.9 Overriding global default values

```
/* Override the default settings for all max length instances.
   @param  options  (object) the new settings to use as defaults
   @return  (MaxLength) this object */
setDefaults: function(options) {
    $.extend(this._defaults, options || {});
    return this;
},
```

You'd call this function as follows, prior to invoking the plugin on any elements:

```
$.maxlength.setDefaults({max: 300, truncate: false});
```

5.5.2 *Localisations/localizations*

To make your plugin available to widest audience, you must take into account differences due to users' locale (the *allow for localisation/localization* principle). The obvious difference here is language—not everyone speaks English—but it also extends to date, number, and currency formats, and even whether the page reads from left to right or from right to left. You can make the localization process much easier for users of your plugin by grouping options affected by locale.

Within the singleton, you define an array of localizations that's indexed by the desired language (and optional region). The default language (English) is accessed by a blank string, and these settings are automatically added to the defaults for the plugin.

Users who wish to create a localization for your plugin then need to define a new set of values for the options in the `regional` settings, make it available in the `regional` array, and add it to the defaults for all instances of the plugin.

For example, the French localization for this plugin is shown in the following listing. The localization should appear in a file named for the plugin, but with a language extension—jquery.maxlength-fr.js in this case.

Listing 5.10   French localization for the MaxLength plugin

```
/* http://keith-wood.name/maxlength.html
   French initialisation for the jQuery Max Length extension        ❶ Encapsulate
   Written by Keith Wood (kbwood{at}iinet.com.au) April 2012. */       internal code
(function($) { // hide the namespace                            ◁┘

$.maxlength.regional['fr'] = {                                  ◁┐  Declare
    feedbackText: '{r} de caractères restants ({m} maximum)',      │  localization
    overflowText: '{o} de caractères trop ({m} maximum)'        ❷  values
};
$.maxlength.setDefaults($.maxlength.regional['fr']);            ◁┐  Apply as defaults
                                                                ❸  for all instances
})(jQuery);
```

As for the main plugin, you create a new scope for the localization to ensure that `$` is the same as `jQuery` and to hide any implementation details ❶. Then create the new entry in the plugin `regional` array, indexed by the language code ❷. By overriding the plugin default settings with the new localized settings, you simplify the use of the localization ❸. The user only needs to include the plugin code, followed by the localization, and then use the plugin in its default mode to have the desired language appear, as shown in figure 5.2. Listing 5.11 shows how to load and use the French localization.

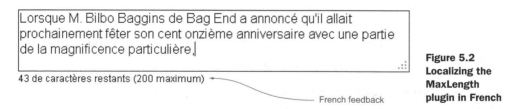

Lorsque M. Bilbo Baggins de Bag End a annoncé qu'il allait prochainement fêter son cent onzième anniversaire avec une partie de la magnificence particulière.

43 de caractères restants (200 maximum) ◀── French feedback

**Figure 5.2
Localizing the
MaxLength
plugin in French**

Listing 5.11   Loading a localization

```html
<script type="text/javascript" src="js/jquery.maxlength.js"></script>
<script type="text/javascript" src="js/jquery.maxlength-fr.js"></script>
<script type="text/javascript">
$(function() {
    $('#text1').maxlength(); // Automatically in French
});
</script>
```

If you want to use a particular localization after loading one or more others, refer to the plugin's `regional` array and use that as your new option:

```
$('#text').maxlength($.maxlength.regional['fr']);
```

Or it can be combined with other settings:

```
$('#text').maxlength($.extend({max: 400}, $.maxlength.regional['fr']));
```

5.5.3 *Reacting to option changes*

Recall that you want to *anticipate customizations* to allow the widest use of your plugin with minimal effort for the user. Options may be set on the plugin during initialization and may also be changed throughout the plugin's lifetime. These options may affect the appearance and/or behavior of the plugin and so need to be immediately applied. You might also want to retrieve the value of one or more options from the plugin. All of these abilities are provided by the `option` method.

In retrieval mode, the `option` method lets you specify the name of an option and returns its current value (taking default values into account). If you don't provide a name, the entire set of options is returned.

```
var maxChars = $('#text1').maxlength('option', 'max');
var options = $('#text1').maxlength('option');
```

In setter mode, the `option` method can change a single named value or multiple options from a given map.

```
$('#text1').maxlength('option', 'max', 400);
$('#text1').maxlength('option', {max: 400, truncate: false});
```

The particular mode of operation is determined by the number and type of parameters supplied in the call, as seen next.

Listing 5.12   Reading and writing option values

```
/* Retrieve or reconfigure the settings for a control.
   @param  target   (element) the control to affect
   @param  options  (object) the new options for this instance or
                     (string) an individual property name
   @param  value    (any) the individual property value
                     (omit if options is an object or
                     to retrieve the value of a setting)
   @return (any) if retrieving a value */
_optionPlugin: function(target, options, value) {          ← ❶ Define option
    target = $(target);                                          function
    var inst = target.data(this.propertyName);
    if (!options || (typeof options == 'string' && value == null)) {  ←┐
      // Get option                                        Retrieve current
      var name = options;                                  instance settings ❷
      options = (inst || {}).options;
      return (options && name ? options[name] : options);
    }
```

❸ Retrieving an option value

```
    if (!target.hasClass(this.markerClassName)) {        ◁─┐    Check that plugin
        return;                                            ④    has been initialized
    }
    options = options || {};
    if (typeof options == 'string') {                    ◁─┐    Handle single
        var name = options;                                ⑤    named option
        options = {};
        options[name] = value;
    }
    $.extend(inst.options, options);                     ◁─┐    Update with
    // Plugin specific code to implement these options ...  ⑥    new options
},
```

First you define a function to respond to the `option` method call ❶. The function name follows the pattern established in section 5.4.3, where method calls are automatically mapped onto functions with a name consisting of an underscore (_), followed by the method name, and the text `Plugin`.

Within this function, you retrieve the current instance settings for the target control (a `textarea`) ❷. Then check whether the user has requested the retrieval of one or more option values ❸—in which case no name nor any options are supplied, or only a name is given. Return either all of the instance's options or the value of the single named one.

Otherwise the `option` method is being used in setter mode. As with other functions, check that the plugin has been initialized for this `textarea` ❹ and exit if it hasn't initialized. If the call is to set a single named option ❺, you convert that one option into a map so that the remaining processing can proceed without duplication.

Save the new options against the current instance ❻. Because these options may affect the appearance or behavior of the plugin, the changes need to be applied to the target element immediately.

The code presented here applies to all collection plugins that need to maintain some state for the affected elements. When changing the value of one or more options, you then need to apply those to the current element, which is specific to the functionality that the plugin offers. The details for the MaxLength plugin are discussed in the next section.

5.5.4   *Implementing MaxLength options*

Options supplied for the MaxLength plugin change its appearance and/or behavior. As these values are updated, they need to be reapplied to the affected elements, removing previous applications if necessary. The code specific to this plugin, as shown in listing 5.13, appears at the end of the `_optionPlugin` function from section 5.5.3, after the standard option processing has completed.

Listing 5.13   Handling specific MaxLength options

```
if (inst.feedbackTarget.length > 0) {                    ◁─┐    Remove previous
    // Remove old feedback element                         ❶    feedback
    if (inst.hadFeedbackTarget) {
        inst.feedbackTarget.empty().val('').
```

```
                    removeClass(this._feedbackClass + ' ' +
                        this._fullClass + ' ' + this._overflowClass);
        }
        else {
            inst.feedbackTarget.remove();
        }
        inst.feedbackTarget = $([]);
    }
    if (inst.options.showFeedback) {
        // Add new feedback element
        inst.hadFeedbackTarget = !!inst.options.feedbackTarget;
        if ($.isFunction(inst.options.feedbackTarget)) {
            inst.feedbackTarget =
                inst.options.feedbackTarget.apply(target[0], []);
        }
        else if (inst.options.feedbackTarget) {
            inst.feedbackTarget = $(inst.options.feedbackTarget);
        }
        else {
            inst.feedbackTarget = $('<span></span>').insertAfter(target);
        }
        inst.feedbackTarget.addClass(this._feedbackClass);
    }
    target.unbind('mouseover.maxlength focus.maxlength ' +
        'mouseout.maxlength blur.maxlength');
    if (inst.options.showFeedback == 'active') {
        // Additional event handlers
        target.bind('mouseover.maxlength', function() {
                inst.feedbackTarget.css('visibility', 'visible');
            }).bind('mouseout.maxlength', function() {
                if (!inst.focussed) {
                    inst.feedbackTarget.css('visibility', 'hidden');
                }
            }).bind('focus.maxlength', function() {
                inst.focussed = true;
                inst.feedbackTarget.css('visibility', 'visible');
            }).bind('blur.maxlength', function() {
                inst.focussed = false;
                inst.feedbackTarget.css('visibility', 'hidden');
            });
        inst.feedbackTarget.css('visibility', 'hidden');
    }
    this._checkLength(target);
```

❷ Add new feedback abilities

❸ Handle feedback only when active

❹ Rerun the length check

The MaxLength plugin allows feedback to be shown in either an element managed by the plugin or in an existing element. In the event that feedback isn't required any longer, or has changed from internal to external, you'd initially undo/remove any previous feedback usage ❶. Then, taking the new options into account, you'd set up the appropriate feedback element as requested ❷.

NOTE The !! construct is explained in section 3.2.1.

Similarly, you remove any previous events that dealt with only showing the feedback when the textarea is active and add that functionality back in if it's still required ❸.

5.6.2 *Triggering an event handler*

The event handler is triggered at the end of the _checkLength function in the MaxLength plugin, once you've applied the maximum length restriction, as shown in the following listing. In other plugins you'd trigger events at other appropriate points in the code.

Listing 5.16 Triggering an event callback

```
/* Check the length of the text and notify accordingly.
   @param  target  (jQuery) the control to check */
_checkLength: function(target) {
    var inst = target.data(this.propertyName);          Test trigger and  ❶
    var value = target.val();                           callback option
    var len = value.replace(/\r\n/g, '~~').replace(/\n/g, '~~').length;
    ...
    if (len >= inst.options.max && $.isFunction(inst.options.onFull)) {   ◁┘
        inst.options.onFull.apply(target, [len > inst.options.max]);     ◁┐
    }
},                                                      Invoke callback  ❷
```

You check that the triggering condition is true and that the callback option refers to a function ❶, before calling that function appropriately ❷. The standard JavaScript apply function lets you set the context of the function call as well as provide any parameters for that call. Its first parameter is assigned to the this variable within the callback function.

5.7   Adding methods

Other functionality within the plugin is implemented as custom methods. Because of the framework, all you need to do is to name a function in a particular way to connect it to a method request from the user. If the method returns some value other than the current jQuery collection, it should also be registered in the getters array, as shown in section 5.4.4.

5.7.1 *Getting the current length*

The MaxLength plugin allows the user to retrieve the current character counts for a particular instance. Using the curLength method, shown in the next listing, you obtain an object with the attributes used, indicating the number of characters entered, and remaining, to hold the number of characters still allowed. Note that used may be greater than the max setting and remaining will be negative, if the text-area is allowed to overflow the imposed limit.

Listing 5.17 Retrieving the current length

```
/* Retrieve the counts of characters used and remaining.
   @param  target  (jQuery) the control to check
   @return  (object) the current counts with attributes
            used and remaining */                       ❶ Function for method
_curLengthPlugin: function(target) {                    curLength  ◁┘
```

```
    var inst = target.data(this.propertyName);
    var value = target.val();
    var len = value.replace(/\r\n/g, '~~').replace(/\n/g, '~~').length;
    return {used: len, remaining: inst.options.max - len};        ◁────  Return current
},                                                                        ❷ lengths
```

Follow the naming convention for method functions ❶: an underscore (_), followed
by the method name, and the text `Plugin` to link this function with the calling mechanisms shown in section 5.4.4. Return the appropriate value for the given element ❷,
which is then passed directly back to the user.

5.8 Removing the plugin

Your plugin enhances the elements found on the page by adding functionality to
them, and therefore enriches the user's experience. But sometimes you may want to
remove all that extra capability and return the elements to their original states. The
`destroy` method indicates to the plugin that it should remove all traces of itself.

5.8.1 The destroy method

The `_destroyPlugin` function, shown in the following listing, provides the implementation of the `destroy` method. As with other methods, it's invoked via the main plugin
function, which we covered in section 5.4.3, and receives a reference to the affected
`textarea` as its only parameter.

Listing 5.18 Removing the plugin functionality

```
/* Remove the plugin functionality from a control.
   @param  target  (element) the control to affect */      ❶ Define destroy
_destroyPlugin: function(target) {                            function
    target = $(target);
    if (!target.hasClass(this.markerClassName)) {          ◁──
        return;                                               ❷ Check that plugin
    }                                                          has been initialized
    var inst = target.data(this.propertyName);
    if (inst.feedbackTarget.length > 0) {                  ◁──
        if (inst.hadFeedbackTarget) {                        ❸ Remove any
            inst.feedbackTarget.empty().val('').               feedback controls
                css('visibility', 'visible').
                removeClass(this._feedbackClass + ' ' +
                    this._fullClass + ' ' + this._overflowClass);
        }
        else {
            inst.feedbackTarget.remove();
        }
    }                                                      ❹ Remove plugin
    target.removeClass(this.markerClassName + ' ' +          functionality
            this._fullClass + ' ' + this._overflowClass).
        removeData(this.propertyName).
        unbind('.maxlength');
}
```

As in other functions, you name the function so that it can be processed from the `destroy` method call ❶. Next, you check that the `textarea` has been initialized with this plugin, and exit without any action if that isn't the case ❷. Otherwise you have to undo everything that was done in the `_attachPlugin` and `_optionPlugin` functions.

You start by checking for a feedback element and restore that to its original state (if provided as an option) or remove it altogether (if created by this plugin) ❸. Then remove any marker classes on the `textarea`, remove the instance data attached to it, and remove any event handlers attached to it ❹. By using a namespace when initially binding the event handlers, it's easy to remove them all by referring to that namespace. Any other event handlers connected to the `textarea` are unaffected.

Your page has now been returned to its initial state, and the MaxLength functionality no longer applies.

5.9   *Finishing touches*

The framework portion of the plugin is now complete. Most of that framework code can be reused in other plugins to provide the basic functionality expected of a collection plugin. But you can apply a couple of finishing touches to improve this plugin:

- Implementing the main purpose of the plugin
- Styling it to define its appearance

5.9.1   *The plugin body*

The purpose of the MaxLength plugin is to restrict the amount of text that may be entered into a `textarea`. Previous sections have shown how to implement the main plugin function that integrates with jQuery and have that farm out specific methods to their corresponding internal functions. When initializing the plugin or when changing its options, the path eventually leads to the `_checkLength` function, which does the work. The next listing shows how it works.

Listing 5.19   Restricting the `textarea` length

```
/* Check the length of the text and notify accordingly.
   @param  target  (jQuery) the control to check */
_checkLength: function(target) {                                    Normalize ❶
    var inst = target.data(this.propertyName);                      line endings
    var value = target.val();
    var len = value.replace(/\r\n/g, '~~').replace(/\n/g, '~~').length;   ◁──┘
    target.toggleClass(this._fullClass, len >= inst.options.max).
        toggleClass(this._overflowClass, len > inst.options.max);
    if (len > inst.options.max && inst.options.truncate) {          ◁──┐ Apply text
        // Truncation                                               ❸ truncation
        var lines = target.val().split(/\r\n|\n/);
        value = '';
        var i = 0;
        while (value.length < inst.options.max && i < lines.length) {
            value += lines[i].substring(
                0, inst.options.max - value.length) + '\r\n';
            i++;
```

❷ Set current state on textarea

```
        }
        target.val(value.substring(0, inst.options.max));
        // Scroll to bottom
        target[0].scrollTop = target[0].scrollHeight;
        len = inst.options.max;
    }
    inst.feedbackTarget.
        toggleClass(this._fullClass, len >= inst.options.max).
        toggleClass(this._overflowClass, len > inst.options.max);
    var feedback = (len > inst.options.max ? // Feedback
        inst.options.overflowText : inst.options.feedbackText).
            replace(/\{c\}/, len).
            replace(/\{m\}/, inst.options.max).
            replace(/\{r\}/, inst.options.max - len).
            replace(/\{o\}/, len - inst.options.max);
    try {
        inst.feedbackTarget.text(feedback);
    }
    catch(e) {
        // Ignore
    }
    try {
        inst.feedbackTarget.val(feedback);
    }
    catch(e) {
        // Ignore
    }
    if (len >= inst.options.max && $.isFunction(inst.options.onFull)) {
        inst.options.onFull.apply(target, [len > inst.options.max]);
    }
},
```

4 Set current state on feedback

Populate and show feedback **5** message

Invoke **6** callback when appropriate

After retrieving the instance details for this textarea, you determine the current length of its text content, taking into account browser differences regarding line-ending characters **1**. Based on that value and the options set for the plugin, you apply one or two classes to the textarea to indicate its current status—full or overflowing **2**.

If the text length is greater than the maximum specified and the user has requested that extra text be truncated **3**, then you compute the shortened value, once more normalizing line endings. When the text is assigned back into the textarea, it automatically scrolls back to the top. Assuming that most text entry happens at the end of the content, you move back to the bottom to assist the user. Because you've truncated the text, the calculated length must change to reflect that.

Now you apply one or two classes to the feedback control **4**, based on the new length of the text. As the length may have been reduced in the previous processing, there might appear to be a disjoint between the textarea and its feedback when truncation occurs. This is intentional, as the feedback has to represent the updated status, whereas the textarea can show that additional text entry was attempted but failed.

The status of the textarea is shown in any feedback control, using one of two messages determined by the overflow state of the plugin **5**. To allow for maximum flexibility, you let the feedback control be a div, span, paragraph, or an input field. But these elements have their text set differently, and invoking the wrong one can generate errors in some browsers. Hence, the two `try/catch` statements push the status into the specified control in a protected manner.

Lastly, you notify the user via any `onFull` callback when the `textarea` has filled or overflowed ❻. Section 5.6.2 provides greater detail on this subject.

5.9.2   *Styling the plugin*

With the plugin code complete, you have a fully functioning addition to jQuery's abilities. But it may not look nice. You should provide an external CSS file to accompany your plugin and set its appearance, in keeping with the principle of *styling your plugin with CSS*. The file is named the same as the plugin code, but with a different extension—jquery.maxlength.css in this case. By using CSS rather than passing in options to the plugin that are then applied to its components, you allow the user to override or customize the plugin's appearance with minimal effort.

The following listing shows the CSS for the MaxLength plugin. It uses the classes associated with the elements created and managed by the plugin to apply the appropriate styles. For example, the error conditions denoted by the `maxlength-full` and `maxlength-overflow` classes are highlighted by changing the field's background color.

> **Listing 5.20   Styles for the MaxLength plugin**

```css
/* Styles for Max Length plugin v2.0.0 */
.maxlength-feedback {
    margin-left: 0.5em;
    font-size: 75%;
}
.maxlength-full {
    background-color: #fee;
}
.maxlength-overflow {
    background-color: #fcc;
}
.maxlength-disabled {
    opacity: 0.5;
}
```

Based on the classes assigned to the controls managed by the plugin, the CSS generates the desired look. With a few lines of CSS the user can change that appearance, as shown in figure 5.3.

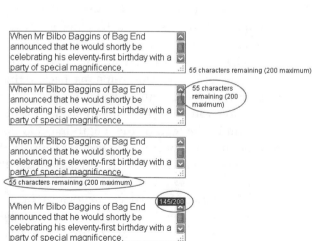

Figure 5.3   Styling the MaxLength plugin: default style, compact styling, feedback beneath, and feedback overlaid

5.10 *The complete plugin*

You've now finished the implementation of a complete plugin that provides maximum length functionality for textarea fields to complement the built-in functionality for input fields. You've seen my plugin framework and how it applies the guidelines and design principles described in chapter 4. The complete code for the plugin is available for download from the book's website.

> **NOTE** Also available on the book's website is a stripped-down file (jquery.framework.js) containing only the basic framework structure and code. You can use this as the basis for your own plugins.

To use the new plugin in a web page, you load jQuery, then the plugin code and styles, before attaching the plugin to a particular element. The following listing shows a minimal page.

Listing 5.21 Using the MaxLength plugin

```
<html>                                                               Load the ❶
<head>                                                           plugin styles
<title>jQuery Max Length Basics</title>
<link type="text/css" href="jquery.maxlength.css" rel="stylesheet">
<script type="text/javascript"
    src="http://ajax.googleapis.com/ajax/libs/jquery/1.8.3/jquery.min.js">
</script>
<script type="text/javascript" src="jquery.maxlength.js"></script>
<script type="text/javascript">                                  Load plugin
$(function() {                                                        code ❸
    $('#maxLength').maxlength();          Attach the plugin
});                                    ❹ to an element
</script>
</head>
<body>
<h1>jQuery Max Length Basics</h1>
<p>This page demonstrates the very basics of the
    <a href="http://keith-wood.name/maxlength.html">jQuery
    Max Length plugin</a>.
    It contains the minimum requirements for using the plugin and
    can be used as the basis for your own experimentation.</p>
<p>For more detail see the <a href="http://keith-wood.name/
➥ maxlengthRef.html">documentation reference</a> page.</p>
<p><span class="demoLabel">Default max length:</span>
    <textarea id="maxLength" rows="5" cols="50"></textarea></p>    Target
</body>                                                         ❺ element
</html>
```

Load jQuery code ❷

In the header of your HTML document, load the MaxLength plugin styles ❶, followed by the jQuery library code ❷ (often from a CDN, as shown here) and the MaxLength plugin code ❸. Within a document.ready callback (to ensure that the DOM has loaded before trying to access it), attach the plugin functionality to the target field ❹. The field appears in the body of the document ❺.

What you need to know

Create a collection plugin to operate on the set of elements resulting from a selection or traversal process.

Using a framework as the basis for your code provides the common plugin abilities, allowing you to concentrate on the plugin-specific functionality.

Extend $.fn to add a collection plugin.

Protect your code and prevent name clashes through scoping.

Allow your plugin to be chained to further jQuery calls.

Provide flexible configuration through options, but always initialize them with sensible default values.

Use named methods to provide additional functionality within the plugin.

Allow a plugin to be removed by adding a destroy method.

Try it yourself

Use the basic framework file (jquery.framework.js) as the basis for a new plugin. Re-implement the Watermark plugin from chapter 2 in this context. Add an option to identify the attribute to use when retrieving the label text. Add a method instead of a separate plugin to clear the label.

5.11   *Summary*

A collection plugin operates on a set of elements resulting from a selection and/or traversal in jQuery. Such plugins are easily added by extending $.fn to define a new function that applies the plugin's capabilities, and they're immediately integrated into jQuery's standard processing.

The sample plugin built in this chapter illustrates how a plugin framework can address the various guidelines and design principles described in chapter 4. And as a result, you have a fully functional plugin that provides useful abilities to complement the features built into normal input fields.

In the next chapter you'll build a different type of plugin—one that doesn't operate on collections of elements.

Function plugins

6

This chapter covers

- Defining a function plugin
- Localizing content via a function plugin
- Accessing cookies via a function plugin

The collection plugins from the previous chapter worked by operating on a set of elements retrieved from the page via a selection and/or traversal process, but you can also create plugins that don't apply to such collections but provide utility functions within the jQuery framework. These are *function plugins.*

Examples of this type of plugin include the Debug plugin (http://jquery.glyphix.com/), which provides logging output for debugging purposes, and the Cookie plugin, which provides interactions with the cookies for a website (covered in detail in section 6.2). As with the earlier plugins, you're only limited by your imagination in what you can create.

Because function plugins don't work with sets of elements from the page and often work without any UI component, they're considerably simpler to implement. Although you could define these functions as standalone JavaScript functions, there are benefits to creating them within the jQuery namespace. Doing so reduces the clutter in the global namespace and reduces the risk of a name clash. Often they make use of jQuery itself, and their inclusion there offers a consistent approach when using jQuery. They also aim to make the provided abilities easier to use and to hide any cross-browser differences: key principles behind jQuery itself.

In chapter 5, you extended `$.fn` to define your collection plugin, allowing it to be integrated into the collection processing built into jQuery. For function plugins, you extend `jQuery ($)` directly, and invoke them from there as well.

6.1   Defining your plugin

As a concrete example of a function plugin, you can develop a tool to assist in the localization of your web pages, loading in only the necessary JavaScript files to customize your site for a particular language and region.

6.1.1   Localization plugin

Based on the localization scheme described in section 5.5.2, this tool assumes the presence of several related JavaScript files distinguished only by their language or region code. When requested, the plugin loads in these localization files in order of increasing language and region specificity, each overwriting the one before, resulting in the best possible match for a given language and region.

For example, suppose you have the files shown in table 6.1. Each one represents a different language and region combination and sets a common variable (`greeting`) to the message shown.

Table 6.1   Localization setup

File	Language/Region	Message
greeting.js	Default	Hello
greeting-en.js	English	Good day
greeting-en-US.js	English (US)	Hi
greeting-en-AU.js	English (Australia)	G'day
greeting-fr.js	French	Bonjour

To localize your page with a greeting in a particular language, you can use this code:

```
$.localise('greeting', 'en-AU');
$('#greet').text(greeting);
```

The plugin would load the following files in order, from least specific to most specific—greeting.js, greeting-en.js, greeting-en-AU.js—to arrive at the best possible match for a greeting in Australian English: "G'day". If the language requested were Canadian English (`en-CA`), the chain would stop at the second file (standard English), because there is no greeting-en-CA.js file, and it would produce a greeting of "Good day". And if you happened to ask for Xhosa (`xh`), you'd get the default greeting: "Hello".

Figure 6.1   Datepicker localization: French, Japanese, and Arabic

Once the files are loaded and executed, you can access the variables that they set in the usual manner.

If the `localise()` call is made without any language specified, it uses the default language as indicated by the browser. To enable easy access to this default language, it's made available via `$.localise.defaultLanguage`.

Localization isn't limited to text displayed to the end user. It can affect other aspects of the display and behavior, as shown in some localizations for the Datepicker plugin (see figure 6.1).

There are several differences between these versions, other than the obvious textual changes:

- The drop-downs for selecting month and year appear in different orders.
- Each calendar starts on a different day of the week: Monday for French, Sunday for Japanese, and Saturday for Arabic.
- Arabic reads from right to left, but the other two read left to right.

Now that you know what the plugin is designed to do, you can use the principles and framework from the previous two chapters to help implement it.

6.1.2   Framework code

Although most of the plugin framework presented in the previous chapter doesn't apply to function plugins, a couple of its features should be retained. You should still *hide the implementation details by using scope* and *not rely on $ being the same as jQuery*. The solution is the same as that presented before.

Listing 6.1   Encapsulating the plugin code

```
(function($) { // Hide scope, no $ conflict
    ... the rest of the code appears here
})(jQuery);
```
❶ Declare anonymous function
❷ Immediately invoke it

Create a scope by defining an anonymous function ❶, calling it immediately to establish its scope and execute its contained code ❷. By declaring a parameter of `$` and then supplying a reference to `jQuery` when invoked, you ensure that both refer to the same object within the body of the function.

The plugin also follows the principles of *only claiming a single name and using that for everything* and *placing everything under the jQuery object*. There can be no chaining here, as there's no jQuery collection to work with. The principle of *using sensible defaults* is followed by using the default language from the browser if no specific language is given.

The next section addresses all of these points as you write the main plugin function.

6.1.3   *Loading localizations*

The `localise` function, shown in the following listing, implements the main action of this plugin: loading one or more localization files for a particular package based on the language and region requested.

Listing 6.2   Declare the plugin function

```
$.localise = function(                          ◁────❶ Declare the localise function
       packages, language, loadBase, path, timeout, async, complete) {
   ...
};
```

Attach the function directly to the jQuery object by declaring it as an attribute ❶. The function is then accessible via the jQuery object within your pages, without needing to select any elements for it to operate upon, because it applies to the page as a whole.

The function accepts multiple parameters to alter its behavior. All except for the first parameter are optional and will use appropriate default values if not provided. The parameters are distinguished by their types when deciding what they represent. The following listing shows how the parameters are handled.

Listing 6.3   Defaulting and standardizing parameter values

```
if (typeof language != 'object' && typeof language != 'string') {     ◁────┐
    complete = async;
    async = timeout;
    timeout = path;                                    Handle an optional
    path = loadBase;                                   language code ❶
    loadBase = language;
    language = '';
}
if (typeof loadBase != 'boolean') {                    ◁──┐ Handle an optional
    complete = async;                                   ❷ load base flag
    async = timeout;
    timeout = path;
    path = loadBase;
    loadBase = false;
}
if (typeof path != 'string' && !$.isArray(path)) {     ◁──┐ Handle an
    complete = async;                                   ❸ optional path
    async = timeout;
    timeout = path;
    path = '';
```

```
}
if (typeof timeout != 'number') {
    complete = async;
    async = timeout;
    timeout = 500;
}
if (typeof async != 'boolean') {
    complete = async;
    async = false;
}
var settings = (typeof language != 'string' ? $.extend(
    {loadBase: false, path: '', timeout: 500, async: false},
    language || {}) :
    {language: language, loadBase: loadBase, path: path,
    timeout: timeout, async: async, complete: complete});
var paths = (!settings.path ? ['', ''] :
    ($.isArray(settings.path) ? settings.path :
    [settings.path, settings.path]));
var opts = {async: settings.async, dataType: 'script',
    timeout: settings.timeout};
```

④ **Handle an optional timeout**

⑤ **Handle an optional asynchronous flag**

⑥ **Standardize references to settings**

⑦ **Standardize the path references**

⑧ **Prepare options for the Ajax calls to follow**

You must supply either a single package name (`string`) or a set of them (`string[]`) for the function to work with. Because the remaining parameters are optional, the code must then determine which is which. The second parameter is an optional language code (`string`) or a collection of settings (`object`) with attributes named for the individual parameters. To make further processing simpler, any individual parameter values are collected into a single settings object, as if it had been supplied originally. If the second parameter is neither of these items, the parameters are shifted along ❶ and processing continues with the next one.

Additional optional parameters include a flag indicating that the base localization should be reloaded (`boolean`) ❷, an optional path (`string`) or paths (`string[]`) denoting where to find the base and localization files ❸, an optional timeout value (`number`) ❹, an optional asynchronous flag (`boolean`) ❺, and an optional callback function on completion of the load. Missing parameters are set to their default values.

You create an accumulated settings object from one that's supplied (overriding any default values), or from the individual parameter values ❻. Check the `path` setting to see whether it's a single path or many, and convert it into the latter format if necessary ❼. Collect together various options applying to the forthcoming Ajax calls for later ease of use ❽.

Once the parameters have been defaulted and standardized, the plugin continues to process all the specified packages in turn.

Listing 6.4 Loading localization files

```
var localisePkg = function(pkg, lang) {
    var files = [];
    if (settings.loadBase) {
        files.push(paths[0] + pkg + '.js');
    }
```

❶ **Localize a single package**

❷ **Load base file if required**

```
    if (lang.length >= 2) {
        files.push(paths[1] + pkg + '-' +
            lang.substring(0, 2) + '.js');
    }
    if (lang.length >= 5) {
        files.push(paths[1] + pkg + '-' +
            lang.substring(0, 5) + '.js');
    }
    var loadFile = function() {
        $.ajax($.extend(opts, {url: files.shift(),
        complete: function() {
            if (files.length == 0) {
                if ($.isFunction(settings.complete)) {
                    settings.complete.apply(window, [pkg]);
                }
            }
            else {
                loadFile();
            }
        }}));
    }
    loadFile();
};
var lang = normaliseLang(
    settings.language || $.localise.defaultLanguage);
packages = ($.isArray(packages) ? packages : [packages]);
for (var i = 0; i < packages.length; i++) {
    localisePkg(packages[i], lang);
}
```

❸ **Load a language localization**

❹ **Load a language and region localization**

❺ **Load files in order**

❻ **When all are loaded, trigger complete**

❼ **Load next file in sequence**

❽ **Standardize the language to use**

❾ **Standardize package list and process each in turn**

You define an internal function ❶ to process a single package. Each one is loaded as the base file (if the loading of the base was requested) ❷, then with a two-character language code ❸, and finally with a five-character language and region code (if available) ❹. The files are placed in a queue to be read sequentially.

Loading of the individual files ❺ uses the built-in jQuery `ajax` function, starting with the first file in the queue, specifying that the returned content is "script" and should be executed as such. Because a synchronous load is used by default (to ensure that subsequent code can rely on the returned values), a timeout is included to continue in a timely manner. Alternatively, you can use the additional parameters to the `localise` call to indicate that asynchronous loads should be performed and to provide a callback function to be invoked once they're all completed ❻. If there are further files in the queue, the function is reinvoked to load the next one ❼.

Once the process for a single package and subsequent files has been defined, you find the language and region required ❽, and load each package in turn ❾.

To implement what the plugin is preaching, a second function is defined to provide a localized version of the original:

```
$.localize = $.localise;
```

The complete plugin code is available for download from the book website.

6.2   jQuery Cookie plugin

Another good example of a function plugin is the Cookie plugin (https://github.com/carhartl/jquery-cookie) written by Klaus Hartl. It allows you to read or write the cookies associated with a web page in a simple way without having to know anything about the format and encoding used by those cookies. You can retain some state information for a website on each user's computer to personalize and enhance their experience. As such, it doesn't operate on collections of elements on the page.

6.2.1   Cookie interactions

Cookies are small amounts of data that are stored on a user's machine and are associated with one or more web pages. The information in the cookies for a web page is accessible on that page and is sent back to the server with each request, allowing some state to be maintained on the client machine. Cookies expire after a certain time, and are then removed from the user's machine.

To set a cookie for the current web page using the Cookie plugin, you need to provide its name and value. For example, to track whether you've shown an introduction to each user when they first visit your website, you could save a cookie with that information:

```
$.cookie('introShown', true);
```

You can also provide additional parameters to customize the cookie, setting its expiry period (by default, cookies expire at the end of the current session), the domain and path to which it applies, whether the cookie requires secure transmission, and whether the cookie value is encoded:

```
$.cookie('introShown', true, {expires: 30, domain: 'example.com',
    path: '/', secure: true, raw: true});
```

Retrieving a cookie value is just a matter of providing its name. If there's no cookie with the given name, a null is returned. In the website introduction example, you'd test this value and only show the introduction if it's null:

```
var introShown = $.cookie('introShown');
```

Delete a cookie by setting its value to null:

```
$.cookie('introShown', null);
```

As you can see, the plugin follows the principle of *only claiming a single name (within jQuery) and using that for everything*. Different functionality is provided based on the number and types of parameters provided in each call.

Now that you know what the Cookie plugin can do, you'll see how it implements its functionality. Although the Cookie plugin doesn't use my framework, the basic structure and principles still apply.

6.2.2   *Reading and writing cookies*

As for the previous plugins, the body of the code is protected from the rest of the JavaScript world, and the only access point is via the `jQuery` object itself.

Listing 6.5   Encapsulating the plugin code

```
(function($, document) {                              ← ❶ Declare anonymous
                                                          function
    $.cookie = function(key, value, options) {        ← ❷ Declare
        ... // Rest of Cookie code appears here            the cookie
    };                                                      function
                            ❸ Immediately invoke
})(jQuery, document);       ← definition
```

An anonymous function ❶ hides the plugin from external JavaScript and follows the principles of *hiding the implementation details by using scope* and *not relying on $ being the same as jQuery* ❸. This plugin makes minimal use of jQuery itself, and only defines a single function—cookie—which is added to the `jQuery` object ❷, applying two more principles: *only claiming a single name and using that for everything*, and *placing everything under the jQuery object*.

The plugin has two modes of operation—reading or writing cookies—and which one applies is determined by the number and type of parameters supplied to the call. The initial case handled here is writing a cookie value.

Listing 6.6   Writing a cookie value

```
// key and at least value given, set cookie...        ❶ Check for
if (arguments.length > 1 && (!/Object/.test(      ←      writing a cookie
        Object.prototype.toString.call(value)) || value == null)) {
    options = $.extend({}, $.cookie.defaults, options);

    if (value == null) {                              ❷ Check for deleting
        options.expires = -1;                    ←       a cookie
    }

    if (typeof options.expires === 'number') {        ❸ Standardize/default
        var days = options.expires,              ←       options
            t = options.expires = new Date();
        t.setDate(t.getDate() + days);
    }

    value = String(value);
                                                      ❹ Write the cookie value
    return (document.cookie = [                  ←       with settings and exit
        encodeURIComponent(key), '=', options.raw ?
            value : encodeURIComponent(value),
        options.expires ? '; expires=' +
            options.expires.toUTCString() : '',
        // use expires attribute, max-age is not supported by IE
        options.path    ? '; path=' + options.path : '',
        options.domain  ? '; domain=' + options.domain : '',
```

```
            options.secure  ? '; secure' : ''
    ].join(''));
}
```

If more than one parameter is provided, and the second isn't an object, then a cookie is written ❶. Deleting a cookie is indicated by setting a null value. If that's the case ❷, the expiry time is set to -1, which means the cookie has already expired and will be discarded. Otherwise, if the expires option is a number, it's treated as a number of days from today ❸. Finally, the cookie value is converted into a string, and the cookie and its settings are written to the browser ❹. As expected, the principle of *using sensible defaults* applies, resulting in a cookie that applies to the current domain and path and expires at the end of the current session. The encoded cookie name and value are returned as the result of the function call, although most times you wouldn't need to know or do anything with that value.

If the cookie value is being retrieved, the plugin processing continues as shown in the following listing.

Listing 6.7 Reading a cookie value

```
// key and possibly options given, get cookie...          ❶ Process options
options = value || $.cookie.defaults || {};
var decode = options.raw ? raw : decoded;                 ❷ Separate
var cookies = document.cookie.split('; ');                  cookie values
for (var i = 0, parts;
        (parts = cookies[i] && cookies[i].split('='));   ❸ Retrieve
        i++) {                                              cookie value
    if (decode(parts.shift()) === key) {
        return decode(parts.join('='));
    }
}                                                         ❹ Return null
return null;                                                 if not found
```

First, any options passed as the second parameter to the call are read ❶, with default values being used if none were provided explicitly. The current cookie values (all cookies for this web page) are retrieved and split into individual name/value pairs ❷. Each pair is examined to find the one with the requested name ❸ and the corresponding value returned. If no matching value is found, a null is returned ❹.

You can set default options for all cookies by updating $.cookie.defaults:

```
$.extend($.cookie.defaults, {expires: 7});
```

The full code for the Cookie plugin is available for download from the book's website.

What you need to know

Develop function plugins to add abilities not directly applied to selected elements.

Extend $ directly to add extra functionality.

Protect your code and prevent name clashes by using scoping.

(continued)

Accept parameters to modify the plugin's behavior, but provide sensible default values if they're not supplied.

Try it yourself

Write a function plugin to format a time, to be called as shown here:

```
var time = $.formatTime(new Date(0, 0, 0, 12, 34, 0));
```

Accept a `Date` object to extract the time from, or use the current time if nothing is provided. Format the time as hh:mmAP. For more of a challenge, add an optional first parameter (Boolean) that indicates whether the format should be 12-hour time, as above, or 24-hour time.

Hints: The `Date` object has functions `getHours` and `getMinutes`. Find the current date/time with `new Date()`.

6.3   *Summary*

Whereas collection plugins operate on the set of elements resulting from a selection and/or traversal process, function plugins don't apply to such collections. Instead they offer utility functions that serve to simplify various interactions on the web page. They hide the intricacies of the inner workings of some web page functions and remove the need to worry about cross-browser differences in these processes.

Two examples, the Localization and Cookie plugins, showed how function plugins are created in practice. They demonstrate how the plugin framework applies to this new type of plugin and why you should still follow the best practice principles.

Once you've built your own plugin, you need to ensure that it works correctly and that others can easily obtain it and understand its use. The next chapter examines how to test, package, deploy, and document your plugin to make it ready for the wider jQuery community.

Test, package, and document your plugin

This chapter covers

- Testing your plugin
- Packaging your plugin for distribution
- Documenting and demonstrating your plugin

Once you've written your new plugin, you probably want to make it available to the wider jQuery community. To give it the best chance of competing with other plugins that provide similar functionality, you should ensure that it works as expected in all situations. Using a testing suite such as QUnit lets you create a series of repeatable tests for a wide range of scenarios for your plugin, in the familiar environment of a web browser.

You should also provide potential users with a package that includes everything they need to implement your plugin. As well as the plugin code itself, you may need to include associated stylesheets, images, localizations, and perhaps even a simple demonstration page. To reduce network requirements when the plugin is being used, it's also helpful to include a minimized version of your plugin code, as provided by one of several online packing tools. All of the related files are then collected into a single archive file for ease of distribution.

Finally, you need to document your plugin thoroughly so your users know what to expect and can adapt it to their varying needs. Describe each option that can be set, each callback that can be registered, and each method that can be invoked. You should also show off your plugin's abilities with a demonstration page, preferably with corresponding code snippets that can be easily copied and applied by a user.

The sections in this chapter address each of these issues to help you publish a plugin that works correctly and can be easily implemented by end users.

7.1   Testing your plugin

Testing your plugin may seem like an obvious requirement, but doing it properly can be an art form. Even with only a few options available to change your plugin's behavior, the possible combinations quickly grow and can become unwieldy.

Initially, you might start with a simple page and adjust options manually to check their functionality, but as the complexity of the plugin increases, this is no longer practical and leads to inconsistent testing of various situations. A set of repeatable unit tests overcomes this problem, allowing you to easily run a full suite of tests without missing anything.

A standard set of tests (following the *create a repeatable test case suite* principle) also lets you refactor your code more easily, as you can confirm after each change that the plugin still works as expected.

This section looks at what you should be testing, and then at how you'd implement this using the QUnit testing suite. As an example, you'll create unit tests for the MaxLength plugin you created in chapter 5.

7.1.1   What to test?

Ideally, you should test everything—all methods for all combinations of options, applied to varying elements in diverse positions upon the page, in all the major browsers (one of the guiding principles). But this isn't practical for most plugins, so concentrate on testing each option or method separately or in small groups of related settings.

Start with the basics of setting default values for all plugin instances (`$.plugin-name.setDefaults`), followed by the setting and retrieval of individual or groups of options (`$(selector).pluginname('option')...`). Next, test the instantiation (`$(selector).pluginname()`) and destruction (`$(selector).pluginname('destroy')`) of your plugin to ensure that it makes the necessary DOM modifications and then removes them completely. If your plugin can be enabled and disabled, then test that this happens as expected (`$(selector).pluginname('disable')`). Check that other operations don't work when the plugin is in its disabled state.

Test each option individually to check that it correctly affects the targeted elements. For options that accept different types of values, include tests for each of these types separately. For options that are event callbacks, add tests for each one and ensure that the parameters passed to it are correct.

For each method and utility function offered by the plugin, test that it operates as expected. Check that chaining occurs for methods that don't return a special value from the plugin.

Test user interactions with the elements affected by the plugin using jQuery's event methods. Trigger a normal, bubbling event (one that's passed on to the containing elements up through the DOM hierarchy) with `$(selector).trigger('eventname')`. To invoke an event without bubbling, use `$(selector).triggerHandler('eventname')` instead. You can also use the named jQuery event functions to initiate events, such as `$(selector).click()`. If you need to pass additional information with the event, such as the position of a mouse click or the key pressed, use the `trigger` function but pass it an `Event` object instead of only the event name.

```
var e = $.Event('click');
e.pageX = 10;
e.pageY = 20;
$(selector).trigger(e);
```

7.1.2 Using QUnit

QUnit is a JavaScript test suite developed by John Resig and now maintained by the jQuery team (http://qunitjs.com/). It's used by the jQuery and jQuery UI teams to test jQuery and jQuery UI themselves, and can be applied to any JavaScript code. A QUnit page contains a suite of tests that you can easily run to verify the functionality of your plugin.

To run a QUnit test, you start with an HTML template as shown in listing 7.1. You load in the QUnit CSS and JavaScript, and add your tests in a separate `script` element. In the body of the page, you add two specific `div`s—one to hold the test results (`#qunit`) and the other to hold any elements needed by the tests themselves (`#qunit-fixture`). The latter is hidden by moving it off the screen, thus allowing its contents to be "visible" while not affecting the display of the test outcome. Figure 7.1 shows the results of loading this sample page—a failed test, because the supplied value doesn't match the expected one.

Listing 7.1 QUnit page template

```html
<html>
<head>
  <title>QUnit basic example</title>
  <link rel="stylesheet"
    href="http://code.jquery.com/qunit/qunit-git.css"/>
  <script src="http://code.jquery.com/qunit/qunit-git.js"></script>
  <script>
    test('a basic test example', function() {
      var value = 'hi';
      equal(value, 'hello', 'We expect value to be hello');
    });
  </script>
</head>
<body>
  <div id="qunit"></div>
  <div id="qunit-fixture"></div>
</body>
</html>
```

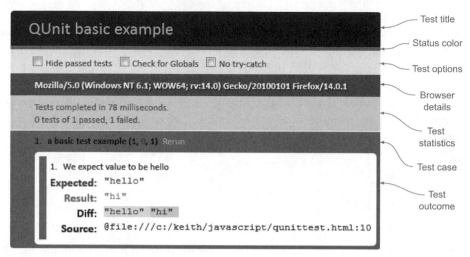

Figure 7.1   Running the QUnit basic example

Your test code consists of one or more calls to the test function, each of which contains a set of related *assertions* (statements of expected results). Each section includes code to set up the appropriate environment and then one or more assertions regarding the outcome of that test. Each time a test is invoked, the test environment is re-established, with the contents of the #qunit-fixture div being restored to their original state, protecting tests from each other and allowing each to start from a known state.

Within the page header is the page title, a status bar colored either green indicating a successful test run or red indicating some sort of failure, the current browser identification, and various checkboxes to change the test behavior. The body of the document shows the results of running the tests. By default, tests that pass are collapsed, whereas those that fail are expanded to show individual assertions. You can toggle a test by clicking on its header. Click Rerun or double-click a test header to rerun just that test.

You can also filter individual tests by matching a portion of their name (ignoring case) as a parameter to the test page, such as

```
test.html?filter=basic
```

Alternately, you can exclude tests matching a filter by prefixing the value with an exclamation mark (!):

```
test.html?filter=!event
```

Checking the Check for Globals checkbox in the header reruns the tests but throws an error if any global variables are declared. Use this option to monitor the global namespace and assist in preventing interference with other libraries. Checking the No Try-Catch checkbox reruns the tests but doesn't trap any exceptions that may be raised, allowing them to fall through to the browser and stop the tests at that point. Normally exceptions are caught and appear as failure messages within the output.

Run your test page on all the major browsers to ensure compatibility across all of these platforms.

To illustrate how you'd test a plugin, you can create a test suite for the MaxLength plugin from chapter 5.

7.1.3 *Testing the MaxLength plugin*

To ensure that the MaxLength plugin works as expected, you should write a QUnit test suite to validate it.

For this plugin, you start off testing the `setDefaults` function. After checking that the initial value of a default option is as expected, you call the function to change that value, and check it again to confirm the update. A message provided to the checking call is logged as is on success, and on fail-

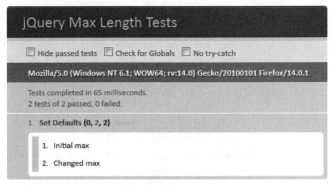

Figure 7.2   Running the first MaxLength test

ure is concatenated with the unequal values being compared. Figure 7.2 shows the (successful) result of running this initial test; the next listing shows the initial page setup and the code behind this first test.

Listing 7.2   Setting up MaxLength tests

```
<!DOCTYPE HTML PUBLIC "-//W3C//DTD HTML 4.01//EN"
    "http://www.w3.org/TR/html4/strict.dtd">
<html>
<head>
<meta http-equiv="Content-Type" content="text/html;charset=utf-8">
<title>jQuery Max Length Tests</title>
<link type="text/css" rel="stylesheet"                        ❶ Load QUnit
    href="http://code.jquery.com/qunit/qunit-git.css">
<script type="text/javascript"
    src="http://code.jquery.com/qunit/qunit-git.js"></script>  ❷ Load jQuery
<script type="text/javascript"                                   and plugin
    src="http://ajax.googleapis.com/ajax/libs/jquery/1.8.0/jquery.min.js">
</script>
<script type="text/javascript" src="js/jquery.maxlength.js"></script>
<script type="text/javascript">
$(function() {                                       ❸ Define a test
    test('Set Defaults', function() {
        expect(2);                                            Set number
        init();                                               of assertions
        equal($.maxlength._defaults.max, 200, 'Initial max'); ❹ to be made
        $.maxlength.setDefaults({max: 300});
        equal($.maxlength._defaults.max, 300, 'Changed max');
```

Make an
assertion ❺

```
        $.maxlength.setDefaults({max: 200});
    });
});

function init(settings) {
    return $('#txa').val('').maxlength('destroy').maxlength(settings);
}
</script>
</head>

<body>
<div id="qunit"></div>
<div id="qunit-fixture">
    <input type="text" id="fbk1"><span id="fbk2"></span>
    <textarea id="txa" rows="3" cols="30"></textarea>
</div>
</body>
</html>
```

6 Area for QUnit
controls and results

7 Area for elements
used by tests

The testing page starts by loading in the QUnit styling and code **1**, followed by jQuery and the plugin code **2**.

The body of the page contains the two standard divs: the first (#qunit) to hold the QUnit interface and the results of running the tests **6** and the second (#qunit-fix-ture) to hold any elements required by the tests themselves **7**. The latter is cloned and re-created at the beginning of each set of tests to provide a clean environment for those tests, and is styled to move it out of the normal viewport so that its contents remain "visible" without overlaying the QUnit results.

The test appears within a call to the QUnit test function **3**. This function defines a name for the set of assertions that it contains and a callback function to run them. A test should be targeted at a particular aspect of the plugin, and may be run on its own to focus on that one area. Any changes you make to the environment during a test will apply until that test is completed.

To ensure that any code failures are correctly handled, you should start each test with a call to the expect function, to specify how many assertions are being made within this set **4**. This way, if a problem arises that prevents the remaining code from executing, you'll still be informed of an error (instead of it failing silently) because the number of assertions run won't match what was expected. Alternatively, you can supply the number of expected assertions as the second parameter to the test function, push-ing the callback function into third position. Finally, you should initialize the environ-ment for your test, run the code, and make assertions about the outcome **5**.

When testing the setDefaults function, you call the function to alter the value and check that it did in fact change. The calls to equal are assertions provided by QUnit. Each one compares the actual value with an expected value (the first two parameters) and succeeds if these are equal (after type conversion, if necessary). A descriptive message is provided to the call as its third parameter for logging purposes.

The init function in the code initializes the textarea within the #qunit-fixture div by resetting its value, removing any existing MaxLength functionality, and then adding it back in again. Although it's not necessary for this particular test, which relates to global functionality, the `init` function will be used by later sets of tests. The `input` field and `span` within the fixture `div` will be used to contain feedback information in later tests.

7.1.4 Testing option setting and retrieval

Having checked the setting of default options for the plugin, you can continue by testing the setting and retrieval of options. You can set individual options, or collections of them, in the one call. Similarly you can retrieve one or all option values from a call. All of these possibilities should be tested, as shown in the following additional test.

Listing 7.3 Testing MaxLength options

```
test('Options', function() {                    ◄──────❶ Define the options test
    expect(12);
    var txa = init();                                              ❸ Initialize the
    deepEqual(txa.maxlength('option'), {max: 200, truncate: true,     testing element
        showFeedback: true, feedbackTarget: null,
        feedbackText: '{r} characters remaining ({m} maximum)',     Make an
        overflowText: '{o} characters too many ({m} maximum)',    assertion
        onFull: null}, 'Initial settings');                        about
                                                                 an object ❹
    equal(txa.maxlength('option', 'max'), 200,
        'Initial max setting');                          Make an assertion
    equal(txa.maxlength('option', 'truncate'), true,   ❺ about a value
        'Initial truncate setting');
    txa.maxlength('option', {feedbackText: 'Used {c} of {m}'});
    deepEqual(txa.maxlength('option'), {max: 200, truncate: true,
        showFeedback: true, feedbackTarget: null,
        feedbackText: 'Used {c} of {m}',
        overflowText: '{o} characters too many ({m} maximum)',
        onFull: null}, 'Changed settings');
    equal(txa.maxlength('option', 'max'), 200,
        'Unchanged max setting');
    equal(txa.maxlength('option', 'truncate'), true,       ❼ Test multiple
        'Unchanged truncate setting');                        options are
    txa.maxlength('option', {max: 100, showFeedback: false});  changed
    deepEqual(txa.maxlength('option'), {max: 100, truncate: true,
        showFeedback: false, feedbackTarget: null,
        feedbackText: 'Used {c} of {m}',
        overflowText: '{o} characters too many ({m} maximum)',
        onFull: null}, 'Changed settings');
    equal(txa.maxlength('option', 'max'), 100,
        'Changed max setting');
    equal(txa.maxlength('option', 'truncate'), true,      ❽ Test individual
        'Unchanged truncate setting');                       option is changed
    txa.maxlength('option', 'truncate', false);
    deepEqual(txa.maxlength('option'), {max: 100, truncate: false,
        showFeedback: false, feedbackTarget: null,
        feedbackText: 'Used {c} of {m}',
        overflowText: '{o} characters too many ({m} maximum)',
        onFull: null}, 'Changed named setting');
    equal(txa.maxlength('option', 'max'), 100,
```

Set number of assertions to be made ❷

Change an option and retest ❻

```
        'Unchanged max setting');
    equal(txa.maxlength('option', 'truncate'), false,
        'Changed truncate setting');
});
```

Define a new test to probe the option capabilities of the plugin ❶. As done previously, specify the number of assertions to be made in this test so you're sure you're not missing any ❷.

Initialize the test elements with a call to `init` ❸, and then confirm that the initial state is as expected. A call to the `option` method without any other parameters results in an object being returned containing all the current option values. Use the `deep-Equal` function provided by QUnit to compare the returned value with the expected one ❹. This function differs from `equal` by comparing each attribute of the two objects separately (and recursively if necessary), rather than only checking that the two objects are the same one. Use the `equal` function to check a single simple option value retrieved when using the `option` method with a named option ❺.

Continue the test by changing an option value, again with the `option` method ❻, and check for the changes that should have resulted. Also test the situations where several option values are changed at the one time by providing a collection of new values to the `option` method ❼, and where an individual option is altered by providing its name and new value ❽.

7.1.5   *Simulating user actions*

The behavior of the MaxLength plugin depends on interactions with the user, in particular their entry of text into the affected `textarea`. You need to test this behavior by simulating these exchanges. Other plugins may need to test mouse clicks or drags. The following listing shows how the MaxLength tests handle this requirement.

Listing 7.4   Testing text entry

```
test('Text', function() {
    expect(28);                                          ◁──  Define the text
    var txa = init({max: 20});                           ❶   entry test
    var rem = txa.nextAll('.maxlength-feedback');
    keyboard(txa, 'abcdefghij');                         ❷  Simulate
                                                         ◁──┘ entering text
    equal(txa.val(), 'abcdefghij', 'Entered short text');
    ok(!txa.hasClass('maxlength-full'), 'Not full with short text');   ◁──
    ok(!txa.hasClass('maxlength-overflow'),
        'Not overflow with short text');                     Make a
    equal(rem.text(), '10 characters remaining (20 maximum)',  true/false
        'Feedback for short text');                          assertion ❹
    keyboard(txa, 'klmnopqrstuvwxyz');
    equal(txa.val(), 'abcdefghijklmnopqrst', 'Entered full text');
    ok(txa.hasClass('maxlength-full'), 'Full with full text');
    ok(txa.hasClass('maxlength-overflow'), 'Not overflow with full text');
    equal(rem.text(), '0 characters remaining (20 maximum)',
        'Feedback with full text');
    backspace(txa);
    equal(txa.val(), 'abcdefghijklmnopqrs', 'BS');
```

Test the entered text ❸

```
ok(!txa.hasClass('maxlength-full'), 'Not full with BS');
ok(!txa.hasClass('maxlength-overflow'), 'Not overflow with BS');
equal(rem.text(), '1 characters remaining (20 maximum)',
    'Feedback with BS');
keyboard(txa, 'u');
equal(txa.val(), 'abcdefghijklmnopqrsu', 'More text');
ok(txa.hasClass('maxlength-full'), 'Full with more text');
ok(!txa.hasClass('maxlength-overflow'), 'Not overflow with more text');
equal(rem.text(), '0 characters remaining (20 maximum)',
    'Feedback with more text');
// Truncate off
txa = init({max: 20, truncate: false}).val('');          ⬅  Reinitialize with different
...                                                     ❺  settings and retest
});

function keyboard(input, chars) {                       ⬅      Simulate
    for (var i = 0; i < chars.length; i++) {            ❻  keyboard events
        var ch = chars.charCodeAt(i);
        input.simulate('keydown', {charCode: ch}).
            simulate('keypress', {charCode: ch}).
            val(function(index, value) {
                return value + chars.charAt(i);
            }).
            simulate('keyup', {charCode: ch});
    }
}
                                                           ❼  Simulate
                                                              backspace key
function backspace(input) {                             ⬅
    input.simulate('keydown', {keyCode: $.simulate.VK_BS}).
        simulate('keypress', {keyCode: $.simulate.VK_BS}).
        val(function(index, value) {
            return value.replace(/.$/, '');
        }).
        simulate('keyup', {keyCode: $.simulate.VK_BS});
}
```

As in the earlier tests, you define the test and give it a name ❶. The usual setting of the expected number of assertions and field initialization follow. Then enter text as though it had been typed via the keyboard ❷ and check the resulting content of the field ❸. You can also make assertions about the state of the plugin by using the ok function provided by QUnit ❹. This function takes a Boolean value as its first parameter and asserts it to be true. In this case, you test that certain marker classes haven't yet been applied to the textarea.

Having run through a series of actions and assertions, you reinitialize the textarea with a different option setting and rerun the tests to observe the change in behavior ❺.

Two helper functions assist in the simulation of events normally triggered by the user. The keyboard function ❻ generates keydown, keypress, and keyup events for each character in the given string, whereas the backspace function ❼ does the same for a single backspace character. Both use the Simulate plugin (https://github.com/eduardolundgren/jquery-simulate) to send the events.

It's easy to replicate most other user interactions with elements on the page via jQuery's standard event handler functions. You can simulate a mouse click by calling click on that element, or via the `trigger` function (for all matched elements with event bubbling) or `triggerHandler` function (for just the first element without any bubbling).

```
$('#button1').click();
$('#button1').triggerHandler('click');
```

7.1.6 *Testing event callbacks*

Many plugins use event callbacks to notify the user of significant events within the plugin, such as values changing or timeouts expiring. The conditions triggering these events and the content of any parameters provided to the callback should be tested. In the MaxLength plugin, an event is triggered when the `textarea` reaches or exceeds its allowed limit. This listing shows the event callback tests.

Listing 7.5   Testing callbacks

```
var count = 0;                                              ┌── ❶ Initialize tracking
var overflowing = null;                                     │       variables
function filled(overflow) {          ┌── Define the
    count++;                          ❷   callback function
    overflowing = overflow;
}

test('Events', function() {          ┌── ❸ Define the
    expect(10);                              events test
    var txa = init({max: 20, onFull: filled});       ┌── ❹ Check no activity
    keyboard(txa, 'abcdefghijklmnopqrs');                    until expected
    equal(count, 0, 'No event');
    keyboard(txa, 't');                               ┌── ❻ Check its occurrence
    equal(count, 1, 'Full event');                           and parameters
    equal(overflowing, false, 'Not overflowing');
    keyboard(txa, 'u');
    equal(count, 2, 'Full event');
    equal(overflowing, false, 'Not overflowing');
    // Truncate off                                   ┌── ❼ Reinitialize with different
    count = 0;                                               settings and retest
    overflowing = null;
    txa = init({max: 20, truncate: false, onFull: filled});
    keyboard(txa, 'abcdefghijklmnopqrs');
    equal(count, 0, 'No event');
    keyboard(txa, 't');
    equal(count, 1, 'Full event');
    equal(overflowing, false, 'Not overflowing');
    keyboard(txa, 'u');
    equal(count, 2, 'Full event');
    equal(overflowing, true, 'Overflowing');
});
```

Trigger the callback condition ❺

Start by declaring some variables to track the callback invocations ❶ and the actual function to be called ❷. You can use a simple counter to record how often the callback is invoked and another variable to capture its single parameter.

Define the new test as before ❸, set the expected number of assertions, and initialize the test elements. You can make some initial assertions to ensure that the callback isn't triggered before it should be ❹. Then perform the triggering action ❺ and verify that the callback was called and received the expected parameter value ❻.

Finally, reinitialize the test environment, change an option and check the callback behavior under the new conditions ❼.

The complete test page for the MaxLength plugin is available for download from the book's website. As well as the tests described earlier, it includes tests for enabling and disabling the plugin, for removing its functionality, and for presenting feedback.

You've seen how to create a unit test suite for the MaxLength plugin, using the abilities of the QUnit package. But QUnit offers much more than was shown in this chapter. Additional features include grouping tests into modules, running asynchronous tests, other assertions, and event hooks to monitor QUnit's progress. For more information on its capabilities, read the QUnit API documentation (http://api.qunitjs.com/) and the "Introduction" and "Cookbook" articles on the main website (http://qunitjs.com/).

7.2 Packaging your plugin

Now that you're satisfied your plugin works correctly in various scenarios, you want to make it available to the wider jQuery community. To do this, you should package up everything that the plugin requires to make it simple to distribute and easy for a potential user to obtain.

You need to collect all the relevant files, create a minimized version of your code to reduce download times, and provide a simple implementation of your plugin to start users off. Then combine all these files in a single archive for a one-step download. Each of these steps is described in this section.

7.2.1 Collating all the files

Often a complete plugin consists of more than just a JavaScript file—you may also have any or all of the following:

- Additional JavaScript modules for less-used functionality
- Minimized versions of the JavaScript modules (see section 7.2.2)
- Localization files to adapt your plugin to other languages and countries
- CSS files to style your plugin in various ways
- Image and other resource files that are used by the CSS or that may be used via options of the plugin
- A basic example of how to use the plugin (see section 7.2.3)
- Documentation on the plugin (see section 7.3)

As an example, my Datepicker plugin has all of the types of files listed here, except the documentation, which is available separately. The file list shown in figure 7.3 identifies the various components.

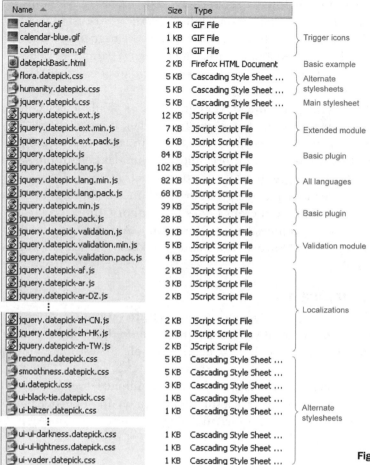

Name ▲	Size	Type	
calendar.gif	1 KB	GIF File	⎫
calendar-blue.gif	1 KB	GIF File	⎬ Trigger icons
calendar-green.gif	1 KB	GIF File	⎭
datepickBasic.html	2 KB	Firefox HTML Document	Basic example
flora.datepick.css	5 KB	Cascading Style Sheet ...	⎫ Alternate
humanity.datepick.css	5 KB	Cascading Style Sheet ...	⎭ stylesheets
jquery.datepick.css	5 KB	Cascading Style Sheet ...	Main stylesheet
jquery.datepick.ext.js	12 KB	JScript Script File	⎫
jquery.datepick.ext.min.js	7 KB	JScript Script File	⎬ Extended module
jquery.datepick.ext.pack.js	6 KB	JScript Script File	⎭
jquery.datepick.js	84 KB	JScript Script File	Basic plugin
jquery.datepick.lang.js	102 KB	JScript Script File	⎫
jquery.datepick.lang.min.js	82 KB	JScript Script File	⎬ All languages
jquery.datepick.lang.pack.js	68 KB	JScript Script File	⎭
jquery.datepick.min.js	39 KB	JScript Script File	⎫ Basic plugin
jquery.datepick.pack.js	28 KB	JScript Script File	⎭
jquery.datepick.validation.js	9 KB	JScript Script File	⎫
jquery.datepick.validation.min.js	5 KB	JScript Script File	⎬ Validation module
jquery.datepick.validation.pack.js	4 KB	JScript Script File	⎭
jquery.datepick-af.js	2 KB	JScript Script File	⎫
jquery.datepick-ar.js	3 KB	JScript Script File	⎪
jquery.datepick-ar-DZ.js	2 KB	JScript Script File	⎪
⋮			⎬ Localizations
jquery.datepick-zh-CN.js	2 KB	JScript Script File	⎪
jquery.datepick-zh-HK.js	2 KB	JScript Script File	⎪
jquery.datepick-zh-TW.js	2 KB	JScript Script File	⎭
redmond.datepick.css	5 KB	Cascading Style Sheet ...	⎫
smoothness.datepick.css	5 KB	Cascading Style Sheet ...	⎪
ui.datepick.css	3 KB	Cascading Style Sheet ...	⎪
ui-black-tie.datepick.css	1 KB	Cascading Style Sheet ...	⎪
ui-blitzer.datepick.css	1 KB	Cascading Style Sheet ...	⎬ Alternate
⋮			⎪ stylesheets
ui-ui-darkness.datepick.css	1 KB	Cascading Style Sheet ...	⎪
ui-ui-lightness.datepick.css	1 KB	Cascading Style Sheet ...	⎪
ui-vader.datepick.css	1 KB	Cascading Style Sheet ...	⎭

Figure 7.3   Files that make up the Datepicker plugin

Place all of your files in a single zip archive. As well as reducing the size of the package through compression, the archive keeps all the required files together in one package, making it easier to distribute without forgetting anything.

7.2.2   *Minimizing your plugin*

To reduce your plugin's download requirements, you can make it smaller by removing unnecessary text, such as comments and whitespace. This process is known as *minimizing* the code.

By including both the original source code and the minimized version in your download, you make it easy for potential users to use whichever suits their needs—debugging or learning with the full code or production use with the minimized one. The minimized version should be named the same as your original plugin file, but with a `.min` addition after the plugin name; for example, `jquery.maxlength.min.js`.

Once you've minimized the code itself, you should copy over the header comments from the original code, because these identify the plugin, its version, and author, and should provide a URL for the plugin website so that users can find updates, examples, and documentation.

Several websites offer to minimize your JavaScript code, including the following:

- Dean Edwards' Packer (http://dean.edwards.name/packer/)
- YUI Compressor (http://developer.yahoo.com/yui/compressor/)
- Google Closure Compiler (https://developers.google.com/closure/compiler/)

DEAN EDWARDS' PACKER

Dean Edwards' Packer is available online and lets you generate the standard minimized code by removing comments and whitespace. It also lets you generate a Base62 encoded file, which is usually smaller than the minimized code, but requires additional processing on the client to reconstruct the original code. The Base62 version also doesn't compress further as much as the straight minimized version, so you get better performance from the minimized code in conjunction with a gzip filter on your server. In both cases, you can opt to shrink variable names. In addition to further reducing the file size, this setting provides a measure of code obfuscation.

To use Dean Edwards' Packer, open the website, paste your code into the top panel, select your options, and click the Pack button, as shown in figure 7.4. Then copy the resulting code from the panel at the bottom and save it locally.

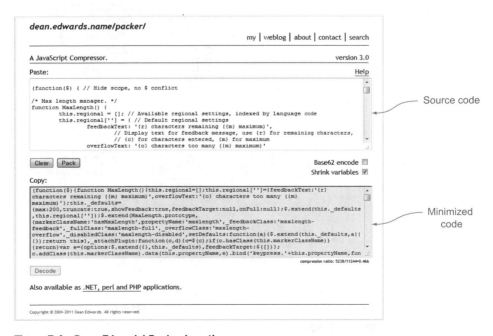

Figure 7.4 Dean Edwards' Packer in action

YUI COMPRESSOR

YUI Compressor is available as a Java (1.4+) application that you download and run locally. This makes it possible to include the minimization step in a local build process. It analyzes the source code via the Rhino JavaScript implementation in Java, and then rewrites it while omitting comments and unessential whitespace, at the same time replacing internal variable names with shorter values.

```
>java -jar \path\to\yuicompressor-2.4.7.jar -o jquery.maxlength.min.js
 jquery.maxlength.js
```

GOOGLE CLOSURE COMPILER

The Google Closure Compiler takes a different approach. In addition to removing unnecessary comments and whitespace, it can scan the code using compiler-like analysis with the aim of rewriting it for equivalent functionality with less code. As a byproduct, it also generates warnings and error messages for (potential) problems found while parsing the code. The compiler is available as an online tool (see figure 7.5) or for download as a Java application (http://closure-compiler.appspot.com/home).

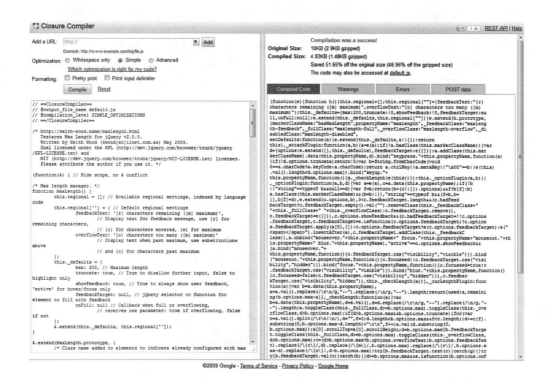

Source code   Minimized code

Figure 7.5   Google Closure Compiler in action

When using the former, paste your code in the box on the left, select your options, and click Compile. Copy the resulting code from the box on the right and save it locally.

Closure Compiler options

The Closure Compiler offers three levels of optimization. The basic level is Whitespace Only, which removes comments, line breaks, unnecessary spaces, and other whitespace. The next level is Simple, which removes whitespace as in the previous option and renames internal variables to use shortened names. Both of these options are safe to use on any code, provided you don't access local variables via string names.

The third level is Advanced, which performs the previous optimizations and then examines the code to determine whether it can be rewritten to achieve the same result. This level requires that your code conform to certain assumptions that the compiler makes, and the resulting code *may not run* if these aren't adhered to. See Google's "Closure Compiler Compilation Levels" documentation (https://developers.google.com/closure/compiler/docs/compilation_levels) for more details.

When checked, the Pretty Print option adds back line breaks and indents to make the code human-readable again, although this does increase the file size a little. When checked, the Print Input Delimiter option adds a comment into the output indicating where each of multiple input files starts.

COMPARISON

As a comparison, applying these three tools to the MaxLength plugin results in the savings shown in table 7.1. There's not a lot of difference between them for this plugin, particularly when further zipped, but the Google Closure Compiler does come out on top.

Table 7.1 Comparing minimization implementations

Product	Minimized size (bytes)	% saving	After zip (bytes)	% saving
Dean Edwards' Packer	5238	53.4%	1551	86.2%
YUI Compressor	5192	53.8%	1566	86.1%
Google Closure Compiler	4949	56.0%	1497	86.7%

7.2.3 *Providing a basic example*

Try to include a complete basic example of your plugin's operations alongside the code and other supporting files. Such an example demonstrates that the plugin works before users start experimenting with changing options and invoking methods. The page should be able to be run as soon as your distribution package is unpacked.

Keep the page as minimal as possible to reduce confusion as to what's required to use your plugin. You should load jQuery (and jQuery UI if applicable) from a CDN to avoid having to include the jQuery library in your download or worry about where jQuery might be kept in relation to this page. Show the default configuration for your plugin in this page, and allow users to add options later as they explore the plugin's possibilities. Include a link to your plugin's main demonstration page and any documentation on the plugin's abilities.

The basic page for the MaxLength plugin is shown in the following listing.

Listing 7.6   A minimal MaxLength page

```
<!DOCTYPE HTML PUBLIC "-//W3C//DTD HTML 4.01//EN"
    "http://www.w3.org/TR/html4/strict.dtd">
<html>                                                          Load plugin CSS  ❶
<head>
<meta http-equiv="Content-Type" content="text/html;charset=utf-8">
<title>jQuery Max Length Basics</title>
<link type="text/css" href="jquery.maxlength.css" rel="stylesheet">   ◄─
<script type="text/javascript"
    src="http://ajax.googleapis.com/ajax/libs/jquery/1.8.0/jquery.min.js">
</script>
<script type="text/javascript" src="jquery.maxlength.js"></script>   ◄─  Load
<script type="text/javascript">                                          plugin
$(function() {                                                      ❸   code
    $('#maxLength').maxlength();
});                                        ◄─     Basic plugin
</script>                                     ❹  initialization
</head>
<body>
<h1>jQuery Max Length Basics</h1>
<p>This page demonstrates the very basics of the          ❺  Link to plugin
    <a href="http://keith-wood.name/maxlength.html">          website
    jQuery Max Length plugin</a>.                      ◄─
    It contains the minimum requirements for using the plugin and
    can be used as the basis for your own experimentation.</p>
<p>For more detail see the
    <a href="http://keith-wood.name/maxlengthRef.html">
    documentation reference</a> page.</p>              ❻  Elements
<p><span class="demoLabel">Default max length:</span>     used by
    <textarea id="maxLength" rows="5" cols="50"></textarea></p>  ◄─  the plugin
</body>
</html>
```

Load jQuery from CDN ❷

Start by loading any CSS required by your plugin ❶ followed by the jQuery library ❷ and your plugin code ❸. Invoke your plugin with a minimum of configuration ❹. To further assist your prospective users, include links to the documentation for the plugin and to the plugin's website that demonstrates more of its abilities ❺. Finally, include the elements upon which your plugin operates ❻, again in their simplest form.

> ## jQuery content delivery network
>
> Google provides a CDN that contains multiple versions of jQuery, both in full source and in minimized format. Change the version number as necessary, and omit the `.min` if you want the full source code:
>
> ```
> <script type="text/javascript" src="http://ajax.googleapis.com/
>   ajax/libs/jquery/1.8.2/jquery.min.js">
> ```
>
> It also hosts jQuery UI versions:
>
> ```
> <script type="text/javascript" src="http://ajax.googleapis.com/
>   ajax/libs/jqueryui/1.9.2/jquery-ui.min.js">
> ```
>
> It even provides jQuery UI ThemeRoller themes. Change the version number and theme name as required:
>
> ```
> <link type="text/css"
>   rel="stylesheet" href="http://ajax.googleapis.com/ajax/libs/
>   jqueryui/1.9.2/themes/south-street/jquery-ui.css">
> ```
>
> Microsoft and jQuery (via MediaTemple) also provide CDNs for jQuery, jQuery UI, and the standard ThemeRoller themes.

7.3   Documenting your plugin

Your plugin may be fantastic and highly configurable, but if users don't know about its abilities, they won't be able to use it to its fullest extent. Most developers include some comments within the code (at least they should), and the plugin framework does collect all the available options together, but users don't want to have to wade through the code to find those descriptions.

By documenting your plugin and publishing it on the web, you make it easy for users to evaluate the possibilities offered by your plugin, and then to configure the plugin for their own use. Clear documentation with examples can reduce your maintenance burden, as users can find the answers to many of their questions without having to contact you directly.

7.3.1   Documenting options

All the options available to configure your plugin need to be documented. Each one should list the option's name, its expected type or types, its default value, and an explanation of its purpose and effect. Figure 7.6 shows documentation for some options of the MaxLength plugin.

For more complicated options, especially those that accept objects or functions, you should provide a code snippet to illustrate how that option could be used. List each of the attributes of an object value, along with its expected type, default value, and description. Similarly, list each parameter passed to a function value with its

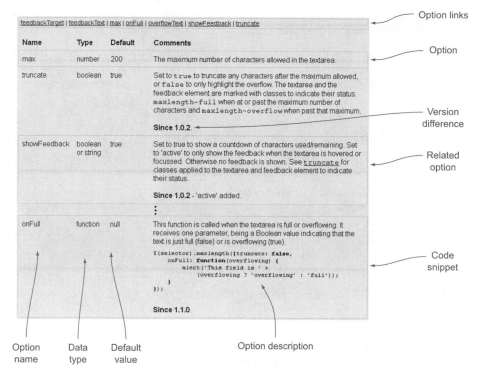

Figure 7.6   Documentation for some MaxLength options

expected type and purpose. For a function, you should also detail what `this` refers to within the body of the function, and what return value, if any, is expected back.

Provide links to related options as appropriate when describing interactions between them. If the set of possible options is extensive, consider providing an alphabetical list of links at the top and/or bottom of the page to provide quick access to particular settings.

As your plugin evolves over time, record in which version an option was added or changed. This will enable users of older versions to easily see what to do when upgrading to the latest version, or provide a reference if they want to continue using their existing version.

7.3.2   *Documenting methods and utility functions*

Any methods recognized by your plugin also need to be documented, along with any utility functions provided by it.

Each method or function should detail the manner in which it's invoked, showing all the parameters as well as the value returned by the call and a description of its purpose. Be sure to note any methods that don't return the jQuery object and so can't be used for further chaining. Figure 7.7 shows documentation for the first few functions and methods of the MaxLength plugin.

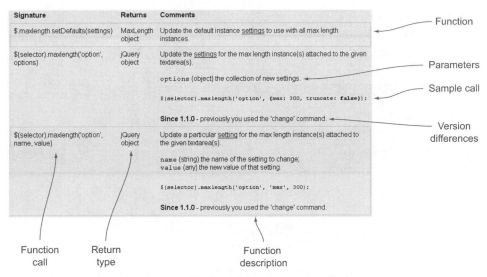

Signature	Returns	Comments
$.maxlength.setDefaults(settings)	MaxLength object	Update the default instance settings to use with all max length instances.
$(selector).maxlength('option', options)	jQuery object	Update the settings for the max length instance(s) attached to the given textarea(s). `options` (object) the collection of new settings. `$(selector).maxlength('option', {max: 300, truncate: false});` **Since 1.1.0** - previously you used the 'change' command.
$(selector).maxlength('option', name, value)	jQuery object	Update a particular setting for the max length instance(s) attached to the given textarea(s). `name` (string) the name of the setting to change; `value` (any) the new value of that setting. `$(selector).maxlength('option', 'max', 300);` **Since 1.1.0** - previously you used the 'change' command.

Function · Parameters · Sample call · Version differences · Function call · Return type · Function description

Figure 7.7 Documentation for some MaxLength functions and methods

List each parameter and indicate its expected type, its optionality, any default value, and its purpose. Provide examples of how to invoke each function or method. Include links to other methods or back to options as appropriate, and note in which version items were introduced or changed.

7.3.3 *Demonstrating your plugin's abilities*

First impressions count for a lot, so present your plugin in the best possible light by providing a web page that demonstrates most, if not all, of its abilities.

First, show the plugin in its default configuration, and then add examples of customizing it by setting various options. Where possible, include the code that you run to produce these examples, allowing users to find a sample that is close to what they want and to copy the relevant script to achieve that.

As well as serving as a showpiece and a repository of examples for potential users, your demonstration page also provides a valuable testing tool for your plugin, especially its visual aspects that are difficult to test with an automated tool. Open the page and put it through its paces on all the major browsers.

You can also include any or all of the following:

- Instructions on how to implement the plugin on the user's page
- Feedback from other users
- A list of websites that already use the plugin
- A quick reference to all the options available
- A link to more detailed documentation for the plugin
- Access to localizations for the plugin (with appropriate credits)
- A list of previous versions and the changes therein

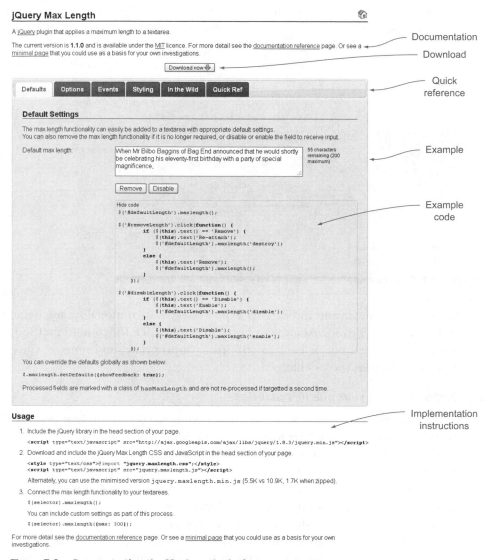

Figure 7.8   Demonstrating the MaxLength plugin

Figure 7.8 shows the main part of the demonstration page for the MaxLength plugin.

What you need to know

Having a unit test suite for a plugin helps ensure that it works correctly in most situations and browsers.

QUnit provides a JavaScript unit test framework that allows you to comprehensively test your plugin.

(continued)

Package all the files for your plugin into one archive for ease of distribution.

Provide minimized versions of your code in your distribution package to reduce network traffic for potential users.

Document your plugin's options and methods to assist users in customizing it for their own needs.

Provide demonstrations of your plugin's functionality, preferably with code examples, to help convince users to try it.

Try it yourself

Write tests for the Watermark plugin you developed as an exercise in chapter 5, following the pattern of the MaxLength tests shown in this chapter. Make sure you test the option to change where the label text comes from and the `clear` method to erase a label.

7.4 Summary

It's all well and good to have written the best plugin ever, but if users can't easily find, deploy, and configure it, they may bypass it for another offering.

Users expect the plugin to be (relatively) bug free when it's made publicly available. To assist in your testing efforts, the QUnit package enables you to write repeatable unit tests for your code. Try to test every option, method, and function offered by your plugin. Having a set of repeatable tests makes it easier to refactor your plugin code while ensuring that it continues to work as expected.

Package all of the plugin files into a single zip archive to make it easier to distribute and to ensure that nothing gets missed. Provide a minimized version of the plugin code to assist users in reducing the download requirements of your code.

A demonstration page for the plugin serves as a visual test bed for your own use, and it highlights all of the possibilities offered by your plugin. Include code samples to give users a helping hand toward producing similar effects in their own websites.

Document everything so that users know the full range of the plugin's abilities and what to expect when they configure it or interact with it. Describe all of the configuration options available, including event handlers, all of the methods that the plugin recognizes, and any other functions that the plugin offers. Well-written and comprehensive documentation can reduce your maintenance burden as users can often find the answers to problems themselves.

In the next part of the book, you'll see how the jQuery UI package offers its own plugin framework and how to tap into that to write compatible plugins. This chapter on testing, packaging, and documenting your plugin applies to any plugins you produce.

Part 3

Extending jQuery UI

The jQuery UI is a collection of user interface plugins built on top of jQuery. These plugins provide basic behaviors, visual effects, and UI widgets to enhance your web pages. jQuery UI has its own extension points and its own plugin framework.

Chapter 8 examines the widget framework of jQuery UI. This framework also applies the best practice principles described in the previous part and assists in creating a consistent appearance and behavior for all jQuery UI widgets. You'll see how to develop a complete plugin using the framework.

A common requirement for UI widgets is to interact with the mouse through a drag operation. jQuery UI has built-in support for this through its Mouse module. Chapter 9 describes how this provided functionality is integrated into your plugin.

jQuery UI also provides visual effects for highlighting or showing or hiding elements on the page. In chapter 10 you'll see how you can create your own effects using jQuery UI's abilities, as well as how to create a new *easing*, or rate of acceleration of a change, for an animation.

jQuery UI widgets

In the previous part of the book, you saw how to create a collection plugin by using a framework to manage basic interactions with jQuery. Now you'll see how jQuery UI provides a similar framework to ensure that the collection of plugins that make up this package work in a standard manner.

jQuery UI "is a curated set of user interface interactions, effects, widgets, and themes built on top of the jQuery JavaScript Library" (http://jqueryui.com). It's an official jQuery add-on that includes several UI components known as *widgets*. It uses the ThemeRoller tool (http://jqueryui.com/themeroller/) to generate a consistent look and feel for all the widgets that it manages.

If you want to create visual components that integrate with the existing jQuery UI widgets, you need to write your plugin based upon its widget framework. Both the jQuery UI widget framework and the framework presented in chapter 5 let you

131

concentrate on creating your plugin's unique functionality, without having to worry unduly about the underlying infrastructure. They each allow for the storage of state against an element and manage the setting and retrieval of options for each instance of the plugin to customize its appearance and behavior. Both let you invoke additional actions on the plugin by naming the required method and supplying any required parameters to complete that action. And each framework can remove the applied functionality to return the affected elements to their original states.

For a comparison with the previous framework, you'll re-create the MaxLength plugin as a jQuery UI widget. Recall that this plugin limits the amount of text accepted in a `textarea` and provides valuable feedback along the way. By the end of this chapter, you'll have a new plugin with the same look and feel as the standard jQuery components.

8.1   *The widget framework*

jQuery UI is highly modularized, allowing you to choose which parts of the package you want to use, thus reducing the code requirements. You can build a custom download for yourself that takes dependencies between the modules into account (http://jqueryui.com/download).

After reviewing the modules that make up the jQuery UI package, we'll focus on the Widget module and you'll start to reimplement the MaxLength plugin based on the widget framework, which is included in the package.

8.1.1   *jQuery UI modules*

A quick review of the modules that make up jQuery UI will help to orient you and make you aware of the options it provides. Basic functionality required by all of jQuery UI comes from the Core module, which must always be included on your page. It incorporates the `zIndex` function, which lets you retrieve or set the z-index of an element, denoting its position in front of or behind other elements.

The Widget module is the subject of this chapter, providing infrastructure that's used by all of the jQuery UI components. If a widget or behavior relies on mouse drag operations for its functionality, the Mouse module makes that process much easier by converting the mouse movements into callbacks that can be overridden. Chapter 9 examines the Mouse module in more detail. The Position module is a standalone utility that simplifies the placement of one element in relation to another.

jQuery UI includes several lower-level behaviors in their own modules. The Draggable module lets you drag an element across the page using your mouse, whereas the Droppable module allows you to define which other elements will accept and process the dragged element when it's released.

You can use the Resizable module to enable dragging the border of an element to alter its size. The Selectable module lets you choose items from a list, either individually or via dragging the mouse across them. To reorder items in a list, apply the functionality from the Sortable module, once again using the mouse to drag the items into position.

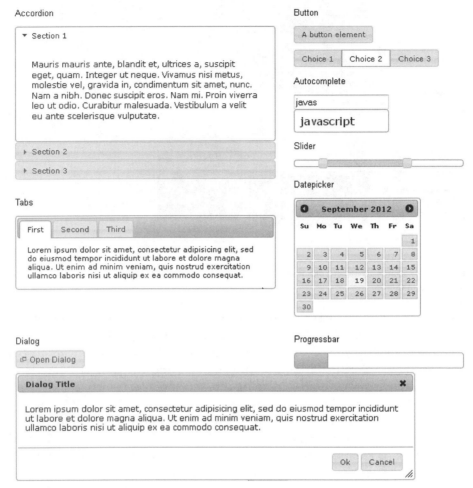

Figure 8.1   The jQuery UI widgets with ThemeRoller styling

Several widgets are currently available as part of jQuery UI (as shown in figure 8.1), and others are planned and in development to be included in future jQuery UI releases.

The Accordion module allows for vertically expanding content beneath sectional headings, whereas the Tabs module stacks multiple content sections and activates one of them from labels across the top. You can use the Dialog module to display a pop-up dialog box over the page, and optionally, to prevent any other interactions with that page.

To obtain a consistent appearance and functionality for action components, such as buttons and links, you can use the Button module. You can use the Autocomplete module to suggest values to populate a field, or the Slider module to visually select a value or range of values within defined limits. To select a date from a pop-up calendar,

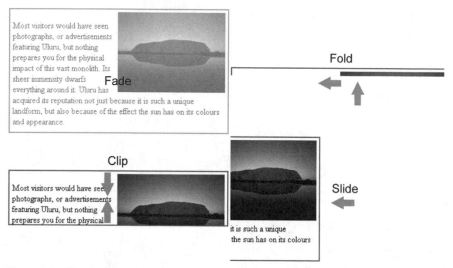

Figure 8.2   jQuery UI effects about 60% through their duration. Clockwise from top left: fade, fold, slide, and clip.

you can use the Datepicker module, or you can place a calendar inline instead. The Progressbar module allows you to display progress through a task in a visual fashion.

New in jQuery UI 1.9 are the Menu module (which provides navigation abilities for your website), the Spinner module (which allows the selection of numeric values by adjusting them up or down), and the Tooltip module (which adds customizable, themeable floating tips for your elements).

A number of visual effects enhance the basics provided by jQuery itself. Most of these can be applied to explicitly show or hide an element or to toggle its visibility, such as Clip or Explode, whereas some serve to draw attention to an element, such as Highlight or Shake. Common functionality used by several effects is contained within the Effects Core module. Figure 8.2 shows several effects partway through their animations. Chapter 10 looks at jQuery UI effects in more detail.

This chapter looks in detail at the jQuery UI widget framework, which is encapsulated in the Widget module.

8.1.2   *The Widget module*

The Widget module is the key one when you develop a UI component for use with jQuery UI. It defines the $.Widget "class" that forms the basis for any new component. (Although JavaScript doesn't have classes as a formal construct, you can create objects that resemble classes as defined in other languages, and I'll refer to them as such.) This class provides the basic functionality that's common to all widgets to ensure that they operate in the same manner: the *widget framework*.

Among the standard abilities are

- Attaching the widget to an element
- Processing initial options for a widget instance

- Retrieving and setting option values after initialization
- Retaining state for a widget instance
- Handling enabling and disabling the widget
- Registering and invoking event handlers
- Invoking custom methods on the widget
- Integrating with ThemeRoller for a consistent look and feel
- Removing the widget if no longer required

The lifecycle of a widget (as it applies to the MaxLength plugin) is described in greater detail in section 8.1.4.

8.1.3　*The MaxLength plugin*

As mentioned earlier, in this chapter you'll redevelop the MaxLength plugin from chapter 5 using the jQuery UI widget framework. This plugin will provide a maximum length restriction for `textarea` fields, similar to the built-in `maxlength` attribute for input fields. It will be called in the same manner as before, either with default settings or with customized options:

```
$('#text1').maxlength();
$('#text1').maxlength({max: 400});
```

As well as limiting the text that can be entered, the plugin will provide feedback on how many characters have been used or remain available for input, as shown in figure 8.3. The feedback will use the current ThemeRoller theme to integrate its appearance with the rest of the page.

The plugin will include the same functionality as before:

- Warn users only when they reach the maximum number of characters
- Suppress feedback altogether
- Show feedback only when the `textarea` is active
- Trigger a callback when reaching or exceeding its maximum

This plugin will follow the principle of *providing progressive enhancements*. Without Java-Script, you can still enter text and the length restriction will be imposed on the server upon submission. With JavaScript, the plugin will restrict the amount of text that may be entered prior to submission and provides valuable feedback along the way.

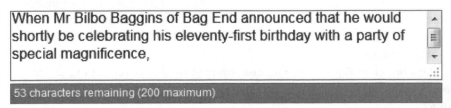

Figure 8.3　The MaxLength jQuery UI plugin in operation

8.1.4 MaxLength plugin operation

The plugin code consists of a number of functions that override or enhance the abilities provided by the widget framework. These are shown in the following listing, and the way that these are invoked during the lifecycle of the widget is described after the listing.

> **Listing 8.1 Plugin function outline**

```
var maxlengthOverrides = {                          ❶ Widget defaults
    options: {...},                                               ❷ Initialization
    _create: function() {...},                                      for an element
    _setOption: function(key, value) {...},         ❹ Custom
    _setOptions: function(options) {...},              options handling
    refresh: function() {...},                                   Refresh widget
    curLength: function() {...},                               ❺ appearance
    _checkLength: function() {...},        ❻ Retrieve current length
    _destroy: function() {...}                      Remove maxlength
};                                                   ❽ functionality
$.widget('kbw.maxlength', maxlengthOverrides);
```

Custom option handling ❸

Enforce length restrictions ❼

As usual, you apply the plugin to one or more `textarea` elements on the page using jQuery's select-and-operate approach. The widget framework creates an instance object for each affected element to hold the current state of the plugin, and stores that against the element. Attributes of that instance object include the set of default options (`options` in the listing at ❶) and customized option overrides supplied in the initialization call. These settings control the plugin's appearance and behavior. After performing the necessary setup, the framework calls the `_create` function ❷ to allow you to complete the initialization for an element.

If at a later time the user wants to change the options for an instance of the plugin, they use the `option` method. This triggers one call to the `_setOptions` function ❹ to deal with the options as a group, and multiple calls to the `_setOption` function ❸ to handle individual option changes.

Both the initialization and option change processes end up calling the custom `refresh` function ❺, which synchronizes the plugin's appearance and behavior with the new option values.

As part of the custom initialization for the plugin, it attaches event handlers to the `textarea` to monitor its keystrokes. Each keystroke triggers a call to the `_checkLength` function ❼, which enforces the current maximum length on the entered text and updates any associated feedback element to reflect the new status. If the `textarea` is full and the user has registered a callback for this event, they're notified of the situation immediately.

The user may request the current count of used and remaining characters at any time by invoking the `curLength` method, which is mapped onto the `curLength` function ❻:

```
var lengths = $('#text1').maxlength('curLength');
```

NOTE Functions with names that don't start with an underscore (_) may be called directly via the widget framework by supplying the name of that function when invoking the plugin, as shown in the curLength sample here. Those that do start with an underscore are hidden by the framework and aren't accessible.

The user may remove the MaxLength functionality altogether by calling the destroy method, which is passed through to the _destroy function **8**. This process undoes all the changes made in the initialization steps.

To begin developing your plugin, you need to declare your new widget so that you can use the widget framework functionality.

8.2 *Defining your widget*

You still need to complete a few basic steps before you can start developing the specific functionality of your plugin. These are

- Claiming a name for the widget
- Protecting your code from the wider JavaScript environment, and vice versa
- Declaring the new widget

Let's look at these in turn.

8.2.1 *Claiming a name*

Your plugin needs some way to be identified, and it needs to stay separate from other plugins. The widget framework helps to apply the principle of *only claiming a single name and using that for everything* through its widget definition call. Even so, you still need to choose an appropriate name and namespace for your plugin.

The namespace is designed to help isolate plugins from one another, but only the plugin name is used to access the functionality, so that name must be unique on its own. As discussed previously, if two plugins with the same name are included on one page, only one (the last one loaded) will be accessible.

In this example, you'll use the same plugin name as before (maxlength) and add a namespace of kbw (my initials). The plugin name and namespace should contain only lowercase characters, digits, and hyphens (-) or underscores (_). The ui namespace is reserved for official jQuery UI plugins and shouldn't be used for your own plugins. Other than that, the namespace should indicate where the plugin comes from and whether it forms part of a collection of plugins.

The plugin code should appear in a file named jquery.<pluginname>.js. To distinguish this plugin from the one developed in chapter 5, name the file jquery.maxlengthui.js, while keeping the plugin name itself maxlength. The associated CSS uses the same file name, but with a different extension.

8.2.2 *Encapsulating the plugin*

Although the widget framework provides a lot of common functionality, you must still use the same anonymous function construct seen in chapter 5 to apply the principles of *hiding the implementation details by using scope* and *don't rely on $ being the same as jQuery.* This serves to protect your plugin's implementation from the rest of the JavaScript environment and vice versa, and it can be seen in the following listing.

Listing 8.2   Encapsulating the plugin code

```
(function($) { // Hide scope, no $ conflict          ◁┐  Declare
    ... the rest of the code appears here               │  anonymous
})(jQuery);                           ◁──❷ Immediately invoke it   ❶ function
```

The anonymous function ❶ serves as a new *scope*—variables and functions defined within this function aren't visible externally. Internal code won't interfere with any external code. You can use the jQuery object itself to provide access to the functionality of your plugin in a controlled manner.

   The wrapper function ensures that within its body, $ refers to the jQuery object, by declaring $ as a parameter and then supplying jQuery as the value when invoking it immediately ❷. Within this function, you include the code for your new widget, which starts with the declaration of the widget itself.

> **NOTE**   As noted previously, do *not* wrap your plugin code in a $(document).ready(function() {...}) callback, or its shorthand form $(function() {...}). You want the code to execute immediately when it's loaded, and to be available subsequently when the normal jQuery initialization is run.

8.2.3   *Declaring the widget*

The widget framework manages the creation of widgets, allowing it to add standard functionality to all of them. Common abilities include initializing the plugin for a collection of elements, handling option setting and retrieval, and removing plugin functionality when it's no longer needed. You create your widget as follows.

Listing 8.3   Declaring the widget

```
var maxlengthOverrides = {                      ◁┐  Define widget
                                                 ❶ functionality
    // Global defaults for maxlength
    options: {                         ◁┐  Provide
        max: 200, // Maximum length     ❷ default options
        ... Other default settings
    },

    _create: function() {...},

    // Other widget code
};

/* Maxlength restrictions for textareas.
   Depends on jquery.ui.widget. */              ❸ Declare
$.widget('kbw.maxlength', maxlengthOverrides);  ◁┘ new widget
```

The widget framework lets you override or enhance its inherited abilities, so you start by defining an object with attributes that provide those overrides ❶, including default option values and custom methods. The contents of this object are described in detail throughout the rest of this chapter.

As in chapter 5, you allow the behavior of the widget to be customized by passing optional settings to it. Following the principle of *using sensible defaults*, you define an `options` object as part of the widget to hold the default values ❷. Most of the options for the MaxLength plugin are identical to those defined in chapter 5. The one difference is the callback function triggered when the `textarea` reaches or exceeds its specified maximum. In chapter 5 it was named `onFull`, but the standard practice in jQuery UI is to omit the `on` part, so here it's just named `full`. Part of the reason behind this change is that jQuery UI allows you to attach an event handler to these internal events via the standard `bind` or `on` functions and connects it to the appropriate event automatically. The event is named from a combination of the plugin name and the option name. You can then provide an event handler as follows:

```
$('#text1').maxlength().bind('maxlengthfull', function(event, ui) {
    ...
});
```

jQuery UI doesn't have a standard localization strategy, so don't worry about incorporating localization support into this widget.

You must declare your widget by invoking the `$.widget` function ❸ and provide the name of the widget, including its namespace, separated by a period (`.`). The last parameter is the object that overrides or extends the inherited widget abilities.

An optional second parameter for this call defines which other widget "class" to use as the basis for the new one. Because you're creating a new widget with only basic inherited functionality, this parameter can be omitted here, and the default `$.Widget` is used. Chapter 9 describes a jQuery UI widget that uses this parameter to include mouse interactions by specifying `$.ui.mouse` as the class to inherit from.

Following your widget declaration, the widget framework creates a new function for jQuery element collections named with the plugin name (`$.fn.maxlength` in this case) and connects it to your overrides as provided in the code. Behind the scenes, the `$.widget.bridge` function performs the mapping between jQuery's collection processing and your custom widget.

Now that your new widget is named and inherits the standard widget functionality, you can start customizing its behavior to meet your requirements.

8.3 Attaching the plugin to an element

The widget framework automatically handles attaching the plugin to a collection of elements, but you probably want to perform some processing when that occurs. To add your own code, you extend the basic widget as part of its definition, overriding the inherited implementation that does nothing.

8.3.1 Basic attachment and initialization

The framework intercepts the plugin initialization call and performs some standard processing around that. It creates a widget instance object and assigns that to the selected element via the data function as an attribute named for the plugin. The name combines the namespace and plugin name separated by a dash, from jQuery UI 1.9 onwards (kbw-maxlength in this case), or it's just the plugin name, prior to jQuery UI 1.9 (maxlength). Within that object are two key attributes: element and options. The former is a reference to the element to which the plugin is applied, and the latter is a copy of the default options for the plugin, overridden by any customized option values.

During the initialization process, the framework calls the _create function, which you can provide in your plugin code by supplying it as part of the overrides in the widget declaration, as shown in the next listing. Within the _create function, this refers to the current widget instance object.

> **Listing 8.4 Attachment and initialization**

```
/* Initialise a new maxlength textarea. */
_create: function() {                                    ← ❶ Override the
    this.feedbackTarget = $([]);                              _create function
    var self = this;
    this.element.addClass(this.widgetFullName || this.widgetBaseClass).
        bind('keypress.' + this.widgetEventPrefix, function(event) {    ←
            if (!self.options.truncate) {
                return true;                                 Add event
            }                                                handlers ❸
            var ch = String.fromCharCode(event.charCode == undefined ?
                event.keyCode : event.charCode);
            return (event.ctrlKey || event.metaKey || ch == '\u0000' ||
                $(this).val().length < self.options.max);
        }).
        bind('keyup.' + this.widgetEventPrefix, function() {
            self._checkLength($(this));
        });                                              ❹ Refresh the widget
    this.refresh();                                         appearance
},
```

❷ Add a marker class

To have the widget framework call your code at the appropriate time, you define the _create function ❶. You should add a marker class to the currently selected element ❷ to help identify affected elements within your page. In chapter 5 this was also done to indicate that the element had already been initialized for this plugin. The widget framework uses the presence of the widget instance object as data to indicate the same thing. The framework provides the this.widgetFullName value (this.widgetBase-Class prior to jQuery UI 1.9) for your use in this and similar circumstances. Its value is the plugin namespace and name separated by a hyphen (-).

The remainder of the code in this function applies processing specific to the plugin. For the MaxLength plugin, you add keystroke handlers to the main element (the textarea) ❸ to allow its state to be updated as soon as the text content changes. You should add a namespace to the events to enable them to be easily identified later on by appending the this.widgetEventPrefix value provided by the framework. Note the reference to the widget options provides the maximum length given for this textarea, and that an internal function is called (_checkLength). Both are part of the widget instance object this, which is aliased by self within the event handlers.

Finally, you should call the custom refresh function ❹ to modify the plugin based on the options currently set. Section 8.4.3 has more details on this function, but first you'll see how the options' default values are defined and how the framework reacts to changes in their values.

8.4 Handling plugin options

You can customize a plugin instance by providing options to alter its appearance or behavior. Recall the guiding principle to *anticipate customizations*. Attempt to predict what users might want to change, so that you can supply an option to let them do that. Then consider the principle to *use sensible defaults,* and assign an initial value to the option that's likely to satisfy most users.

To achieve these goals, you need to

- Define default values for all options.
- Handle retrieving and setting option values.
- Apply any option changes immediately.
- Allow the plugin to be enabled or disabled.

8.4.1 Widget defaults

The widget framework automatically handles the initial setting of options for a plugin instance and assigns them to the widget instance object's options attribute, which is usually accessed via this. It copies any default values specified in the widget declaration and overrides these with any values that are supplied in the initialization call.

The following listing shows how to define the default option values. Recall that this object forms part of the custom overrides in the widget declaration.

Listing 8.5 Default option values

```
// Global defaults for maxlength
options: {                                          ┌─── Define global default
    max: 200, // Maximum length                     ❶    option values
    truncate: true, // True to disallow further input,
        // false to highlight only
    showFeedback: true, // True to always show user feedback,
        // 'active' for hover/focus only
    feedbackTarget: null, // jQuery selector or function for
        // element to fill with feedback
    feedbackText: '{r} characters remaining ({m} maximum)',
        // Display text for feedback message,
        // use {r} for remaining characters,
        // {c} for characters entered, {m} for maximum
    overflowText: '{o} characters too many ({m} maximum)',
        // Display text when past maximum,
        // use substitutions above and {o} for characters past maximum
    full: null // Callback when full or overflowing,
        // receives two parameters: the triggering event and
```

```
                 // an object with attribute overflow set to true
                 // if overflowing, false if not
          },
```

The default values end up as an attribute of the widget prototype ❶. To make them more accessible, you can map an attribute directly within the plugin onto the set of default values:

```
// Make some things more accessible
$.kbw.maxlength.options = $.kbw.maxlength.prototype.options;
```

You'd then override defaults for all plugin instances as follows, prior to invoking the plugin on any elements:

```
$.extend($.kbw.maxlength.options, {max: 300, truncate: false});
```

8.4.2 *Reacting to option changes*

The widget framework also automatically handles retrieving and updating option values throughout the plugin's lifetime. In retrieval mode, the `option` method lets you specify the name of an option and returns its current value (taking default values into account). If you don't provide a name, the entire set of options is returned:

```
var maxChars = $('#text1').maxlength('option', 'max');
var options = $('#text1').maxlength('option');
```

In setter mode, the `option` method can change a single named value, or multiple options from a given map:

```
$('#text1').maxlength('option', 'max', 400);
$('#text1').maxlength('option', {max: 400, truncate: false});
```

The particular mode of operation is determined by the number and type of parameters supplied in the call.

You can hook into the setting process to observe changes and react to them by providing either or both `_setOption` and `_setOptions` functions as part of the widget overrides supplied during the widget declaration. The following listing shows how to react to individual option changes.

> **Listing 8.6   Handling individual options**

```
/* Custom option handling.
   @param key    (string) the name of the option being changed          ❶ Override
   @param value  (any) its new value */                                     _setOption
_setOption: function(key, value) {                                          function
   switch (key) {                                             ❷ Take action specific
      case 'disabled':                                           to an option
         this.element.prop('disabled', value);
         this.feedbackTarget.toggleClass('ui-state-disabled', value);
         break;
   }
   // Base widget handling                              ❸ Call default
   this._superApply(arguments);                            option handling
},
```

The _setOption function ❶ receives two parameters: the name and new value of the option being changed. If multiple options are supplied in one call from the user, they're processed individually through this function. Depending on the name of the option ❷, decide what changes need to be made. For the MaxLength plugin, you should monitor the `disabled` status of the widget and adjust its appearance and behavior accordingly.

Make sure you call the basic widget handler for setting an option value ❸ to have it update the value that's stored in the widget instance object. Prior to calling this handler, you can access both the new option value (`value`) and the old option value (`this.options[key]`) if you need to compare the two.

As previously mentioned, the _setOption function is called for each changed option in turn. If you want to add some processing before or after a set of options is altered, you can provide a _setOptions function for that purpose, as follows.

Listing 8.7   Handling any option change

```
/* Custom options handling.
   @param  option  (object) the new option values */          ❶ Override
_setOptions: function(options) {                                 _setOptions function
   // Base widget handling
   this._superApply(arguments);                                ❷ Call default
   this.refresh();                          ❸ Refresh widget      options handling
},                                              appearance
```

The _setOptions function ❶ receives one parameter: the new option names and values as an object. You should always invoke the standard processing of these options, which includes the individual processing just described, by calling the same function in the base widget ❷. Then you can refresh the appearance and behavior of the widget based on its new option values ❸. By refreshing the widget in this function rather than the previous one, you reduce the performance cost, because it's only done once after a collection of changes is made, instead of repeatedly for each separate option. The `refresh` function is described in the next section.

Prior to jQuery UI 1.9

The way an inherited function is called changed in jQuery UI 1.9. In the newer jQuery UI versions, you call the function through a reference to the parent class, like this:

```
this._superApply(arguments);
```

In the older versions, you refer to the widget prototype and invoke the same function there, like this:

```
$.Widget.prototype._setOption.apply(this, arguments);
```

Or like this:

```
$.Widget.prototype._setOptions.apply(this, arguments);
```

(continued)

To allow your widget to work in the current and earlier jQuery UI versions, you can test for the presence of the new function and act accordingly, as in this example:

```
// Base widget handling
if (this._superApply) {
    this._superApply(arguments);
}
else {
    $.Widget.prototype._setOption.apply(this, arguments);
}
```

8.4.3   *Implementing MaxLength options*

You can change the appearance and/or behavior of the MaxLength plugin by supplying options to it. Figure 8.4 shows the effect of some option changes.

These values need to be reapplied to the affected elements as they change, potentially removing the consequences of a previous usage. The custom `refresh` function performs this task and is called upon initialization (see section 8.3.1) and when an option is altered (see section 8.4.2). The first half of its definition is shown in listing 8.8.

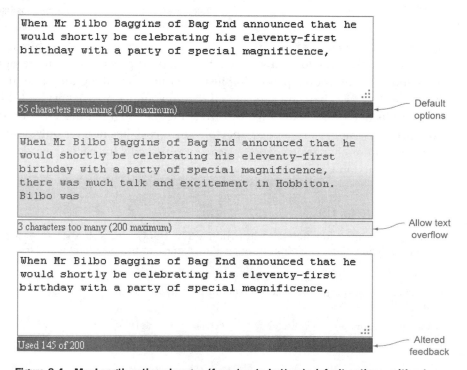

Figure 8.4   MaxLength option changes (from top to bottom): default options, without truncation, and changing feedback text

Listing 8.8　Refresh the widget appearance and behavior

```
/* Refresh the appearance of the maxlength textarea. */        ➊ Define refresh
refresh: function() {                                               function
    if (this.feedbackTarget.length > 0) {
        // Remove old feedback element                             If there was
        if (this.hadFeedbackTarget) {                              feedback
            this.feedbackTarget.empty().val('').             ➋ previously...
                removeClass((this.widgetFullName ||
                    this.widgetBaseClass) + this._feedbackClass + ' ' +
                    this._fullClass + ' ' + this._overflowClass);
        }
        else {                                                  ➍ Remove built-in
            this.feedbackTarget.remove();                          feedback
        }                                              ➎ Clear feedback
        this.feedbackTarget = $([]);                      target reference    If feedback  ➏
    }                                                                      required, do 7-11
    if (this.options.showFeedback) { // Add new feedback element
        this.hadFeedbackTarget = !!this.options.feedbackTarget;
        if ($.isFunction(this.options.feedbackTarget)) {
            this.feedbackTarget =
                this.options.feedbackTarget.apply(this.element[0],[]);
        }
        else if (this.options.feedbackTarget) {
            this.feedbackTarget = $(this.options.feedbackTarget);
        }                                                               Find external
        else {                                                       feedback element ➒
            this.feedbackTarget =
                $('<span></span>').insertAfter(this.element);
        }
        this.feedbackTarget.addClass(                                   Configure
            (this.widgetFullName || this.widgetBaseClass) +             feedback
            this._feedbackClass + ' ui-state-default' +         ⓫ element
            (this.options.disabled ? ' ui-state-disabled' : ''));
    }
    ...
},
```

…reset external feedback element ➌

Remember if external feedback ➐

Evaluate external feedback ➑ function

Create internal feedback ➓ element

You declare the `refresh` function ➊ as part of the widget overrides supplied during the widget definition. By using a name without a leading underscore (_), you allow this function to also be invoked directly as a method:

```
$('#text1').maxlength('refresh');
```

Because the feedback options may have changed, any existing feedback element is removed first. After checking that feedback was previously shown via a reference to that element ➋, the feedback element is reset and cleared if it was externally provided ➌, or it's removed altogether if it was internally generated ➍. In both cases, you clear the reference to the old feedback element ➎.

The new settings are then evaluated to determine whether feedback is now required, based on the `showFeedback` option ➏. If so, you should first remember whether an external feedback element is provided ➐ so that it can be reset correctly in the future. If external feedback is given as a function ❽, you must call it to retrieve the actual element. Otherwise an external feedback element is retrieved via jQuery ❾, allowing it to be specified as a selector string, a DOM element, or an existing jQuery object. If no external feedback element is supplied, you need to create one yourself and add it after the `textarea` ❿. In each case, the resulting feedback element is stored in the `feedbackTarget` attribute of the instance object (`this`) for later access, and is configured with the appropriate ThemeRoller classes ⓫ to fit its appearance with the rest of the page.

NOTE   The `!!` construct is explained in section 3.2.1.

The second half of the `refresh` function mainly deals with handling the option to show feedback only when the element is active.

Listing 8.9   Refresh the widget event handlers

```
/* Refresh the appearance of the maxlength textarea. */
refresh: function() {
    ...
    this.element.unbind('mouseover.' + this.widgetEventPrefix +
        ' focus.' + this.widgetEventPrefix +
        ' mouseout.' + this.widgetEventPrefix +
        ' blur.' + this.widgetEventPrefix);
    if (this.options.showFeedback == 'active') {
        // Additional event handlers
        var self = this;
        this.element.
            bind('mouseover.' + this.widgetEventPrefix, function() {
                self.feedbackTarget.css('visibility', 'visible');
            }).bind('mouseout.' + this.widgetEventPrefix, function() {
                if (!self.focussed) {
                    self.feedbackTarget.css('visibility', 'hidden');
                }
            }).bind('focus.' + this.widgetEventPrefix, function() {
                self.focussed = true;
                self.feedbackTarget.css('visibility', 'visible');
            }).bind('blur.' + this.widgetEventPrefix, function() {
                self.focussed = false;
                self.feedbackTarget.css('visibility', 'hidden');
            });
        this.feedbackTarget.css('visibility', 'hidden');
    }
    this._checkLength();
},
```

Callout labels:
- **Remove previous event handlers** ❶
- **If showing feedback when active, do 3–6** ❷
- **Show feedback when mouseover** ❸
- **Hide feedback when mouseout** ❹
- **Show feedback when focused** ❺
- **Hide feedback when blurred** ❻
- **Initially hide feedback** ❼
- **Apply actual length check** ❽

As with the feedback element in listing 8.8, any previous events that dealt with showing the feedback only when the `textarea` is active are removed first ❶. By using a namespace for all events when setting them up, you can prevent them interfering with other handlers on that element and make their removal here much simpler. You just can't remove all such namespaced events here, as the keystroke events created during initialization must remain.

If the user has opted to have only active feedback ❷, you attach handlers for the events that indicate its active status. You should show the feedback when the mouse moves over the `textarea` ❸, and hide it again when the mouse leaves ❹, but only if the user hasn't moved focus to that element. Similarly, feedback should be shown when the `textarea` receives focus ❺ and hidden when it loses focus ❻. As noted earlier, you should specify a namespaced event name, using the `widgetEventPrefix` value because it's unique to each widget, to simplify the later removal of the handlers. In each case, the `visibility` of the feedback element is altered so as to show or hide the text, while still reserving the space that it occupies. Initially the feedback is hidden ❼.

Finally, you apply the maximum length restriction to the `textarea` by invoking the `_checkLength` function ❽. See section 8.8.1 for details about this function.

8.4.4 *Enabling and disabling the widget*

Within the widget framework, enabling and disabling a widget is standard functionality and doesn't require any action on your part.

The widget status is controlled by the `disabled` option being set to `true` (disabled) or `false` (enabled). The framework also maps the `enable` and `disable` methods onto changes of this option value:

```
$('#text1').maxlength('disable');
...
$('#text1').maxlength('enable');
```

Internally, the framework toggles two classes on the main element—`<namespace>-<plugin name>-disabled` and `ui-state-disabled`—and sets the `aria-disabled` attribute appropriately. You can add extra processing around enabling and disabling by watching for changes to the `disabled` option in a custom `_setOption` function (as shown in section 8.4.2).

Now that users can configure your new widget, let's look at how they can respond to changes in its state via events.

8.5 *Adding event handlers*

You can allow users to react to significant incidents within your plugin's lifecycle by providing custom events to which they can subscribe. Sometimes situations arise during the plugin's processing that the user may want to know about immediately, such as the `change` event for an input field being triggered whenever new content is accepted. By listening for such an event, the user can instantly update the page according to the new state of the plugin. The widget framework provides support for invoking events in the form of the `_trigger` function.

To add event callbacks to your plugin, you need to do two things:

- Allow the user to register handlers for an event.
- Trigger those events at the appropriate time.

Let's look at those two steps.

8.5.1   *Registering an event handler*

Only one event is provided by this plugin: `full`. It occurs when the `textarea` has reached or exceeded the maximum number of allowed characters. A flag is passed as one of the event parameters to indicate whether the limit has been exceeded (because of the `truncate` option being `false`), requiring the text to be shortened before submission.

The `full` handler appears as just another option for the plugin, as shown in listing 8.10, and defaults to `null` when no callback is required. To use it, the user assigns a function that accepts two parameters, in keeping with other jQuery UI event handlers. The first parameter is the triggering event and the second is a custom `ui` object, which here holds the overflow flag. Within that callback function, the `this` variable refers to the main element to which the plugin is applied, possibly allowing the user to reuse a handler across several instances.

Listing 8.10   Defining an event handler

```
// Global defaults for maxlength
options: {
    ...
    full: null // Callback when full or overflowing,
        // receives two parameters: the triggering event and
        // an object with attribute overflow set to
        // true if overflowing, false if not
},
```

Users register their event handler during the plugin initialization, as shown in the next snippet, or by updating options at a later stage:

```
$('#text1').maxlength({full: function(event, ui) {
    $('#warning').show();
}});
```

The plugin framework automatically maps a custom event onto this handler so that you can use the standard `bind` or `on` functionality of jQuery to subscribe to the event. The event is named from the plugin name combined with the option name (`maxlengthfull` in this case).

```
$('#text1').maxlength().on('maxlengthfull', function(event, ui) {
    $('#warning').show();
}});
```

Once the event handler has been set, you need to invoke it at the proper time within the lifecycle of the plugin.

8.5.2   *Triggering an event handler*

The `full` event is triggered at the end of the `_checkLength` function in the MaxLength plugin, once you've applied the maximum length restriction, as shown in the following listing. In other plugins you'd trigger events at other appropriate points in the code.

Listing 8.11   Triggering an event

```
/* Check the length of the text and notify accordingly. */
_checkLength: function() {
    var value = this.element.val();
    var len = value.replace(/\r\n/g, '~~').replace(/\n/g, '~~').length;
    ...
    if (len >= this.options.max) {
        this._trigger('full', null, $.extend(this.curLength(),
            {overflow: len > this.options.max}));
    }
},
```

Test trigger ❶ **condition**

Invoke event ❷

You check that the triggering condition is true ❶ before generating the event via the widget's _trigger function ❷. The parameters for the latter are the name of the event, the original event that caused this trigger to fire, and a custom `ui` object that holds information relevant to this widget. Providing a `null` original event causes jQuery to create a custom event object with a type named from the plugin name and the event name: `maxlengthfull`. Note that if the plugin name is the same as the event name, then the event type isn't the doubling of that name, but just a single copy. For example, the `drag` event within the `drag` plugin just has a type of `drag`.

If you want the user to be able to cancel an action via a callback, they must call `event.preventDefault()` within their handler. This causes the `_trigger` call that invoked the handler to return `false`, allowing you to test the response and act accordingly. For example, your plugin code may look like this:

```
if (this._trigger('myevent', null, {value: this.value})) {
    ... // Only if not cancelled
}
```

The user would cancel the event when the value is greater than 10 as follows:

```
$(selector).myplugin({myevent: function(event, ui) {
        if (ui.value > 10) {
            event.preventDefault();
        }
    }
});
```

Event callbacks allow you to react to changes initiated by the widget itself. To initiate other behaviors yourself, you add custom methods to the widget that can be invoked when necessary by providing their name and possibly some parameters to adjust their functionality.

8.6   *Adding methods*

To implement other functionality within the plugin, you use custom methods, passing that method's name as part of the widget call, such as enabling or disabling the widget:

```
$('#text1').maxlength('enable');
$('#text1').maxlength('disable');
```

The widget framework supports this by allowing any function that doesn't start with an underscore (_) to be invoked directly as a method. If that function returns a value, it's passed through to the caller. Otherwise the current jQuery collection is returned, allowing the call to be chained.

Any function that starts with an underscore is considered an internal one and can't be accessed in this manner. But these functions can be accessed directly on the widget instance object. For example, from jQuery UI 1.9 onward,

```
$('#text1').data('kbw-maxlength')._setOptions({...});
```

or prior to jQuery UI 1.9,

```
$('#text1').data('maxlength')._setOptions({...});
```

8.6.1   *Getting the current length*

As an example of a custom method, you can allow the user to retrieve the current character counts for a particular instance of the MaxLength plugin by using the cur-Length method, as shown in the next listing. It returns an object with attributes used (indicating the number of characters entered) and remaining (to hold the number of characters still allowed). Note that if the textarea is allowed to overflow the imposed limit, then used may be greater than the max setting, and remaining will be negative.

Listing 8.12   Retrieving the current length

```
/* Retrieve the counts of characters used and remaining.
   @return  (object) the current counts with attributes
            used and remaining */                               ❶ Function for
curLength: function() {                                            method curLength
    var value = this.element.val();
    var len = value.replace(/\r\n/g, '~~').replace(/\n/g, '~~').length;
    return {used: len, remaining: this.options.max - len};    ❷ Return current
},                                                               lengths
```

To link the custom method to an implementing function, you must name that function the same as the method to be used ❶. When appropriate, you return the requested value from the function ❷, which is then passed directly back to the user. If you return nothing from a custom method function, the widget framework automatically returns the original jQuery object, allowing calls to such methods to be chained in the usual manner.

You'd call this method as follows:

```
var lengths = $('#text1').maxlength('curLength');
alert(lengths.remaining + ' characters remaining');
```

Custom methods on other plugins may allow or require parameters to control how they operate, such as setting a new position on a slider:

```
$('#slider').slider('value', 25);
```

To implement this, you'd list the parameters in the function definition as usual and use them in the body of the function, and the widget framework will pass through any additional values supplied with the method call.

The code presented so far allows the user to attach the MaxLength plugin to specified elements, set or retrieve its option values, and register handlers for significant events. But the user may want to remove the MaxLength functionality at some stage, as described in the next section.

8.7 Removing the widget

To remove all trace of your widget, the user invokes the destroy method. Like other methods, this generates a call to the function with the same name within the plugin—destroy.

8.7.1 The _destroy method

To add your own processing to the destroy method, you must provide a _destroy function as part of the widget overrides during its declaration. The built-in widget destroy function automatically calls this to implement the widget-specific behavior. Within _destroy, you undo whatever was done in the _create and refresh functions, as follows.

> **Listing 8.13 Removing the widget**

```
/* Remove the maxlength textarea functionality. */          ❶ Define the destroy
_destroy: function() {                                           function
    if (this.feedbackTarget.length > 0) {
        if (this.hadFeedbackTarget) {                       ❷ If there was
            this.feedbackTarget.empty().val('').              feedback, do 3–5
                css('visibility', 'visible').
                removeClass((this.widgetFullName ||
                    this.widgetBaseClass) +
                    this._feedbackClass + ' ' +
                    this._fullClass + ' ' +
                    this._overflowClass);
        }
        else {                                              ❹ Remove built-in
            this.feedbackTarget.remove();                     feedback
        }
    }
    this.element.removeClass(                               ❺ Remove plugin
            (this.widgetFullName || this.widgetBaseClass) + ' ' +   functionality
            this._fullClass + ' ' + this._overflowClass).
        unbind('.' + this.widgetEventPrefix);
}
```

Reset external feedback element ❸ (points to the `this.feedbackTarget.empty().val('')` line)

You start by declaring the function to enhance the destroy method ❶. For the MaxLength plugin, you first check to see whether feedback was being shown by testing the attribute that references any feedback element ❷. If so, you then need to determine whether it was an external element, in which case it must be reset to its original state ❸, or was an internal element that can be removed totally ❹.

You should then remove the marker class and any status classes that were added, and remove any event handlers that were attached ❺. Clearing the event handlers is greatly simplified by the use of a namespace when adding them. Just refer to that same namespace to safely delete all matching handlers, leaving any other handlers intact.

After executing this method, the MaxLength functionality no longer applies to the selected elements and your page has been returned to its initial state.

Prior to jQuery UI 1.9

Prior to jQuery UI 1.9, you had to override the destroy function instead of _destroy and had to invoke the inherited functionality by referring to the widget prototype. To allow your plugin to operate in the current and earlier versions of jQuery UI, you should extend your plugin overrides to add the destroy function in those earlier versions and have it call _destroy, like the latest version does. You also need to call the inherited destroy function from the widget framework. The full code for this is shown here:

```
if (!$.Widget.prototype._destroy) {
    $.extend(maxlengthOverrides, {
        /* Remove the maxlength textarea functionality. */
        destroy: function() {
            this._destroy();
            // Base widget handling
            $.Widget.prototype.destroy.call(this);
        }
    });
}
```

8.8 *Finishing touches*

Interactions between the plugin and the widget framework are now complete. But there are a couple of finishing touches to make to this plugin:

- Implementing the widget body
- Styling it to define its appearance

The widget body implements the main purpose of this plugin—restricting text in a textarea.

8.8.1 *The widget body*

The MaxLength plugin is designed to limit the amount of text that may be entered into a textarea. Up until now, you've been integrating the plugin with the widget framework to provide and then customize the standard widget functionality. Eventually all paths lead to the _checkLength function, which does the actual work of determining the content length and truncating it if necessary. The following listing shows the code for this function.

Listing 8.14 Checking the field length

```
/* Check the length of the text and notify accordingly. */
_checkLength: function() {
    var value = this.element.val();
    var len = value.replace(/\r\n/g, '~~').replace(/\n/g, '~~').length;
    this.element.toggleClass(this._fullClass, len >= this.options.max).
        toggleClass(this._overflowClass, len > this.options.max);
    if (len > this.options.max && this.options.truncate) {
        // Truncation
        var lines = this.element.val().split(/\r\n|\n/);
        value = '';
        var i = 0;
        while (value.length < this.options.max && i < lines.length) {
            value += lines[i].substring(
                0, this.options.max - value.length) + '\r\n';
            i++;
        }
        this.element.val(value.substring(0, this.options.max));
        this.element[0].scrollTop =
            this.element[0].scrollHeight; // Scroll to bottom
        len = this.options.max;
    }
    this.feedbackTarget.toggleClass(
            this._fullClass, len >= this.options.max).
        toggleClass(this._overflowClass, len > this.options.max);
    var feedback = (len > this.options.max ? // Feedback
        this.options.overflowText : this.options.feedbackText).
            replace(/\{c\}/, len).
            replace(/\{m\}/, this.options.max).
            replace(/\{r\}/, this.options.max - len).
            replace(/\{o\}/, len - this.options.max);
    try {
        this.feedbackTarget.text(feedback);
    }
    catch(e) {
        // Ignore
    }
    try {
        this.feedbackTarget.val(feedback);
    }
    catch(e) {
        // Ignore
    }
    if (len >= this.options.max) {
        this._trigger('full', null, $.extend(this.curLength(),
            {overflow: len > this.options.max}));
    }
},
```

Normalize line endings ❶

Set current state on textarea ❷

Apply text truncation ❸

Set current state on feedback ❹

Populate and show feedback message ❺

Invoke callback when appropriate ❻

You begin by determining the current length of content of the textarea, taking into account browser differences regarding line-ending characters ❶. Then apply one or two classes to the textarea to indicate its current status (full or overflowing) based on that length and the options set for the plugin ❷. Recall that this refers to the current widget instance object and that its main attributes are the original element (element) and the current options (options).

If the user has requested that extra text be truncated and the length exceeds the maximum specified ❸, compute the shortened value, normalizing line endings as necessary. The textarea automatically scrolls back to the top when the text is assigned back into it, so you move back to the bottom to assist the user, assuming that most text entry happens at the end of the content. Update the variable holding the text length if the content has been truncated.

Based on the new length of the text, apply one or two classes to the feedback control ❹. There might appear to be a discrepancy between the status of the textarea and its feedback when truncation occurs, because the length may have been reduced in the previous processing. This is intentional, as the feedback has to represent the updated status, whereas the textarea can show that additional text entry was attempted but failed.

Using a message determined by the overflow state of the plugin, show the status of the textarea in any feedback control ❺. The feedback control may be a div, span, or paragraph, or an input field to allow for maximum flexibility. But these two types of elements have their text set differently, and invoking the wrong one can generate errors in some browsers. Hence the two try/catch statements to push the status into the specified control in a protected manner.

Finally, you notify the user via a provided full callback if the textarea has filled or overflowed ❻. Section 8.5.2 went into greater detail on this subject.

The functionality of the plugin is complete. The next step is to style it appropriately to fit in with other jQuery UI widgets.

8.8.2   Styling the widget

jQuery UI uses the ThemeRoller tool to generate CSS for its widgets, providing a consistent look and feel for all components, and to follow the principle of *styling your plugin with CSS*. Most of your plugin's appearance is produced by the application of standard classes to your elements to invoke the ThemeRoller styles. If you need any additional styling, provide an external CSS file to accompany your plugin, named the same as the plugin code, but with a different extension: jquery.maxlengthui.css in this case.

The plugin code assigns several state classes to the elements it manages. These classes integrate the appearance of the plugin with other jQuery UI components on the page. The feedback control is initially set to have a class of ui-state-default, with the classes ui-state-highlight and ui-state-error being added to it and to the original textarea when the textarea is full or overflowing, respectively. When the widget is disabled, the standard ui-state-disabled is applied to both the textarea and its feedback control.

As a result of reusing the ThemeRoller classes, the custom CSS for the plugin is minimal, providing a default look for any feedback element as shown here.

Listing 8.15 Styles for the widget

```
/* Styles for Max Length UI plugin v1.0.0 */
.kbw-maxlength-feedback {
    margin: 0em 0em 0em 0.5em;
    font-size: 75%;
    font-weight: normal;
}
```

Feedback
element styling

With a few lines of CSS, the user can change the appearance of the widget as shown in figure 8.5.

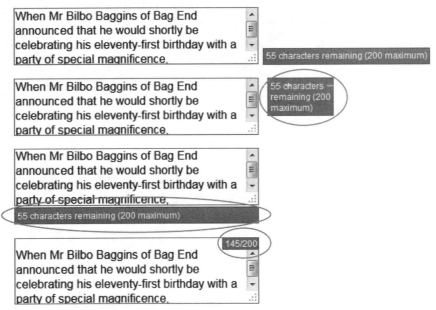

Figure 8.5 Styling the jQuery UI MaxLength plugin (from top to bottom): default style, compact styling, feedback beneath, and feedback overlaid

8.9 *The complete plugin*

The MaxLength jQuery UI widget is now complete, providing maximum length functionality for `textarea` fields to complement the built-in functionality for input fields. The widget framework included in jQuery UI makes the implementation of this plugin simple, and assists in applying the guidelines and design principles described in chapter 4. The complete code for the plugin is available for download from the book's website.

Additional widget functionality

The widget framework provides a few more abilities that were not used or covered in this chapter.

Name constants

You used two name constants in the code of the MaxLength plugin, and the framework provides a couple more. You access each one from the widget instance object (`this`) within your plugin functions.

Name	Purpose	Example
namespace	The namespace you supplied for the plugin in its definition	kbw
widgetBaseClass	A class name used standalone or as a prefix (prior to jQuery UI 1.9)	kbw-maxlength
widgetEventPrefix	The name used as a prefix for event types	maxlength
widgetFullName	A class name used standalone or as a prefix (jQuery UI 1.9 and later)	kbw-maxlength
widgetName	The name of the plugin supplied in its definition	maxlength

Create event

Another way of interacting with the widget's lifecycle is to respond to the `create` event generated as part of the initialization process. It's triggered after the _create function has finished, and it allows you to make further changes for particular instances once the widget is ready

```
$('#text1').maxlength({create: function(event, ui) {
    ...
}});
```

Widget initialization

You overrode the `_create` function to initialize the plugin for a particular element (see section 8.3.1). You can also provide a function to perform further processing for all instances after the initial creation. The _init function is called following _create and the triggering of the `create` event. It receives no parameters, and the `this` variable refers to the widget instance object as usual.

```
$.widget('kbw.maxlength', {
    _init: function() {
        ...
    }
}
```

Metadata support

The widget framework automatically makes use of the Metadata plugin (https://github.com/jquery-orphans/jquery-metadata) if it's available (up until jQuery UI 1.9), allowing you to configure the elements inline rather than via options. For example, you

(continued)

could make a basic initialization call and pick up the required settings from the targeted element like this:

```
$('#text1').maxlength();

<textarea id="text1" rows="5" cols="50"
    class="{maxlength: {max: 300}}"></textarea>
```

From jQuery UI 1.10, the Metadata plugin is no longer supported out of the box. But it's easy to add the functionality back in. You test for the absence of the `_getCreateOptions` function and restore it if it's not there:

```
if ($.Widget.prototype._getCreateOptions === $.noop) {
    $.extend(maxlengthOverrides, {
        /* Restore the metadata functionality. */
        _getCreateOptions: function() {
            return $.metadata && $.metadata.get(
                this.element[0])[this.widgetName];
        }
    });
}
```

Widget access

You can use the `widget` method to retrieve a reference to the main element, which the plugin manages, from outside of the plugin code. By default, this function returns the original element to which the plugin was applied (`this.element`), but you can override this behavior to provide something more useful. For example, the Dialog plugin returns a reference to the `div` that's wrapped around the original element:

```
$('#dialog').dialog({open: function(event, ui) {
    var wrapper = $(this).dialog('widget');
    ...
}});
```

What you need to know

Create a jQuery UI plugin when you need to integrate with other jQuery UI widgets.

jQuery UI includes the widget framework to provide the basic functionality needed by most collection plugins.

Protect your code and prevent name clashes through scoping.

Use the `$.widget` function to define a new widget.

Override inherited widget functions to customize the new widget's behavior; in particular, `_create`, `_setOptions`, `_setOption`, and `_destroy`.

Provide flexible configuration through options, but always initialize them with sensible default values.

Use named methods for additional functionality within the plugin.

Add appropriate ThemeRoller classes to your elements to integrate the plugin into an applied theme.

Try it yourself

Reimplement your Watermark plugin from the exercise in chapter 5 as a jQuery UI widget. As previously, add an option to control where the label text comes from, and a method to clear the label text on demand.

8.10   *Summary*

jQuery UI is an official jQuery extension that provides a number of enhancements for interacting with a web page. It includes basic utility functions, low-level behaviors (such as drag and drop), high-level components or widgets (such as Tabs and Datepicker), and numerous visual effects. The associated ThemeRoller tool allows a consistent look and feel to be applied to all of the package's widgets.

jQuery UI widgets are built on a common infrastructure provided by the widget framework to ensure that they operate in a consistent manner and are easier to maintain. This framework parallels the custom framework presented in chapter 5.

By re-creating the MaxLength plugin using the widget framework, you've seen the similarities and differences between these two approaches. Both allow you to produce a plugin that integrates properly with jQuery, maintains state for each plugin instance, interacts with the user, and clears up after itself. These frameworks enable you to concentrate on the functionality specific to your plugin, instead of getting bogged down in the basic infrastructure underlying it.

In the next chapter, you'll look at another jQuery UI module—one that simplifies interacting with the mouse—and you'll use it to capture a signature.

jQuery UI mouse interactions

9

This chapter covers

- The jQuery UI Mouse module
- Creating a jQuery UI plugin that uses the mouse

The last chapter introduced you to the jQuery UI widget framework and walked you through developing a plugin using its abilities. You saw how the framework provides basic management of the widget and helps to keep jQuery UI components consistent in appearance and behavior. Another important part of a web UI is its interaction with the mouse, and standard jQuery supports this through its numerous mouse event handlers. But these handlers operate at the most basic level, leaving more complex interactions for your own development.

jQuery UI makes use of mouse drag operations in several of its widgets and has developed a separate module to deal with these interactions in an easy-to-use and consistent manner. The jQuery UI Mouse module watches the underlying mouse events and converts these into drag events you can react to. It's similar to your car speedometer, which transforms the individual wheel rotations into an overall speed for you.

To see the Mouse module in action, you'll develop a plugin that lets you capture a signature drawn with the mouse within a web page and convert it into a text representation for further processing. Additional functionality will allow you to check that a signature has been entered (perhaps for validation purposes), clear a signature, and redisplay it at a later time.

9.1   *The jQuery UI Mouse module*

jQuery UI recognizes that interactions with the mouse are a fundamental part of many UI components and provides direct support for drag processing via its `ui.mouse` module. This module is a dependency for the Draggable, Resizable, Selectable, Sortable, and Slider modules, demonstrating the common requirement for such functionality. Basic mouse interactions are provided by the standard jQuery library in the form of various mouse events and their handlers, whereas jQuery UI translates these basic events into higher-level behaviors and lets you customize when they're triggered.

9.1.1   *Mouse-drag actions*

The Mouse module adds wrappers for several mouse events on the targeted element and converts these low-level events into higher-level ones directly associated with a drag operation. The result is that widgets based on this module only have to implement the drag behavior that they want, instead of worrying about how to detect and start a drag in the first place, and then track its progress.

So instead of you having to worry about the underlying `mousedown`, `mousemove`, and `mouseup` events, the widget translates these into calls to the `_mouseCapture`, `_mouseStart`, `_mouseDrag`, and `_mouseStop` functions, as shown in figure 9.1. If you want a new widget to handle a drag, you need only extend the Mouse module and override these functions to have them invoked at the appropriate times.

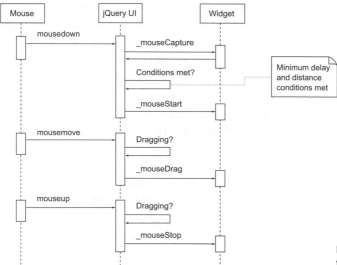

Figure 9.1   Sequence diagram for jQuery UI Mouse widgets

The Mouse module also handles moving the mouse outside of the element where the drag started and still continues to process the drag normally. It prevents more than one element from starting drag operations at the same times, removing the possibility of interference between them.

9.1.2 Mouse options

The Mouse module supports several options to customize its behavior. You can override these for particular widget instances by including them in the normal customization options for that instance, like this:

```
$('div.item').draggable({distance: 5, delay: 100});
```

These are the customization options:

- `cancel`—You can provide a selector that prevents a drag event from being initiated. The selector is applied to the target element's parents, and any match stops further processing. The default is any input field (including `textareas`, select boxes, and buttons) or select option: `:input,option`.
- `distance`—Specify the minimum distance that the mouse needs to move to initiate a drag operation. The default is one pixel.
- `delay`—Specify the minimum time (in milliseconds) that the mouse button must be held down before initiating a drag operation. The default is zero milliseconds.

9.2 Defining your widget

As with the MaxLength widget developed in the previous chapter, you need to do some groundwork before getting into the body of this new widget. First, define the functionality that the plugin will provide and the sequence of operations that will produce it. Then, declare the widget and include the mouse support supplied by jQuery UI.

We'll look at these steps in the following subsections.

9.2.1 Signature functionality

The Signature widget you're going to create lets you capture a signature by monitoring mouse drags over a particular region within a web page (a `div` or `span` element). It uses an embedded `canvas` element to render those movements into a visual image of the signature for immediate feedback and can generate a textual representation of the signature for storage and later reuse.

> ### Canvas element
> JavaScript isn't designed to manipulate images on the fly, but you can create a temporary image of the signature to display immediately. The `canvas` element of HTML5 provides a standard drawing surface within a web page that you can use to display a generated image. It has an API that allows it to be manipulated via JavaScript.

(continued)

Unfortunately, this element isn't supported in older versions of Internet Explorer, so additional code is required to add that functionality in those cases. The `Explorer-Canvas` script (http://excanvas.sourceforge.net/) adds the methods necessary to access and utilize the `canvas` in these browsers. Include it in your page with the following tags:

```
<!--[if IE]>
<script type="text/javascript" src="js/excanvas.js"></script>
<![endif]-->
```

Generating an image file for future processing is outside the scope of JavaScript's abilities, so a textual version of the signature is produced, allowing it to be easily transferred and stored. We chose JSON as the text format, because it can specify the signature with a relatively low overhead and is easily processed by JavaScript.

A signature consists of a number of lines, each of which is made up of a number of connected points. This translates into an array of lines, each of which is an array of points, each containing an *x* and *y* coordinate. For example, the signature shown in figure 9.2 would become the JSON text in listing 9.1.

Figure 9.2 Capture a signature and convert it to JSON

Listing 9.1 JSON version of a signature

```
{"lines":[[[38,85],[38,83],[38,82],[39,80],[40,76],
[41,73],[42,69],[42,65],[43,61],[44,58],[44,54],
[44,51],[45,48],[46,44],[48,41],[48,40],[49,37],
[51,36],[52,35],[53,34],[54,33],[55,33],[56,33],
[57,34],[58,36],[59,39],[61,43],[63,47],[65,52],
[66,55],[66,59],[66,64],[67,67],[67,70],[67,72],
[67,73],[68,74],[69,74],[70,74]],
[[41,62],[42,62],[43,62],[45,60],[48,59],[54,56],
[60,54],[66,52],[71,51],[77,50],[80,50],[83,49]]]}
```

Once the JSON version of the signature is transferred to the server, it could be regenerated into an image by appropriate server-side processing, such as a Java or .NET application, or it could be stored in its textual format. A Java version of image generation is provided on the book's website. The widget also supports the redisplay of a signature from its JSON representation.

The widget allows the signature to be cleared if a mistake has been made or if your users aren't happy with their previous entry. To cater to possible validation requirements, the widget can report back if a signature has been captured.

The Signature widget uses the name `signature`, with a namespace of `kbw` (the same as the MaxLength widget). The plugin code appears in a file named jquery .signature.js, and its associated CSS is in jquery.signature.css. An outline of the plugin code is shown in the next section.

9.2.2 *Signature plugin operation*

The plugin code consists of a number of functions that override or enhance the abilities provided by the widget framework and its Mouse module. These are shown in listing 9.2, and following the listing we'll look at how these are invoked during the lifecycle of the widget.

> **Listing 9.2 Plugin function outline**

```
var signatureOverrides = {
    options: {...},              ⟵⎤ Widget defaults
    _create: function() {...},            ⟵⎤ Initialization for an element
    _refresh: function(init) {...},    ⟵── Refresh widget appearance
    clear: function(init) {...},     ⟵── Clear signature
    _changed: function(event) {...},        ⟵── Synchronize changes and notify
    _setOptions: function(options) {...},      ⟵── Custom options handling
    _mouseCapture: function(event) {...},       ⟵── Determine if dragging can start
    _mouseStart: function(event) {...},    ⟵── Start new line
    _mouseDrag: function(event) {...},          ⟵⎤ Track mouse for a line
    _mouseStop: function(event) {...},     ⟵── End line
    toJSON: function() {...},         ⟵── Convert captured lines to JSON text
    draw: function(sigJSON) {...},          ⟵── Draw signature from its JSON description
    isEmpty: function() {...},     ⟵── Determine whether any drawing has occurred
    _destroy: function() {...}            ⟵⎤ Remove signature
};                                          functionality
$.widget('kbw.signature', $.ui.mouse, signatureOverrides);
```

First, the Signature plugin is applied to one or more `div` elements on the page using the usual jQuery select-and-operate paradigm. At this point, the widget framework creates an instance object to store the state of the plugin for each affected element. Part of that object is the set of options controlling its appearance and behavior, which derive from the widget defaults (`options` variable) and any overrides supplied with the initialization call. Then the `_create` function is invoked to allow you to perform any setup specific to this plugin.

If users want to change options at a later time, they do so via the `option` method, which triggers a call to the `_setOptions` function to let you update the widget accordingly. In this case, you should invoke the `_refresh` function to apply the new settings and redisplay the widget.

When users try to begin a drag operation with the mouse over the widget elements, the `_mouseCapture` function prevents it from starting if the widget is disabled.

Otherwise, the _mouseStart function is called to let you initialize a new signature line, followed by multiple calls to _mouseDrag as the mouse is moved, and a final _mouseStop call when the drag ceases. The plugin stores the captured points in an internal array for later processing. At the end of the drag, the _changed function is also invoked to notify users of the change via a callback event.

To retrieve the JSON representation of the signature, the user makes a method call to the toJSON function. The resulting text value can then be sent to the server or used elsewhere to define the captured lines. Providing that JSON value when making a method call to the draw function redisplays the signature within the widget element.

```
var signature = $('#mysignature').signature('toJSON');
...
$('#mysignature').signature('draw', signature);
```

NOTE Functions with names that don't start with an underscore (_) may be called directly via the widget framework by supplying the name of that function when invoking the plugin, as shown in the toJSON and draw sample here. Those that do start with an underscore are hidden by the framework and aren't accessible.

Users can determine whether or not a signature has been captured via a method call to the isEmpty function, perhaps for validation purposes, whereas a method call to the clear function erases any captured lines.

If users wish to remove the signature functionality altogether, they make a destroy method call that gets passed through to the _destroy function, which undoes everything that was set up in the initialization processing.

To start creating your plugin, you declare your new widget and base it upon the jQuery UI Mouse class.

9.2.3 Declaring the widget

As with the MaxLength widget, you *hide the implementation details by using scope* and *don't rely on $ being the same as jQuery* by declaring an anonymous function and calling it immediately, as the following shows:

```
(function($) { // Hide scope, no $ conflict
    ... the rest of the code appears here
})(jQuery);
```

You then define the new widget, as shown in the following listing, and let the widget framework provide the bridging functionality and basic abilities.

Listing 9.3 Declaring the widget

```
var signatureOptions = {                           Define new
                                                   ❶ widget
    // Global defaults for signature
    options: {
        background: '#ffffff', // Colour of the background    Provide
                                                              ❷ default options
```

```
        ... Other default settings
    },

    _create: function() {...},

    // Other widget code
};

/* Signature capture and display.
   Depends on jquery.ui.widget, jquery.ui.mouse. */
$.widget('kbw.signature', $.ui.mouse, signatureOverrides);
```

❸ Declare new widget

You start by defining an object that provides overrides and enhancements to the built-in widget functionality ❶, including default option values ❷ and custom methods. Then you declare your widget by invoking the $.widget function ❸ and provide the name of the widget, including its namespace separated by a period (.), with the last parameter being your overrides for the inherited widget abilities.

Recall that the second parameter for this call defines which other widget "class" to use as the basis for the new one. For this plugin you want a widget that interacts with the mouse, so you specify $.ui.mouse as the parameter value. The capabilities of the Mouse widget are then included in your new widget, along with those of the base Widget from which Mouse inherits.

Following this declaration, jQuery has a new function for collections ($.fn.signature) and has connected that to your overrides, as provided previously. Included in the basic functionality for this widget is the ability to monitor any mouse drags.

Before you respond to the mouse movements, though, you need to initialize the plugin for particular elements on the page.

9.3   Attaching the plugin to an element

To use the plugin, the user selects an appropriate element on the web page and applies the plugin to it, as is usually done in jQuery. The jQuery UI widget framework provides commonly required functionality automatically before allowing you to customize the affected elements for the specific purposes of the current plugin.

9.3.1   Framework initialization

As with the MaxLength widget in the previous chapter, when the plugin is applied to an element, the widget framework starts by creating an object to hold the state of the plugin for that particular element and attaches the object with the data function. You use a name based on the plugin's name (kbw-signature for jQuery UI 1.9 or later, or signature prior to jQuery UI 1.9) to retrieve that instance object.

Within the instance object, the element attribute refers to the selected element to which the plugin is being applied, and the options attribute contains a copy of the default options for the plugin, overridden by any customized option values supplied in the initialization. In addition, the widget framework checks whether the Metadata plugin (https://github.com/jquery-orphans/jquery-metadata) is included on the page. If so, the framework uses it to check for further configuration within attributes on the selected element, again based on the plugin name. By default, the `class` attribute holds the customizations:

```
<div id="sign" class="{signature: {guideline: true}}"></div>
```

> **NOTE** Automatic support for the Metadata plugin was removed in jQuery UI 1.10, but you can restore this functionality as shown in section 8.9.

In addition to the automatic processing provided by the widget framework, you often need to perform your own initialization steps when attaching the plugin to an element.

9.3.2   *Custom initialization*

As part of the framework's initialization processing, it calls the `_create` function, which you provide in your plugin declaration to perform any custom initialization, as shown in the following listing. Recall that within the `_create` function, `this` refers to the current widget instance object.

Listing 9.4   Attachment and initialization

```
/* Initialise a new signature area. */              ❶ Override _create
_create: function() {                                     function
    this.element.addClass(this.widgetFullName || this.widgetBaseClass);
    try {                                                              ❸ Initialization for
        this.canvas = $('<canvas width="' + this.element.width() +        other browsers
            '" height="' + this.element.height() + '">' +
            this.options.notAvailable + '</canvas>')[0];
        this.element.append(this.canvas);
        this.ctx = this.canvas.getContext('2d');
    }
    catch (e) {                                        ❺ Initialization for IE
        $(this.canvas).remove();
        this.resize = true;
        this.canvas = document.createElement('canvas');
        this.canvas.setAttribute('width', this.element.width());
        this.canvas.setAttribute('height', this.element.height());
        this.canvas.innerHTML = this.options.notAvailable;
        this.element.append(this.canvas);
        if (G_vmlCanvasManager) { // Requires excanvas.js   ❻ Initialize
            G_vmlCanvasManager.initElement(this.canvas);        ExplorerCanvas
        }
        this.ctx = this.canvas.getContext('2d');
    }                                                  ❼ Refresh widget
    this._refresh(true);                                  appearance
    this._mouseInit();                       ❽ Initialize mouse
},                                              interactions
```

Add marker class ❷

Retrieve drawing context ❹

You must define the `_create` function ❶ as part of the widget overrides to have the widget framework call your code as part of the initialization processing. You can use the provided `this.widgetFullName` value (`this.widgetBaseClass` before jQuery UI 1.9) to add a marker class to the currently selected element ❷ to help identify affected elements within your page. Then continue with the processing specific to this plugin.

For browsers that support `canvas` natively ❸, you can create and add the new element in the standard jQuery way. You retain a reference to the underlying `canvas` element within the current widget instance object by assigning it to `this.canvas`. Because you'll be using the `canvas` continually when drawing the signature, you should also save a reference to its drawing context in the widget instance object as the `this.ctx` value ❹.

Because of the differing support for the `canvas` element in IE, it throws an exception and must be handled separately ❺. For IE, you create the new `canvas` element and resize it to fill its parent—the element that's the target of the signature functionality. You should provide some text content for the `canvas` (taken from an option value) to be shown if the browser doesn't support `canvas`, perhaps because the Explorer-Canvas code wasn't loaded correctly. After adding the new element to its container, you initialize the ExplorerCanvas code for it ❻. This last step adds in the `canvas` functions that would be provided natively by a more modern browser. As with the other browsers, you save a reference to the drawing context ❹.

For all browsers, you call the custom `_refresh` function ❼ to modify the plugin based on the options currently set. See section 9.4.3 for more details.

Finally, you must initialize the mouse handling provided by the jQuery UI Mouse module on which this widget is based ❽. The mouse setup wraps handlers around the basic mouse events to convert sequences of these events into the higher-level mouse drag operations, making it much easier to integrate the latter into your widget.

The plugin functionality is now attached to an element on the page. The next step is to allow for the configuration of that plugin instance via options.

9.4 *Handling plugin options*

Users expect to supply options to alter the widget's appearance or behavior as part of its initialization call. You should try to predict what those users might want to alter and *anticipate customizations* by providing an option to let them do that. If you always *use sensible defaults* for the options, you allow the widget to be used with a minimum of configuration.

To achieve these goals you need to

- Define defaults values for all options
- Handle retrieving and setting option values
- Apply any option changes immediately
- Allow the plugin to be enabled or disabled

We'll discuss these points in turn.

9.4.1 *Widget defaults*

Options for a particular instance of the widget are set by the widget framework by copying any default values specified in the widget declaration and overriding these with any values that are supplied in the initialization call. The following listing shows the definition of the default option values.

Listing 9.5   Default option values

```
// Global defaults for signature
options: {
    background: '#ffffff', // Colour of the background
    color: '#000000', // Colour of the signature
    thickness: 2, // Thickness of the lines
    guideline: false, // Add a guide line or not?
    guidelineColor: '#a0a0a0', // Guide line colour
    guidelineOffset: 50, // Guide line offset from the bottom
    guidelineIndent: 10, // Guide line indent from the edges
    notAvailable: 'Your browser doesn\'t support signing',
        // Error message when no canvas
    syncField: null, // Selector for synchronised text field
    change: null // Callback when signature changed
},
```

❶ **Define global default
option values**

By declaring an options attribute ❶ within the overrides provided when first defining the widget, you list all the possible configuration settings and supply their default values. This process also lets you document all the options in one place. The effects of changing some of these options can be seen in the examples in figure 9.3.

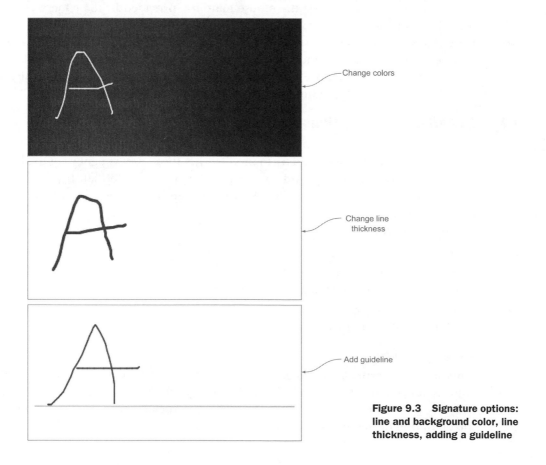

Change colors

Change line
thickness

Add guideline

**Figure 9.3   Signature options:
line and background color, line
thickness, adding a guideline**

The widget framework saves the set of default values as an attribute of the widget prototype. You can map an attribute directly within the plugin onto that set of default values to make them more accessible:

```
$.kbw.signature.options = $.kbw.signature.prototype.options;
```

To override defaults for all plugin instances, you could then use the following code, prior to invoking the plugin on any elements:

```
$.extend($.kbw.signature.options,
    {background: '#FFFFE0', guideline: true});
```

Although the widget framework automatically handles setting and retrieving option values, you often need to perform additional processing when those values change, to keep the plugin synchronized with the new values.

9.4.2 *Setting options*

Two of the abilities provided by the widget framework are setting and retrieving option values. As seen with the MaxLength widget, you can hook into the setting process to add your own functionality as these values change. The Signature widget doesn't need to take any actions specific to individual options, so it won't override the _setOption function. But it should refresh its appearance when any option is updated to reflect the latest values.

Listing 9.6   Handling option changes

```
/* Custom options handling.
   @param options (object) the new option values */
_setOptions: function(options) {                    ❶ Override _setOptions
    // Base widget handling                            function
    this._superApply(arguments);                    ❷ Call default
    this._refresh();                                   options handling
},                                                  ❸ Refresh widget
                                                       appearance
```

You can override the _setOptions function ❶ to refresh the widget's appearance when any option changes. You must invoke the inherited options processing to ensure that the new values are stored against the current element ❷. Then you should call the custom _refresh function to apply the changes to the elements managed by the widget ❸. This function is described in the next section.

Prior to jQuery UI 1.9

The way an inherited function is called changed in jQuery UI 1.9. In the newer jQuery UI versions, you call the function through a reference to the parent class, like this:

```
this._superApply(arguments);
```

In the older versions, you refer to the widget prototype and invoke the same function there, like this:

```
$.Widget.prototype._setOptions.apply(this, arguments);
```

(continued)

To allow your widget to work in the current and earlier jQuery UI versions, you can test for the presence of the new function and act accordingly. Here's an example:

```
// Base widget handling
if (this._superApply) {
    this._superApply(arguments);
}
else {
    $.Widget.prototype._setOptions.apply(this, arguments);
}
```

9.4.3   Implementing Signature options

As option values are changed, you should refresh the widget elements to reflect those changes. For the Signature plugin, the options affect the appearance of the visual rendering of the signature. The custom _refresh function performs this task and is called upon initialization (section 9.3.1) and when an option is altered (section 9.4.2). The following listing shows its workings.

Listing 9.7   Refresh the widget appearance and behavior

```
/* Refresh the appearance of the signature area.
   @param  init  (boolean, internal) true if initialising */   ❶ Define _refresh
_refresh: function(init) {                                          function
    if (this.resize) {
        var parent = $(this.canvas);              ❷ Update canvas
        $('div', this.canvas).css(                   size for IE
            {width: parent.width(), height: parent.height()});
    }
    this.ctx.fillStyle = this.options.background;    ❸ Apply new
    this.ctx.strokeStyle = this.options.color;          graphical
    this.ctx.lineWidth = this.options.thickness;        settings
    this.ctx.lineCap = 'round';
    this.ctx.lineJoin = 'round';
    this.clear(init);                    ❹ Erase canvas
},
```

You start by declaring the _refresh function ❶ as part of the widget overrides supplied during the widget definition. Because of the leading underscore (_), this function can't be invoked directly as a method.

Support for the canvas element in IE isn't as complete as you might like, so you need to reset the size of the canvas to match that of its container when it's shown ❷. This function is an appropriate place to do that, as it's called before any drawing occurs within that element. The this.resize flag was set in _create (see section 9.3.2) when the IE initialization was performed.

Next you should initialize the drawing context with the latest option values ❸, before erasing any existing content by calling the clear function ❹ (see section 9.7.1

for a description of this function). The next time that the `canvas` is drawn upon, it'll use the new settings.

As well as changing the appearance of the widget, you can enable or disable its functionality altogether.

9.4.4   Enabling and disabling the widget

Enabling and disabling a widget is standard functionality provided by the widget framework and doesn't require any action on your part. The `disabled` option controls the widget's status, being set to `true` (disabled) or `false` (enabled). The framework also maps the `enable` and `disable` methods onto changes of this option value.

```
$('#sign').signature('disable');
...
$('#sign').signature('enable');
```

The framework toggles two classes on the main element—`<namespace>-<plugin name>-disabled` and `ui-state-disabled`—and sets the `aria-disabled` attribute appropriately. This widget doesn't add any extra processing around changing the disabled option directly, but checks its value when any mouse drag is about to be started (see section 9.6.1).

You can now configure the plugin and have those changes be reflected in its appearance and behavior. Some of those configuration options may include callback handlers to let you monitor significant events in the plugin's lifecycle, as described in the next section.

9.5   Adding event handlers

The Signature widget allows users to react to changes to the captured signature via an event. The widget framework provides support for creating events in the form of the `_trigger` function.

To add event callbacks to your plugin, you do the following:

- Allow the user to register handlers for an event
- Trigger those events at the appropriate time

The following subsections look at these in detail.

9.5.1   Registering an event handler

The `change` event for the Signature widget occurs when the signature is altered by drawing a new line, by redrawing a complete signature from its textual representation, or by clearing all content.

The `change` handler appears as an option for the plugin, as shown in listing 9.8, and it defaults to `null` to indicate that no callback is required. When used, its value must be a function that accepts two parameters—the triggering event and a custom `ui` object—in keeping with other jQuery UI event handlers. In this case, there's no custom information to return, so the `ui` value will always be an empty object. Within the callback function, the `this` variable refers to the main element to which the plugin is applied.

Listing 9.8 Defining an event handler

```
// Global defaults for signature
options: {
    ...
    change: null // Callback when signature changed
},
```

You can register an event handler during the plugin initialization, as shown in the following code, or by updating options at a later stage:

```
$('#sign').signature({change: function(event, ui) {
    $('#submit').prop('disabled', false);
}});
```

Alternately, you can use jQuery's standard `bind` or `on` functionality to subscribe to that event because the plugin framework automatically maps a custom event onto this handler. The event is named from the plugin name combined with the option name (`signaturechange` in this case).

```
$('#sign').signature().on('signaturechange', function(event, ui) {
    $('#submit').prop('disabled', false);
}});
```

Now that the event handler is known to the plugin, you need to invoke it at the appropriate time within the plugin lifecycle.

9.5.2 *Triggering an event handler*

The `change` event is triggered whenever the captured signature is altered. This occurs when the signature is cleared, when a new line is drawn, or when the entire signature is redrawn from a JSON representation. Each case invokes the `_changed` function defined as part of the widget overrides, as shown in this listing.

Listing 9.9 Triggering an event

```
/* Synchronise changes and trigger change event.
   @param   event   (Event) the triggering event */        ❶ Define _changed
_changed: function(event) {                                   function
    if (this.options.syncField) {
        $(this.options.syncField).val(this.toJSON());      ❷ Synchronize signature
    }                                                         with text field
    this._trigger('change', event, {});                    ❸ Trigger change
},                                                            event
```

You define the `_changed` function to be called whenever the signature changes ❶. If you specify that a text field is to be kept synchronized with the signature, then you should update that field based on the latest changes at the same time ❷. See section 9.7.2 for more details on the `toJSON` function.

Finally you generate the event via the `_trigger` function of the widget ❸. Its parameters are the name of the new event, the original event that caused this trigger to fire, and a custom `ui` object that holds information relevant to this widget. The event is provided to the `_changed` function and will be the appropriate mouse event in the case that a new line is added to the signature. No custom information is sent along for this widget, so an empty object is specified for the last parameter.

Having initialized and configured the plugin, you can proceed to the heart of its functionality—capturing mouse movements over it.

9.6   *Interacting with the mouse*

The jQuery UI Mouse widget automatically intercepts the standard mouse events and converts these into higher-level drag events. At the same time, it applies any minimum distance and time restrictions specified for the widget and only allows one element to capture and track the mouse during this time.

Your widget then only needs to respond to the following events:

- Determining if a drag can start
- Starting a drag operation
- Mouse tracking during a drag
- Ending a drag operation

We'll discuss each of these in turn.

9.6.1   *Can a drag start?*

The Mouse module determines whether a drag operation can commence based on various conditions, including how far the mouse has moved and how long it has been held down. The module also provides a hook that you can use to add your own conditions—the `_mouseCapture` function, as shown in listing 9.10. This function receives one parameter—the triggering mouse event—and must return `true` if a drag is allowed or `false` if it should be aborted. The default implementation always returns `true`.

Listing 9.10   Allowing a drag operation

```
/* Determine if dragging can start.
   @param  event   (Event) the triggering mouse event
   @return (boolean) true if allowed, false if not */
_mouseCapture: function(event) {
    return !this.options.disabled;
},
```

❶ Override `_mouseCapture` function

❷ Can't drag if disabled

To add a custom drag condition, you override the `_mouseCapture` function as part of the widget definition ❶. For the Signature widget, a drag can only commence if the widget hasn't been disabled. The disabled status is maintained by the `disabled` option of the widget, so you can return the negated option value as the function result ❷.

> **NOTE** Within this drag function, as in all the others we'll cover in this chapter, the `this` variable refers to the current widget instance object, which has references to the original targeted element (`this.element`) and the current option values (`this.options`), amongst other attributes.

9.6.2 Starting a drag

You should provide a `_mouseStart` function as part of the widget overrides to add your own functionality when a drag operation commences. Details about the mouse position are supplied by the `event` parameter to this function.

Listing 9.11 Starting a mouse drag

```
/* Start a new line.                                      ❶ Override
   @param  event  (Event) the triggering mouse event */      _mouseStart
_mouseStart: function(event) {                              function
    this.offset = this.element.offset();
    this.offset.left -= document.documentElement.scrollLeft ||   Calculate current
        document.body.scrollLeft;                            ❷ mouse position
    this.offset.top -= document.documentElement.scrollTop ||
        document.body.scrollTop;
    this.lastPoint = [this._round(event.clientX - this.offset.left),
        this._round(event.clientY - this.offset.top)];
    this.curLine = [this.lastPoint];
    this.lines.push(this.curLine);                            Create new
},                                                          ❹ line and save it
```

❸ Create current point (pointing to `this.lastPoint` line)

By default, the `_mouseStart` function does nothing, so you override that to process the start of a mouse drag ❶. The coordinates of the mouse event supplied to this function are relative to the current viewport—the portion of that page that you can see within the browser—so you need to convert these positions into ones that are relative to the canvas managed by the widget.

You start by computing the offset of the originally targeted element within the viewport ❷, taking into account that the underlying web page may have been scrolled. The offset is stored within the widget instance object for later use as the mouse moves (`this.offset`). Based on that offset and the coordinates of the mouse event, create a point that encodes the mouse location relative to the top-left corner of the original element ❸. Create a new signature line containing only that point, because you're starting a new drag operation, and add it to the list of lines for the signature ❹.

Once the new line has been started, you can follow the mouse's progress across the screen and capture its coordinates as it goes.

9.6.3 Tracking a drag

The `_mouseDrag` function lets you track the movement of the mouse during a drag operation. This function is specified as one of the overrides when declaring the widget. Once again, the event parameter contains details about the mouse position. The following listing shows its implementation.

Listing 9.12   Tracking a mouse drag

```
/* Track the mouse.
   @param event (Event) the triggering mouse event */        ❶ Override _mouseDrag
_mouseDrag: function(event) {                                    function
    var point = [this._round(event.clientX - this.offset.left),
        this._round(event.clientY - this.offset.top)];
    this.curLine.push(point);                                 Calculate current
    this.ctx.beginPath();                                     mouse position ❷
    this.ctx.moveTo(this.lastPoint[0], this.lastPoint[1]);
    this.ctx.lineTo(point[0], point[1]);
    this.ctx.stroke();                                        ❹ Save new last
    this.lastPoint = point;                                      position
},
```

Draw from last position ❸ (applies to the `moveTo`/`lineTo`/`stroke` block)

You should override the _mouseDrag function to add your own mouse tracking ❶. Because the location of the mouse obtained from the supplied mouse event is relative to the page, you should convert it to be relative to the containing element, based on the latter's offset as computed at the start of the drag ❷, and add this point into the array defining the current line.

You provide feedback to your users by reflecting their movements on the canvas that fills the containing element ❸. Using the drawing context, move to the last mouse position and draw a line from that to the current position. The styling of the line drawn was set during initialization (or via an option update) and was applied in the _refresh function (see section 9.4.3). Finally, you save the current point as the last point for the next mouse movement ❹.

Monitoring the drag movements lets you capture the lines drawn by your users. Once they complete a line, you have some housekeeping to do.

9.6.4   Ending a drag

At the completion of a mouse drag operation, the _mouseStop function is called. To add your own processing here, override it as part of the widget declaration. Details about the mouse position are provided by the event parameter to this function. The following listing shows the completion processing.

Listing 9.13   Ending a mouse drag

```
/* End a line.
   @param event (Event) the triggering mouse event */        ❶ Override _mouseStop
_mouseStop: function(event) {                                    function
    this.lastPoint = null;
    this.curLine = null;                                      Clear last
    this._changed(event);                                     ❷ point and line
},
```

Invoke signature-changed processing ❸

To add processing at the end of a mouse drag, you define the _mouseStop function ❶. You should tidy up the plugin by clearing out the last point and current line references ❷ before calling the signature-changed processing ❸ to synchronize any associated field and to trigger the change event (see section 9.5.2).

The plugin can now capture a signature based on mouse movements over its canvas and record them into an array of line definitions. But there's more to do yet, as you make use of those captured points in further processing.

9.7 Adding methods

The Signature plugin provides additional custom functionality to allow you to interact with the signatures that are captured. These abilities include clearing a signature, converting a signature to a text format for transfer and storage, redrawing a signature from a saved text version, and determining whether any signature has been entered at all.

Recall that the widget framework provides support for custom methods within a plugin by attempting to invoke such methods by name directly on the widget instance object. Any function that starts with an underscore (_) is deemed to be an internal function and can't be called in this manner. Methods that return a value have that value passed straight through to the caller. Otherwise, the current jQuery collection is returned, allowing the call to be chained.

9.7.1 Clearing the signature

If your users make a mistake when signing the allocated element, or they're unhappy with the result, they can erase their signature and start again. The clear method provides this functionality.

Listing 9.14 Clearing the signature

```
/* Clear the signature area.
   @param  init  (boolean, internal) true if initialising */    ❶ Function for
clear: function(init) {                                            clear method
    this.ctx.fillRect(0, 0,
        this.element.width(), this.element.height());           ❷ Erase canvas
    if (this.options.guideline) {
        this.ctx.save();
        this.ctx.strokeStyle = this.options.guidelineColor;
        this.ctx.lineWidth = 1;
        this.ctx.beginPath();
        this.ctx.moveTo(this.options.guidelineIndent,
            this.element.height() - this.options.guidelineOffset);
        this.ctx.lineTo(
            this.element.width() - this.options.guidelineIndent,
            this.element.height() - this.options.guidelineOffset);
        this.ctx.stroke();
        this.ctx.restore();
    }
    this.lines = [];                                            ❹ Clear line
    if (!init) {                                                   definitions
        this._changed();
    }                             ❺ Trigger change event
},                                   if not initializing
```

❸ Draw requested guideline

Name the function the same as the method to be used, to have the widget framework map from one to the other **❶**. Clear the canvas by drawing a filled rectangle via the saved drawing context, using the background color specified previously (see listing 9.7) **❷**.

If a guideline to write the signature upon is requested, draw that in the specified color and position **❸**. The styling of the signature lines themselves is maintained by saving the current styles of the drawing context (`save()`) before drawing the guideline, and then restoring those styles afterwards (`restore()`).

You then clear any existing lines captured by the widget **❹** and invoke the `_changed` function **❺** to synchronize the textual version of the signature (if required) and to inform users of the change. The changed processing isn't required during initialization of the widget, so it's bypassed here based on the value of the `init` flag passed in. Although this function takes a parameter, it's only intended for internal use, and the end user wouldn't need to provide it.

You'd call this method as follows:

```
$('#sign').signature('clear');
```

9.7.2 *Converting to JSON*

The signature can be represented as a JSON object for ease of transmission and storage. This object contains a single attribute (`lines`) that is an array of the lines that make up the signature. Each line consists of an array of points (the *x* and *y* coordinates). To obtain a textual version of such a JSON object, use the `toJSON` method.

Listing 9.15 Converting to JSON

```
/* Convert the captured lines to JSON text.
   @return  (string) the JSON text version of the lines */
toJSON: function() {                                       ❶ Function for
    return '{"lines":[' + $.map(this.lines, function(line) {    toJSON method
        return '[' + $.map(line, function(point) {          ❷ Add each line
            return '[' + point + ']';
        }) + ']';
    }) + ']}';
},
```

❸ Add each point

You provide the code for the `toJSON` method by defining a function with the same name **❶**. The conversion process starts by defining the outermost object and its `lines` attribute, before processing each line in turn and adding its definition to the JSON text **❷**. For each line, step through each of its points and add them to the JSON text **❸**.

> **NOTE** This is only a partial JSON-to-string implementation. For a full conversion, see the stringifyJSON function on GitHub: https://gist.github.com/JaNightmare/2051416.

You can retrieve the JSON version of a signature as follows:

```
var jsonText = $('#sign').signature('toJSON');
```

The resulting string may look like this, which defines two lines made up of numerous points:

```
{"lines":[[[38,85],[38,83],[38,82],[39,80],[40,76],
[41,73],[42,69],[42,65],[43,61],[44,58],[44,54],
[44,51],[45,48],[46,44],[48,41],[48,40],[49,37],
[51,36],[52,35],[53,34],[54,33],[55,33],[56,33],
[57,34],[58,36],[59,39],[61,43],[63,47],[65,52],
[66,55],[66,59],[66,64],[67,67],[67,70],[67,72],
[67,73],[68,74],[69,74],[70,74]],
[[41,62],[42,62],[43,62],[45,60],[48,59],[54,56],
[60,54],[66,52],[71,51],[77,50],[80,50],[83,49]]]}
```

As an alternative, you can provide a `synchField` option to the widget, which identifies a text field to be kept synchronized with the JSON text for the signature. You can provide a jQuery selector string, a DOM element, or an existing jQuery object as the option value. The synchronization happens as part of the processing in the `_changed` function (see section 9.5.2).

Although you can now capture a signature and convert it to JSON text for storage, at some future time you'll need to redisplay that signature.

9.7.3   Redrawing the signature

If a signature is to be redisplayed, it may need to be redrawn from that JSON representation. The `draw` method accepts a JSON string or object and renders the signature that it defines onto its canvas, as shown in listing 9.16.

Listing 9.16   Redrawing the signature

```
/* Draw a signature from its JSON description.
   @param  sigJSON  (object) object with attribute lines
                     being an array of arrays of points or
                     (string) text version of the JSON */        ❶ Function for
draw: function(sigJSON) {                                            draw method
    this.clear(true);                    ◄── Erase canvas ❷
    if (typeof sigJSON == 'string') {    ◄──
        sigJSON = $.parseJSON(sigJSON);      ❸ Copy line definitions
    }
    this.lines = sigJSON.lines || [];
    var ctx = this.ctx;
    $.each(this.lines, function() {      ◄──
        ctx.beginPath();                     ❹ Draw each line
        $.each(this, function(i) {
            ctx[i == 0 ? 'moveTo' : 'lineTo'](this[0], this[1]);
        });
        ctx.stroke();                    ❺ Trigger
    });                                      change event
    this._changed();                     ◄──
},
```

To implement the `draw` method, you declare the `draw` function ❶. It accepts a single parameter, which is the object that defines the lines that make up the signature or the JSON text representation of that object.

You erase any existing signature by invoking the `clear` function ❷. If the signature value supplied is in a text form, you should convert it to the corresponding JavaScript object ❸. Otherwise use the JSON object as is. Then transfer the new line definitions from that object into the widget instance object and draw each line in turn ❹. Recall that this drawing uses the styles established previously in the `_refresh` function (see section 9.4.3). Once it's drawn, you handle data synchronization and user notification via the `_changed` call ❺ (see section 9.5.2).

9.7.4 *Checking signature presence*

It's likely that a signature block is a required field when it appears on a web page. To assist in the validation process, and to hide the internal workings of the widget, the `isEmpty` method returns a Boolean value indicating the field's status.

Listing 9.17 Checking signature presence

```
/* Determine whether or not any drawing has occurred.      ❶ Function for
   @return  (boolean) true if not signed, false if signed */      isEmpty method
isEmpty: function() {
   return this.lines.length == 0;
},                                     ❷ Return empty status
```

You define the `isEmpty` function to implement the corresponding method ❶. From that function, you return the empty status by comparing the number of captured lines with zero ❷.

Note that this method returns a Boolean value and can't be used in the middle of a jQuery function chain. You could use the method like this, with the outcome shown in figure 9.4:

```
if ($('#sign').signature('isEmpty')) {
    alert('Please enter your signature');
}
```

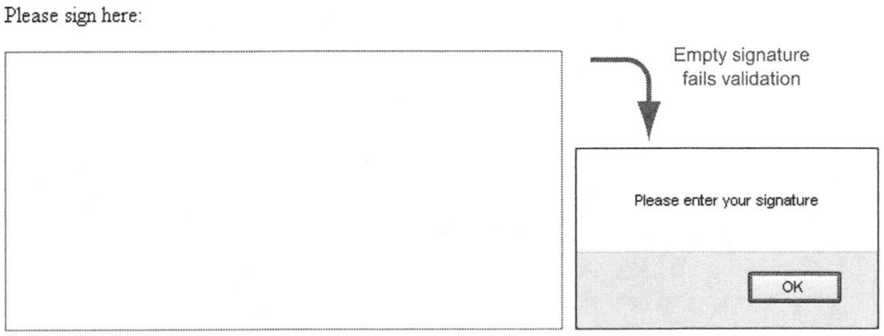

Please sign here:

Figure 9.4 The result of validating a signature

That completes the interactions with the Signature plugin. But you may want to remove the Signature functionality altogether from the affected elements.

9.8 *Removing the widget*

You invoke the `destroy` method to remove all trace of your widget. As with other methods, this generates a call to the function with the same name within the plugin—`destroy`.

9.8.1   The _destroy method

The widget framework contains a destroy function that tidies up any framework initializations. At the appropriate time during that process, it calls the _destroy function, which does nothing by default. By providing a _destroy function as part of the widget overrides during its declaration, you can hook into the destroy method call and undo whatever was done in your _create function.

Listing 9.18   Removing the widget

```
/* Remove the signature functionality. */                    ❶ Define the destroy
_destroy: function() {                                          function
    this.element.removeClass(
        this.widgetFullName || this.widgetBaseClass);        ❷ Remove marker class
    $(this.canvas).remove();                                 ❸ Remove canvas
    this.canvas = this.ctx = this.lines = null;
    this._mouseDestroy();                                    ❹ Tidy up mouse processing
}
```

You declare the _destroy function to intervene in the destroy method call ❶. Within your function, you should remove the marker class ❷, canvas element, and associated references ❸ that were added during setup. Allow the integrated mouse widget to tidy up after itself by calling the _mouseDestroy function ❹.

After executing this method, the affected elements will have been returned to their initial states and the Signature functionality no longer applies.

Prior to jQuery UI 1.9

Prior to jQuery UI 1.9, you had to override the destroy function instead of _destroy, and invoke the inherited functionality by referring to the widget prototype. To allow your plugin to operate in the current and earlier versions of jQuery UI, you should extend your plugin overrides to add the destroy function in those earlier versions and have it call _destroy, like the latest version does. You also need to call the inherited destroy function from the widget framework. The full code for this is shown here:

```
if (!$.Widget.prototype._destroy) {
    $.extend(maxlengthOverrides, {
        /* Remove the maxlength textarea functionality. */
        destroy: function() {
            this._destroy();
            // Base widget handling
            $.Widget.prototype.destroy.call(this);
        }
    });
}
```

9.9   The complete plugin

That completes the jQuery UI Signature widget, allowing you to capture a signature in an area on a web page, encode that signature for further external processing, and decode and redraw it as necessary. Interacting with the mouse to handle drag operations is greatly simplified by the use of the jQuery UI Mouse module. The complete code for the plugin is available for download from the book's website.

What you need to know

Inherit from the jQuery UI Mouse module when you need to incorporate mouse drag operations into your widget.

Call `_mouseInit` to initialize the mouse handling and `_mouseDestroy` to remove its effects.

Override the `_mouseCapture` function to indicate whether to start a mouse drag.

Override the `_mouseStart`, `_mouseDrag`, and `_mouseStop` functions to respond to the drag operation.

The standard widget functionality is still available to handle option processing and setup and teardown of the plugin.

Try it yourself

Create a plugin for a simple sketchpad, also based around the HTML5 `canvas` element. Allow the user to drag across the canvas and draw a rectangle within the bounds of the dragged region. You can use an `Image` element to save the state of the canvas while dragging, to simplify the drawing of a feedback rectangle:

```
this.img.src = this.canvas.toDataURL(); // Save initial state
this.ctx.drawImage(this.img, 0, 0); // Restore initial state
```

9.10 *Summary*

Although jQuery provides support for basic mouse interactions via its mouse event handling, jQuery UI provides a higher-level interaction in dealing with mouse-drag operations. The jQuery UI Mouse module intercepts the basic mousedown, mousemove, and mouseup events and converts these into calls to the _mouseStart, _mouseDrag, and _mouseStop functions, allowing you to concentrate on reacting to the mouse drag, rather than worrying about the underlying infrastructure. jQuery UI makes use of the drag functionality in several of its own modules.

You add the Mouse module to your own widget by using it as the starting point in your widget declaration. Then override the drag functions listed previously to add your own processing. All of the functionality of the basic Widget is still available because the Mouse module extends that component.

The Signature plugin developed in this chapter shows how you can use the mouse interactions to develop useful functionality within your web page. It allows you to capture a signature within an area on the page by dragging the mouse over it, and then converts that signature into a JSON representation for storage and further processing.

The last chapter in this part looks at the jQuery UI effects framework and how this can be extended to provide eye-catching animations for your web pages.

jQuery UI effects 10

This chapter covers

- The jQuery UI effects framework
- Adding a new effect
- What easings are
- Adding new easings

Alongside the various widgets provided by jQuery UI (discussed in the previous two chapters) are additional behaviors, including user interactions, such as `draggable` and `droppable`, and visual effects for presenting elements. These effects enhance the showing or hiding of elements on your web page or serve to highlight a particular element by animating various aspects of their appearance. Underlying the built-in effects is a core of functionality that's useful in creating such animations. As you'd expect, you can add your own effects and have them integrate into jQuery UI along with the built-in ones.

In a similar way, *easings* enhance an animation by modifying the rate of change of an attribute value over the duration of the animation. jQuery UI provides many such easings to greatly expand the range available beyond the two defined in jQuery itself. You can also add your own easings to make the animation behave exactly as you want it to.

Together, these visual effects can liven up a page and provide a unique look and feel for your website. You can make an element disappear by collapsing into its center line, similar to the way television screens used to turn off. Or bring an element that's been updated by an Ajax call to the user's attention by flashing its background color. You can use an easing to simulate a physical process when moving an element, such as having it bounce as if under the effect of gravity. These effects may allow a user to better relate to that element within the context of the rest of the web page.

10.1 The jQuery UI effects framework

The jQuery UI effects framework is modularized, just like the widget framework, allowing you to choose which parts of the package you want to use and reduce the code requirements. You can create a custom download for yourself (http://jque-ryui.com/download), which takes into account dependencies between the modules.

Before looking at how to create a new effect, you should be aware of the other functionality already offered by the jQuery UI effects framework, so that you can use it when developing your own effects.

10.1.1 The Effects Core module

Underlying the individual jQuery UI effects modules is a core of commonly used functionality. These abilities are implemented here so that you don't need to re-invent them and can apply them immediately to your own effects. Along with color animation, you'll find animation from the attributes of one class to another, and several low-level functions that may be useful in developing new effects.

COLOR ANIMATION

The Effects Core module adds custom animation support for style attributes that contain color values: foreground and background colors, and border and outline colors. jQuery itself only allows the animation of attributes that are simple numeric values, with an optional units designator such as px, em, or %. It doesn't know how to interpret more complex values, like colors, or how to increment those values correctly to achieve the desired transition, such as from blue to red via an intermediate purple color.

Color values are made up of three components: the red, green, and blue contributions, each with a value between 0 and 255. They can be specified in HTML and CSS in a number of different ways, as listed here:

- Hexadecimal digits—#DDFFE8
- Minimal hexadecimal digits—#CFC
- Decimal RGB values—rgb(221, 255, 232)
- Decimal RGB percentages—rgb(87%, 100%, 91%)
- Decimal RGB and transparency values—rgba(221, 255, 232, 127)
- A named color—lime

The red, green, and blue components must be separated out and individually animated from their initial values to their final ones, before being combined into the new composite color for the intermediate steps.

jQuery UI adds animation steps for each affected attribute to correctly decode the current and desired colors, and to change the value as the animation runs. In addition to the color formats described in the previous list, the `animate` call can also accept an array of three numeric values (each between 0 and 255) to specify the color. Once these functions are defined, you can animate colors the same way you would do for other numeric attributes:

```
$('#myDiv').animate({backgroundColor: '#DDFFE8'});
```

jQuery UI contains an expanded list of named colors that it understands, from the basic `red` and `green` to the more esoteric `darkorchid` and `darksalmon`. There is even a `transparent` color.

Chapter 11 looks at how you can add animation functions for other non-numeric attribute values.

CLASS ANIMATION

Standard jQuery lets you add, remove, or toggle classes on selected elements. jQuery UI goes one better by allowing you to animate the transition between the before and after states.

It does this by extracting all the attribute values that can be animated (numeric values and colors) from the starting and ending configurations, and then invoking a standard `animate` call with all of these as properties to change. This new animation is triggered by specifying a duration when calling the `addClass`, `removeClass`, or `toggleClass` functions:

```
$('#myDiv').addClass('highlight', 1000);
```

jQuery UI also adds a new function, `switchClass`, which removes a class and adds a class, with the optional transition between the two states (when providing a duration):

```
$('#myDiv').switchClass('oldClass', 'newClass', 1000);
```

10.1.2 *Common effects functions*

To better support the various effects of jQuery UI, the Effects Core module provides several functions that are of use to these effects, and perhaps to your own. To illustrate how several of these functions are used, the following listing shows the relevant parts of the `slide` effect.

> **Listing 10.1   `slide` effect using common functions**

```
$.effects.effect.slide = function( o, done ) {

    // Create element
    var el = $( this ),
        props = [ "position", "top", "bottom",
            "left", "right", "width", "height" ],
        mode = $.effects.setMode( el, o.mode || "show" ),     ❶ Determine mode
        ...;                                                      of operation
```

```
// Adjust
$.effects.save( el, props );                                    Save current
el.show();                                                  ❷ settings
distance = o.distance || el[ ref === "top" ?
    "outerHeight" : "outerWidth" ]( true );

$.effects.createWrapper( el ).css({overflow: "hidden"});        Create
                                                                wrapper for
...                                                         ❸ animation

// Animation
animation[ ref ] = ...;

// Animate
el.animate( animation, {
    queue: false,
    duration: o.duration,
    easing: o.easing,
    complete: function() {
        if ( mode === "hide" ) {
            el.hide();
        }                                               ❹ Restore original
        $.effects.restore( el, props );                     settings
        $.effects.removeWrapper( el );      Remove
        done();                             animation
    }                                   ❺ wrapper
});
};
```

You can use the setMode function ❶ to convert a mode of toggle into the appropriate show or hide value based on the current visibility of the element (el, a jQuery object). If the provided mode is show or hide, it retains that value, and in this case, defaults to show if not given at all.

Before starting the animation for the effect, you might want to use the save function ❷ to remember the original values of several attributes (from the names in props) on the element (el), so that they can be restored when finished. The values are stored against the element using the jQuery data function.

To facilitate the movement of an element for an effect, you can wrap a container around that element with the createWrapper function ❸ to use as the reference point for the motion. Positional information is copied from the specified element (el) onto the wrapper so that it appears directly atop the original element. The element is then positioned within the new container at its top left so that the overall effect is unnoticeable by the user. The function returns a reference to the wrapper. Any changes to the left/right/top/bottom settings for the original element will now be relative to its original position, without affecting the surrounding elements.

Having saved certain attribute values earlier, you'd use the restore function at the completion of the animation to return them to their original settings ❹. At the same time, you should remove any wrapper that you created previously with the remove-Wrapper function ❺. This function returns a reference to the wrapper if it was removed, or to the element itself if there was no wrapper.

There are some other functions provided by the jQuery UI Effects Core module that may be of use:

- `getBaseline(origin, original)`—This function normalizes an `origin` specification (a two-element array of vertical and horizontal positions) into fractional values (0.0 to 1.0) given an `original` size (an object with `height` and `width` attributes). It converts named positions (`top`, `left`, `center`, and so on) to the values 0.0, 0.5, or 1.0, and converts numeric values into the proportion of the relevant dimension. The returned object has attributes `x` and `y` to hold the fractional values in the corresponding directions. For example,

```
var baseline = $.effects.getBaseline(['middle', 20],
    {height: 100, width: 200}); // baseline = {x: 0.1, y: 0.5}
```

- `setTransition(element, list, factor, value)`—To apply a scaling factor to multiple attribute values at once, use this function. For each attribute name in `list`, retrieve its current value for `element`, and update that by multiplying it by `factor`. Set the result into the `value` object under the name of the attribute, and return that object from the function. For example, to reduce certain values by half, you might do this:

```
el.from = $.effects.setTransition(el, ['borderTopWidth',
    'borderBottomWidth', ...], 0.5, el.from);
```

- `cssUnit(key)`—To separate a named CSS attribute (`key`) into its amount and units (`em`, `pt`, `px`, or `%`), returned as an array of two values, use this function. If the units aren't one of these known types, an empty array is returned. For example,

```
var value = el.cssUnit('width'); // e.g. value = [200, 'px']
```

The functions presented in this section are used by many of the effects provided by jQuery UI. These effects are reviewed in the next section, before we look at how you'd create your own effect.

10.1.3 *Existing effects*

Numerous effects are provided by jQuery UI. Most of these are designed to enhance how an element appears or disappears (such as `blind` and `drop`), whereas others serve to bring your attention to an element (such as `highlight` and `shake`). Table 10.1 lists the available effects, along with the options that may be used to alter their behavior.

Table 10.1   jQuery UI effects

Name	Effect	Options
blind	Element expands or contracts vertically (default) or horizontally from its top or left	direction
bounce	Element drops into or out of view and bounces a few times	direction, distance, times
clip	Element expands or contracts vertically (default) or horizontally from its center line	direction

Table 10.1   jQuery UI effects *(continued)*

Name	Effect	Options
drop	Element slides into or out of view from the left (default) or top, and fades to or from full opacity	direction, distance
explode	Element breaks up into sections and flies apart, or reassembles itself from flying parts	pieces
fade	Element fades to or from full opacity	–
fold	Element expands or contracts first in one direction then in the other (horizontally then vertically by default)	horizFirst, size
highlight	Element changes background color briefly	color
puff	Element decreases or increases in size, and fades to or from full opacity	direction, from, origin, percent, restore, to
pulsate	Element fades out and in several times	times
scale	Element expands or contracts from or to its center point by a percentage amount	direction, from, origin, percent, restore, scale, to
shake	Element moves from side to side several times	direction, distance, times
size	Element decreases or increases in size to given dimensions	from, origin, restore, scale, to
slide	Element slides horizontally (default) or vertically from its own edge	direction, distance
transfer	Element is moved and resized to match a target element	className, to

jQuery UI Effects Demo

Click on the objects in the house.

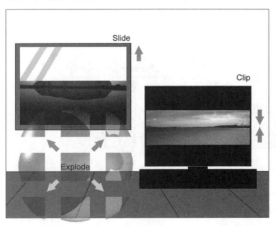

Figure 10.1   Some jQuery UI effects in operation (clockwise from top left): slide, clip, and explode

These effects may be used in conjunction with the enhanced jQuery UI show, hide, and toggle functions by providing the name of the desired effect as the first parameter. You can also supply additional options that change the behavior of the effect, the duration of the animation, and a callback function that's triggered on completion.

```
$('#aDiv').hide('clip');
$('#aDiv').toggle('slide', {direction: 'down'}, 1000);
```

Figure 10.1 shows a sample of the available effects midway through their operation.

Now that you've seen what effects are currently available, it's time to discover how to add your own effect so that it can be used in the same manner.

10.2   Adding a new effect

Adding a new effect to those available in jQuery UI involves extending $.effects.effect to add a function that implements your requirements. As with previous plugins, you need to follow several of the guiding principles to ensure a robust solution.

> **NOTE** Prior to jQuery UI 1.9.0, you extended the $.effects variable with your new effect. The requirements for such a call are somewhat different for jQuery UI 1.9.0 and later versions. The differences are covered in section 10.2.4.

10.2.1 Imploding an element

There's an existing jQuery UI effect called explode that takes an element, breaks it up into several pieces, and then moves these away from each other while fading them out, to simulate it being blasted to pieces. When used to show a hidden element, this effect fades in the various pieces and reassembles the original element. To demonstrate how you can create your own effect, you can write a similar one that implodes an element rather than exploding it. Instead of the component pieces flying out when hiding an element, they'll collapse into the center and fade away, as shown in figure 10.2. When showing an element with the imploding effect, the individual pieces will move out from the center and fade in to recreate the whole element.

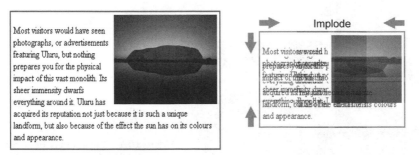

Figure 10.2   The implode effect, showing the initial element (left) and part way through its hiding (right)

You need to choose a name for the effect to be able to identify it to jQuery (keeping in mind the principle of *only claiming a single name and using that for everything*), such as `implode`. Existing effects are contained within files with names of the format jquery.ui.effect-<name>.js. Although this naming convention isn't required, it's good practice to follow it to indicate that the new effect relies on the jQuery UI Effects Core module.

As always, surround your code with an anonymous function to *hide the implementation details by using scope* and to *not rely on $ being the same as jQuery*. Within that function, you define your new effect and integrate it into the standard jQuery effect offerings (*placing everything under the jQuery object*). The following listing shows the declarations for the new effect.

> **Listing 10.2 Defining an implode effect for jQuery UI**

```
(function($) { // Hide scope, no $ conflict

$.effects.effect.implode = function(options, done) {      ◁─┐  ❶ Define implode
    ... // Implement the effect                                     effect
};


})(jQuery);
```

You define the `implode` effect by extending `$.effects.effect` to add a function that accepts two parameters ❶, which encapsulate all the parameters supplied to the effect call (`options`) and provide a callback to process any further animations (`done`). The `options` parameter object has attributes for any user-provided options to customize the effect, for the duration of the animation (`duration`, which has already been converted into a numeric value if provided as a name, such as `slow`), for the mode of operation (`mode`), and for any callback function that's invoked upon completion of the animation (`complete`).

Your effect function is called to run the effect at the appropriate time, because this effect may be part of a sequence of animations applied to the element. The remainder of the processing (shown in listings 10.3 and 10.4) takes place within this context.

10.2.2 Initializing the effect

When an effect is requested, the function defined in listing 10.2 is called for the affected elements. Before it can implement the actual animation, it must interpret any provided options and initialize the environment for its subsequent actions. Listing 10.3 shows this part of the effect processing.

> **Listing 10.3 Implode effect initialization**

```
var rows = cells = options.pieces ?           ◁─┐  Default number
    Math.round(Math.sqrt(options.pieces)) : 3;      ❶ of pieces

options.mode = $.effects.setMode($(this), options.mode);   ◁─┐  Set show/hide
var el = $(this).show().css('visibility', 'hidden');           ❷ mode
```

```
var offset = el.offset();                                    Calculate
// Subtract the margins - not fixing the problem yet      3  offsets
offset.top -= parseInt(el.css('marginTop'), 10) || 0;
offset.left -= parseInt(el.css('marginLeft'), 10) || 0;

var cellWidth = el.outerWidth(true) / cells;
var cellHeight = el.outerHeight(true) / rows;

var segments = $([]);
var remaining = rows * cells;                             4  Completed
var completed = function() { // Countdown to full completion    callback
    if (--remaining == 0) {
        options.mode == 'show' ? el.css({visibility: 'visible'}) :
            el.css({visibility: 'visible'}).hide();
        if (options.complete) {                          Trigger user
            options.complete.apply(el[0]); // Callback   5  callback
        }
        segments.remove();      Tidy up and
        done();              6  continue
    }
};
```

The process starts by providing default values for options that aren't defined ❶. To compress the element you break it up into a number of pieces and move each of these separately, so you need to know how many pieces to use. For this effect, you calculate the square root of the number supplied (options.pieces), rounding to an integer value, to make the effect symmetrical. If no pieces count is given, you default to an appropriate value (in this case, 3).

The jQuery UI effects use a mode option (options.mode) to determine whether the element is being shown or hidden, with a call to show or hide setting the corresponding value. Alternatively the user can toggle the current visibility, so you should translate a mode of toggle into the appropriate show or hide value using the setMode function ❷. The original element has its visibility set to hidden to make it invisible but still occupy the space it normally uses within the page. A reference to that element (el) is saved for later use.

Continue the initialization by calculating several values to be used to render the animated effect ❸, including the offset of the original element within the page and the width and height of each component piece. By computing the values here, you avoid having to recalculate them multiple times later on.

To ensure cleanup of the effect once it has run, you define a completed callback for the animation of each of the individual pieces ❹. This callback is invoked once for each piece that moves, but you only want to tidy up when they have all finished, so you decrement a count of the completed animations (remaining), and only continue when that count reaches zero. When they're all done, you completely show or hide the original element, which was only made invisible previously, according to the requested mode of the effect. If a user-defined callback was supplied for the effect as a whole, you invoke that at this time ❺, providing the current element (el[0]) as the context of that call. Remove the cloned pieces of the original element and invoke the done callback to process any further animations for that element ❻.

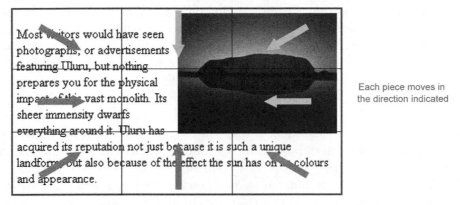

Each piece moves in
the direction indicated

Figure 10.3   Break the element up into pieces, and move them separately toward the center.

10.2.3   *Implementing the effect*

Having prepared the groundwork for the effect, the next step is to implement its functionality, animating the affected element(s) in the desired way. Figure 10.3 shows how the element is broken up into sections, each of which is moved separately toward its common center.

Listing 10.4 shows the code that animates the `implode` effect.

Listing 10.4   Apply the implode effect

```
for (var i = 0; i < rows; i++) {                              ❶ For each imploding piece...
    for (var j = 0; j < cells; j++) {
        var segment = el.clone().appendTo('body').wrap('<div></div>').
            css({position: 'absolute', visibility: 'visible',
            left: -j * cellWidth, top: -i * cellHeight}).        ❹ Access
        parent().addClass('ui-effects-implode').                    the wrapper
        css({position: 'absolute', overflow: 'hidden',
            width: cellWidth, height: cellHeight,                 ❺ Position the
            left: offset.left + j * cellWidth +                     wrapper
                (options.mode == 'show' ?
                -(j - cells / 2 + 0.5) * cellWidth : 0),
            top: offset.top + i * cellHeight +
                (options.mode == 'show' ?
                -(i - rows / 2 + 0.5) * cellHeight : 0),
            opacity: options.mode == 'show' ? 0 : 1}).
        animate({left: offset.left + j * cellWidth +              Animate this
                (options.mode == 'show' ? 0 :                     piece via
                -(j - cells / 2 + 0.5) * cellWidth),            ❻ its wrapper
            top: offset.top + i * cellHeight +
                (options.mode == 'show' ? 0 :
                -(i - rows / 2 + 0.5) * cellHeight),
            opacity: options.mode == 'show' ? 1 : 0
        }, options.duration || 500, completed);
        segments = segments.add(segment);                        Remember
    }                                                          ❼ this segment
}
```

...clone the
original and
❷ wrap in a div

Position the
content within
its wrapper ❸

The implosion effect results from breaking the original element up into smaller sections and having each of those move toward the center, fading as they go. Start by stepping through each of the requested pieces ❶ (rows and cells) and create a wrapped clone of the original element, so you can show a portion of the latter ❷ by positioning the contents (left and top) within the new div ❸. The result is separate divs, each showing a portion of the original element that can be moved independently.

The wrapping div for each piece (parent) is then marked with a class (ui-effects-implode) to help identify it ❹ (in the completed callback in listing 10.3). The wrapper is sized to show just one part of the original element, while hiding anything outside those dimensions, and is positioned absolutely to its starting location ❺. When using the effect to hide an element, each piece starts atop the corresponding section of the original element, as calculated from the current indexes (i and j) and the individual cell width and height. When showing an element with this effect, the starting position is all pieces overlaying each other in the center before they move outward to their original locations to reconstruct the entire element.

Finally, you animate the location of the wrapping div to its final position ❻, which is the inverse of the starting positions. The completed callback from the previous section is invoked at the end of each individual animation to eventually tidy up and remove the segments that are added here ❼.

10.2.4 Implementing an effect prior to jQuery UI 1.9

The implementation of effects changed in jQuery UI 1.9.0, and several changes need to be made to allow the effects code to function in earlier versions. Fortunately, most of the code is directly reusable, as shown in this listing.

Listing 10.5   Implementing an effect for earlier jQuery versions

```
var newEffects = !!$.effects.effect; // Using new effects framework?    ◄─ Using new effects? ❶

if (newEffects) {                                                        ◄─ If so, declare jQuery 1.9 ❷ effect
    $.effects.effect.implode = function(options, done) {
        implodeIt.apply(this, arguments);                                ◄─ Invoke effect ❸ function
    };
}                                                                        Otherwise, ❹ declare earlier jQuery effect
else {
    $.effects.implode = function(o) {
        var options = $.extend({complete: o.callback}, o, o.options);    ◄─ Convert options ❺
        return this.queue(function() {                                   ◄─ Enqueue effect processing ❻
            var el = $(this);
            implodeIt.apply(this, [options, function() {                 ◄─ Invoke effect ❼ function
                el.dequeue();
            }]);
        });
    };
}

/* Apply the implode effect immediately.
   @param options (object) settings for this effect
```

```
           @param  done      (function) callback when the effect is finished */
    function implodeIt(options, done) {
        ... // Same code as for jQuery UI 1.9.0 effect
    }
```

Extracted effect function

You should start by determining whether the new effects framework is available by checking for the existence of $.effects.effect ❶. If it's present, declare the new effect as shown previously ❷, but this time you invoke a common function that implements the actual effect ❸.

If you're not using the new effects framework, you declare the effect under $.effects, still with the same name, and assign it a function that receives only a single parameter (o) ❹ that contains any options to customize the effect. The provided options are structured differently from those given in jQuery 1.9.0, so you need to translate from this format to the newer version for use in the common implementation function ❺. The new options are flattened out, so you bring the user-defined settings (o.options) up to the top level, alongside the attributes already at that level. In addition, the end-user's complete callback has a different name (callback) that needs to be converted.

Your effect function must return a reference to the jQuery collection it's being applied to in this version, and it does this via the queue function ❻. The call to queue adds a callback function to the standard fx queue for each selected element, to run the effect functionality at the appropriate time as the queue is processed. jQuery 1.9.0 handles the queues for you, removing this requirement in the newer version.

The enqueued function invokes the common implementation function, passing along the converted options and a done callback that triggers the next item in the element's standard fx queue by calling dequeue ❼.

The common implementation function is defined using the parameters for a jQuery 1.9.0 effect ❽ and contains exactly the same code as presented earlier to actually animate the effect.

Using the code presented here, your effect will run under all jQuery versions without any effort on the part of the user.

10.2.5 *The complete effect*

That completes the implementation of a new jQuery UI effect that hides or shows an element by collapsing it to or expanding it from its center. All the code for the plugin is available for download from the book's website.

To use the new effect, you need to load both the jQuery and jQuery UI code (at least the Effects Core module) into your page, followed by the plugin code. Then apply the effect to an element by providing its name to the appropriate show, hide, or toggle call. Additional options may be supplied at that time to customize the effect.

```
$('#aDiv').hide('implode');
$('#aDiv').toggle('implode', {pieces: 25}, 1000,
    function() { alert('Done'); });
```

By default, all animations proceed by changing attribute values in a near-constant manner from their start value to their final one. Instead, you can use other ways to vary the values and so achieve interesting and more realistic motion. Such methods are described next.

10.3   Animation easings

Animations work by changing an attribute from one value to another, causing the appearance of the element on the web page to alter accordingly. But varying the value at a constant pace doesn't always match our expectations, as we relate elements on the page to real-world objects. Fortunately, jQuery provides for such nonlinear changes, enabling you to achieve additional effects for your animations.

10.3.1   What's an easing?

Easing is the acceleration or deceleration of an object in motion. In the real world, this could be due to external forces such as gravity or friction. In animation terms, it's a definition of the way that the speed of an attribute change varies over time.

An *ease-in* is an acceleration from a stopped position. An *ease-out* is a deceleration down to a stop. Sometimes these are combined in one easing, an *ease-in-out* that starts slowly, speeds up, and then slows to a halt again.

An easing is implemented as a function that returns the attribute value for a given time period. To cater to user-defined durations for an animation and for any attribute range, the function is normalized to expect a time between 0.0 at the start and 1.0 at the end, and to generate an output value also between 0.0 and 1.0. The following listing shows the definition of the swing easing function.

Listing 10.6   The swing easing function

```
jQuery.easing = {
    ...
    swing: function( p ) {
        return 0.5 - Math.cos( p*Math.PI ) / 2;
    }
};
```

NOTE   The way that animation easing functions operate changed in jQuery 1.7.2 and jQuery UI 1.8.23 to the description given in this section. Prior to those versions, the easing function was responsible for calculating the actual attribute value at a particular point in time, and was supplied with the attribute's starting value and the difference between start and end values as parameters. The rest of the text here concentrates on the newer version only.

To use an easing with your animation, you supply its name as one of the options for that animation. For example, to have the height of an element spring from its current value to a new one, you might use the easeInOutElastic easing:

```
$('#mydiv').animate({height: 200}, 1000, 'easeInOutElastic');
```

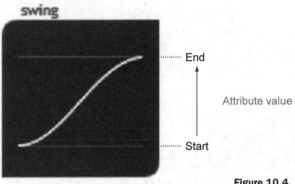

Figure 10.4   An easing graph showing the change in an attribute's value over the duration of an animation

You can apply different easings to different portions of one animation by specifying the required easing on a per-attribute basis. For example, to use the easeInOut-Elastic easing for all attributes except for the background color, which uses a linear easing, you'd use this:

```
$('#mydiv').animate({height: 200, backgroundColor: ['red', 'linear']},
    1000, 'easeInOutElastic');
```

The easiest way to see the effect of an easing is to graph its function. Figure 10.4 shows the easing graph for the swing easing. Time increases from left to right across the graph, while the attribute changes from its initial value at the bottom to its final value at the top (indicated by the horizontal gray lines). In this case, you can see that the attribute value starts out changing slowly, then speeds up, before once more slowing down as it reaches the final value. Hence, it's an ease-in-out type of easing.

10.3.2 Existing easings

jQuery itself defines only two easings, linear and swing, with the latter being the default. The easings offered by jQuery UI come from the jQuery Easing plugin (http://gsgd.co.uk/sandbox/jquery/easing/), which was incorporated into the jQuery UI Effects Core module. These functions are a porting to JavaScript of the easing functions defined by Robert Penner (http://www.robertpenner.com/easing/). The standard jQuery swing easing is renamed as jswing, and the default easing changes to easeOutQuad.

Figure 10.5 shows the graphs for the jQuery and jQuery UI easings.

The linear easing is a constant change from the attribute's starting value to its ending one, whereas the swing easing is based on a cosine curve and has a slight acceleration to start and a corresponding deceleration to finish. The next group of easings (easeInQuad through easeInOutExpo offer ever faster accelerations and decelerations, which are based on mathematical functions of increasing power (quadratic, cubic, quintic, and exponential). Each has an ease-in, ease-out, and combination version.

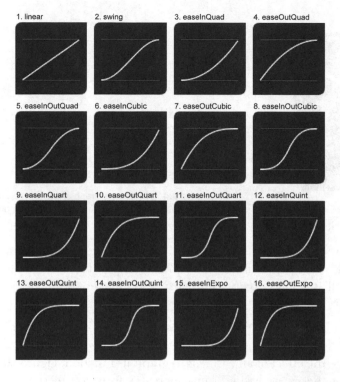

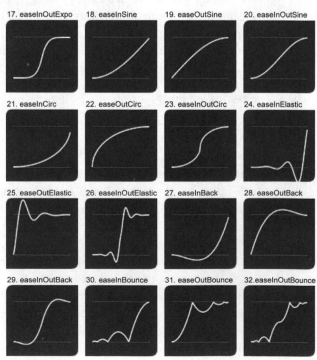

Figure 10.5   jQuery and jQuery UI easing graphs

Next are easings based on a sine function and the shape of a circle. The `elastic` and `back` easings are of interest in that they extend the attribute value outside of its initial range to achieve their effects. The `elastic` easings oscillate an attribute value about its initial or final value, as if it were attached to a spring, whereas the `back` easings briefly roll back or overshoot the starting or ending value. The `bounce` easings simulate an increasing or decreasing bounce effect to reach the desired value. All of these easings have an ease-in, ease-out, and combination form.

10.3.3 Adding a new easing

You can produce some attention-grabbing effects with easings, like the `bounce` easings shown in the previous section. To make your animations stand out from the crowd, you can define custom easings to achieve exactly the outcome you want. One such effect would be to have the attribute value backtrack a little halfway through the transition to add more interest to a standard animation (see the `bump` easing ahead).

To add your own easing, you extend `$.easing` to provide a function named for the new motion. The function takes one parameter representing the portion of the time elapsed in the duration of the animation (from 0.0 to 1.0), and returns the proportion of the attribute value difference that applies at that time (from 0.0 at the start to 1.0 at the end). jQuery converts the calculated proportion into the actual attribute value.

Figure 10.6 shows graphs of the two standard easings, `linear` and `swing`, along with several custom easings; listing 10.7 shows the code behind the latter.

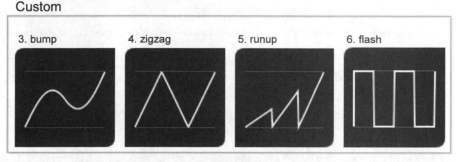

Figure 10.6   Standard and custom jQuery easing graphs

Listing 10.7   Custom easing functions

```
/* Bump easing. */
$.easing.bump = function(p) {
    return (p < 0.5 ? Math.sin(p * Math.PI * 1.46) * 2 / 3 :
        1 - (Math.sin((1 - p) * Math.PI * 1.46) * 2 / 3));
};

/* Zigzag easing. */
$.easing.zigzag = function(p) {
    return 3 * (p < 0.333 ? p : (p < 0.667 ? 0.667 - p : p - 0.667));
};

/* Runup easing. */
$.easing.runup = function(p) {
    return (p < 0.333 ? p :
        (p < 0.667 ? (p - 0.333) * 2 : (p - 0.667) * 3));
};

/* Flash easing. */
$.easing.flash = function(p) {
    return Math.floor(p * 4 + 1) % 2;
};
```

① The bump easing

② The zigzag easing

③ The runup easing

④ The flash easing

The bump easing ① makes an attribute value move toward its final value and then retreat slightly, before continuing on to its end. It links together two portions of a sine curve to achieve this. The zigzag easing ② varies the attribute value linearly up to its final value, back to its initial one, and again up to its final setting, with each transition lasting one third of the overall duration.

The runup easing ③ varies the attribute value linearly, but resets itself to the start after each third of the duration, moving closer to the final value each time. The flash easing ④ switches directly between the initial and final values with no intermediate steps, resulting in a flashing effect.

You use these easings by specifying their name as part of an animation request, either for all animated values,

```
$('#aDiv').animate({height: 300}, 1000, 'runup');
```

or as an override for an individual attribute, following its ending value:

```
$('#aDiv').animate({height: [300, 'bump'], opacity: 0.0}, 1000, 'runup');
```

The complete code for these easings is available for download from the book's website.

Easings in earlier jQuery versions

To convert these easings to support all versions of jQuery, you should define the basic easing function separately and then provide a direct link to that function for newer jQuery versions (when `$.support.newEasing` is `true`). Otherwise, for older versions, include a wrapper function that computes the actual value using the result of the basic easing function, the initial attribute value, and its difference from the final value.

```
(continued)
$.support.newEasing = ($.easing.linear(1.0) == 1.0);

function bumpEasing(p) {
    return (p < 0.5 ? Math.sin(p * Math.PI * 1.46) * 2 / 3 :
        1 - (Math.sin((1 - p) * Math.PI * 1.46) * 2 / 3));
}

if ($.support.newEasing) {
    $.easing.bump = bumpEasing;
}
else {
    $.easing.bump = function(p, n, firstNum, diff) {
        return firstNum + diff * bumpEasing(p);
    };
}
```

What you need to know

Create a custom effect or easing to add a unique visual look to your web pages.

jQuery UI includes effects that alter the appearance of affected elements—either when they're appearing or disappearing, or to bring them to the user's attention.

jQuery UI provides common functionality used by effects.

Extend $.effects.effect to add a new effect ($.effects before jQuery UI 1.9).

Easings control the rate of change of the animated property values over time.

Extend $.easing to add new easings (but it's implemented differently before jQuery 1.7.2 and jQuery UI 1.8.23).

Try it yourself

Develop a new effect called spiral. Break the affected element up into four sections, and have the top-left one slide down, the top-right slide left, the bottom-right slide up, and the bottom-right slide left. Each section fades out as it moves. Reverse the slide directions when showing the element instead of hiding it.

Add a new easing that overshoots the final value by 10% before ending at the correct value. For more of a challenge, implement this easing using a parabolic path instead of a linear one.

10.4 Summary

Included in the jQuery UI modules are some basic utility functions, low-level behaviors (such as drag and drop), high-level components or widgets (such as Tabs and Datepicker), and numerous visual effects. You can use these effects to enhance the presentation of elements on your web page, or to bring a particular element to the user's attention. To assist you in creating your own effects, there's a core of commonly used functions available.

You can add your own effects that operate alongside the existing ones by extending `$.effects.effect` to define the function that implements the desired changes. The implode effect described here complements the existing explode one, causing an element to collapse in upon itself.

Basic jQuery also provides the ability to modify the timing of an attribute change for an animation by specifying an easing. It defines only two such easings, but jQuery UI adds many new ones, allowing you to achieve interesting effects with your own animations. As expected, you can add your own easing functions to define new ways of getting from the start to the end of an attribute change.

That completes our foray into jQuery UI, its modules, and extension points. In the last part of the book, you'll see other aspects of basic jQuery that can be enhanced to provide new abilities, starting with the animation of attributes that don't contain simple numeric values.

Part 4

Other extensions

There are still several extension points provided by jQuery that need covering; this part collects them together.

jQuery can automatically animate simple numeric values, but more complex or multivalued properties are beyond it. In chapter 11 you'll see how to add animation capabilities for these other property values, enabling you to incorporate them into your existing animations.

The use of Ajax to retrieve remote content and process it without requiring a full page refresh is well supported by jQuery. Chapter 12 shows how you can hook into the Ajax processing to enhance the built-in capabilities, from preprocessing a request, through providing an alternate retrieval mechanism, to converting returned data into a more useful format.

Event handling is another aspect of web development that jQuery simplifies by providing cross-browser consistency. The special events framework of jQuery described in chapter 13 lets you augment the event handling process to add new events or alter how existing events are dealt with.

Finally, chapter 14 discusses adding new validation rules for use with the Validation plugin. Although not a part of jQuery itself, this plugin is commonly used and provides its own extension point.

Animating properties

11

This chapter covers

- The jQuery animation framework
- Adding custom property animations

One of the most widely used of jQuery's features is its animation functionality, which provides support for animating various properties of elements, resulting in visual changes on the web page. Besides the basic show and hide functions that provide an animated transition if a duration is specified, several slide and fade animations are also available as standard, such as slideDown and fadeIn. If you want something more exotic, you can request a custom animation to move an element to a particular position or to change its dimensions or font size by using the animate function.

```
$('#myDiv').slideDown('slow');
$('#myDiv').animate({width: '20%', left: '100px'});
```

But the built-in animation functions can only deal with properties that contain simple values: a numeric value followed by an optional units specification, such as 200 (pixels), 2em, or 50%. To enable jQuery to work with more complicated property values, such as colors (#CCFFCC), you must define a custom animation handler that knows how to interpret an existing complex value, compute changes to that value as the animation proceeds, and set the new value back into that property.

jQuery UI includes custom animations for those properties that contain color values, such as `color` and `background-color`. These functions know how to interpret the CSS color values, which may be specified as hexadecimal values, as RGB triplets, or as named colors, to extract the red, green, and blue components. Each component is animated separately, before being combined back into the current composite value at each step of the animation. Using the color animation plugin lets you specify color values alongside the standard format properties when you request an animation.

```
$('#myDiv').animate({fontSize: '20px', backgroundColor: '#DDFFE8'});
```

To be able to animate other non-standard property values, you'll need to find an appropriate animation plugin or develop your own, as described in this chapter. Once you have such a plugin, that property is treated the same as the standard ones, enabling you to apply all of the animation functionality to it as well. For example, you could apply a custom easing to your property animation, or have a callback triggered when its animation is complete.

In this chapter, you'll create an animation handler for the `background-position` style to demonstrate how to provide an animation for a complex value, and how to deal with differences between the animation frameworks in various jQuery versions.

11.1 The animation framework

jQuery's `animate` function lets you animate one or more properties of the selected elements. You specify the list of properties to change and the final values desired for each one. The animation processing then gradually transforms each property from its current value to the new one, altering the appearance of the web page as it proceeds.

Note that jQuery imposes some limitations on what can be animated. Besides the restriction on properties with simple numeric values, jQuery can't interpret some property values that are set from standard named values. For example, when animating an element's border width, you should start with a number value rather than the terms `thin` or `thick`. Also, you shouldn't mix units when animating, such as animating from a starting pixel value to an ending percentage one, because jQuery can't handle the conversion automatically.

The following sections describe the built-in abilities of jQuery animations, such as setting the duration of the change, using alternative easings for additional effects, and being notified when the animation completes, as well as offering a behind-the-scenes look at how jQuery accomplishes these tasks.

11.1.1 Animation capabilities

For common effects, jQuery defines more targeted functions than the basic `animate` call that encapsulate a number of related properties. If you provide a duration to a `show`, `hide`, or `toggle` call, the affected element fades in or out and expands from or contracts to the top-left corner, as shown in figure 11.1. Similarly, the `fadeIn`, `fadeOut`, and

Figure 11.1
Animation progress from a show() call at (from the top) 35%, 85%, and 100% of the duration elapsed

fadeToggle functions reveal or conceal an element by changing its opacity, whereas the slideDown, slideUp, and slideToggle functions alter the element's height.

Multiple animations on the same element, from different animate or related calls, are placed into a queue (named fx) to be executed one after the other. You can request that an animation run immediately by setting its queue option to false.

New property values can be given as a single number (which assumes pixels as the units) or as a number in conjunction with a units specifier, such as 2em or 50%. In addition, you can request a relative change by prefixing the value with -= or +=, whereupon the supplied amount is subtracted from or added to the current value to derive the final quantity.

You can provide additional options to alter the behavior of the animate call.

```
$('#myDiv').animate({left: '50px', width: '-=50px'},
    {duration: 500, easing: 'linear', complete: function() {
        $('#myDivController').attr('src', 'img/expand.gif');
    }});
```

The duration specifies how long the animation takes to complete, as either a numeric amount in milliseconds or one of the named speeds (slow, normal, or fast). Supply an easing to define how the property values vary over time (easings were covered in more detail in chapter 10). Since the release of jQuery 1.4, you can specify per-property easings for more control over your animation.

To be notified when an animation finishes, provide a complete callback as part of the options to the call. This function is triggered once for each element being animated when the animation ends for that element, regardless of the number of properties that are changing. Although no parameters are passed to the callback, within it the this variable refers to the current element.

For callbacks as the animation proceeds, specify a step option and assign it a function that accepts two parameters—the current property value (now) and an object containing details about the property and animation (tween)—and that has the this variable set to the current element. The function is called once for each element for each property at each stage of the animation, allowing you to monitor and/or alter its progress.

But what's jQuery doing when you make an animate call? Read on to find out.

11.1.2 *Stepping an animation*

Behind the scenes, jQuery uses its Deferred objects to manage the animation progress, but ultimately it relies on the standard JavaScript setInterval function to introduce the delay. That delay is set to 13 milliseconds by default, as held in the $.fx.interval variable. At each step of the animation, jQuery calls a function to update the affected properties with their new values. Note that jQuery calculates the elapsed time at each step, rather than relying on counting iterations, allowing it to provide a more accurate rendering of the animation.

> **NOTE** Prior to jQuery 1.8.0, the animation process didn't use the Deferred handling, but called the setInterval function directly.

Deferred objects

jQuery.Deferred(), introduced in jQuery 1.5, is a chainable utility object that can register multiple callbacks into callback queues, invoke callback queues, and relay the success or failure state of any synchronous or asynchronous function (http://api.jquery.com/category/deferred-object/).

jQuery.Deferred() introduces several enhancements to the way callbacks are managed and invoked. In particular, jQuery.Deferred() provides flexible ways to provide multiple callbacks, and these callbacks can be invoked regardless of whether the original callback dispatch has already occurred.

The animation handlers are held in the $.Tween.propHooks object and are indexed by the property name. A standard handler, named _default, is used when no custom override is provided, as shown in listing 11.1. This handler only understands the basic amount and units format for a property value, and can cater to properties that are directly set on the element itself and those that are managed as style settings via the css function.

```
Tween.propHooks = {                                    ❶ Animation extension point
    _default: {
        get: function( tween ) {                       ❸ Retrieve property value
            var result;

            if ( tween.elem[ tween.prop ] != null &&   ❹ Get an attribute value
                    (!tween.elem.style ||
                    tween.elem.style[ tween.prop ] == null)){
                return tween.elem[ tween.prop ];
            }

            // passing any value as a 4th parameter to .css will
            // automatically attempt a parseFloat and fallback to a
            // string if the parse fails so, simple values such as
            // "10px" are parsed to Float. complex values such as
            // "rotate(1rad)" are returned as is.
            result = jQuery.css( tween.elem, tween.prop, false, "" );  // ❺ Get a style value
            // Empty strings, null, undefined and "auto"
            // are converted to 0.
            return !result || result === "auto" ? 0 : result;
        },
        set: function( tween ) {                       ❻ Set property value
            // use step hook for back compat -
            // use cssHook if its there - use .style if its
            // available and use plain properties where available
            if ( jQuery.fx.step[ tween.prop ] ) {      ❼ jQuery 1.8 fallback
                jQuery.fx.step[ tween.prop ]( tween );
            } else if ( tween.elem.style && ( tween.elem.style[  ❽ Update a style
                    jQuery.cssProps[ tween.prop ]] != null ||
                    jQuery.cssHooks[ tween.prop ] ) ) {
                jQuery.style( tween.elem, tween.prop,
                    tween.now + tween.unit );
            } else {
                tween.elem[ tween.prop ] = tween.now;  // ❾ Update an attribute
            }
        }
    }
};
```

❷ Default property handler

The default handler (named _default ❷) is defined as part of the Tween.propHooks object ❶ (and later aliased as $.Tween.propHooks). Each handler is an object that has two attributes: a getter function (get) ❸ to retrieve the current property value, and a setter function (set) ❻ to update and apply the new value during the animation.

NOTE How you define custom animations changed in jQuery 1.8.0. Prior to that you provided a single setter function to extend $.fx.step to cater to your custom property. The main discussion in the next section concentrates on the later versions, but later sections do show how to define the same animation for the earlier versions.

The parameter passed to the getter and setter functions (tween) contains information about the current animation. It has a reference to the current element (tween.elem), the name of the property being animated (tween.prop) ❹ ❾, and the name of the easing being used (tween.easing) for this property. It also has an object (tween.options) that holds the options passed to the animate call, with default values if applicable. These include the duration of the animation (duration), the default easing for the animation (easing), and any completed (complete) or stepping (step) callbacks.

The getter function attempts to retrieve the value as a CSS property ❺ before converting unknown values to 0.

For the setter function ❻, the tween parameter contains additional information concerning the current step in the animation. It provides the initial (tween.start) and final (tween.end) values for the property, as well as the current value (tween.now) ❽, all of which are straight numeric values. The units for these values are found in the tween.unit attribute, whereas the tween.pos attribute contains a value between 0 and 1 indicating the portion of the animation duration that has elapsed.

For backwards compatibility, the function checks for a $.fx.step implementation for the property ❼ and invokes that if found. Otherwise, you calculate the current value for an animation step as the portion of elapsed time multiplied by the difference between the end and start values, plus the starting value.

```
tween.pos * (tween.end – tween.start) + tween.start
```

You'd append the units to the result before setting it back into the nominated property.

An animation handler is found based on the name of the property being animated, and its get and set functions are invoked at the appropriate times throughout the duration of the animation process. jQuery manages this process to calculate initial property values and the differences from the requested final values, to schedule regular updates for the properties, to call the handler at each step, and to tidy up and notify the user (if necessary) at the end of the animation.

To see how you can develop your own animation handler, you'll create one for the background-position style, which isn't a simple numeric value.

11.2　*Adding a custom property animation*

Many property values fall into the category handled by the built-in animation functions, such as a numeric value and an optional units specifier. But you may want to animate other properties that don't fit this format. Without knowing how to interpret and update these property values, jQuery can't provide for their animation. The background-position animation handler described in the next section deals with a composite value made up of two numeric and unit values, and it will let you smoothly change this combined value over a defined period.

Custom property animations must extend `$.Tween.propHooks` to define a getter and a setter for the particular property format. jQuery can then integrate those functions into its standard animation processing to update those properties as well.

11.2.1 *Animating background-position*

The `background-position` CSS property has one of these nonstandard formats. Its value consists of position definitions for the horizontal and vertical offsets of the top-left corner of the background image (if two values are given), or for both offsets (if only one value is given). You can achieve interesting effects through animating the position of a background image, such as scrolling scenery or highlighting a particular part of the image, making your website more attractive to visitors. An example transition is shown in figure 11.2.

In addition to the standard numeric-followed-by-units format, the positions may be specified as named values: `left`, `center`, or `right` for horizontal offsets and `top`, `center`, or `bottom` for vertical ones. These names correspond to `0%`, `50%`, and `100%` respectively in each direction. You must also allow for relative positions, such as those that start with `-=` or `+=`, when specifying a final property value.

```
.uluru { background-image: url(img/uluru.jpg);
    background-position: 'left top'; }
```

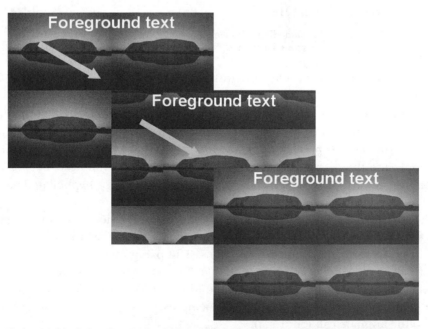

Figure 11.2   Animating the background image's position (in the direction of the arrow) at 0%, 50%, and 100% of the elapsed duration

Once the custom animation is available, you could then move the background image, as follows:

```
$('div.uluru').animate({'background-position': '200px 150px'});
```

> **NOTE** For property names that contain a hyphen (-), you can specify that name using camel-case instead and remove the need to quote it. jQuery automatically converts between the two formats: `$('div.uluru').ani-mate({backgroundPosition: '200px 150px'});`.

First you need to define the animation handler for this property and provide a function to retrieve the current property value.

11.2.2 *Declaring and retrieving the property value*

You start your custom animation plugin by defining the getter function to retrieve the current property value as part of an extension to the jQuery Tween processing. The following listing shows the basic plugin declaration.

Listing 11.2   Defining for jQuery 1.8.x

```
(function($) { // Hide scope, no $ conflict          ① Declare anonymous function

$.Tween.propHooks['backgroundPosition'] = {
    get: function(tween) {
        return parseBackgroundPosition($(tween.elem).css(tween.prop));
    },
    set: setBackgroundPosition
};

})(jQuery);
```

② Add custom property animator

③ Define value getter

④ Define value setter

⑤ Immediately invoke scope function

As with all plugins, you should start with an anonymous function wrapper ① that serves to hide your code from the outside world and ensures that $ is the same as jQuery within your code through the use of its declared and supplied parameter ⑤.

You define the animation functions as an object extending `$.Tween.propHooks`, named for the new property ②. If the property would normally contain a hyphen (-), you should use the corresponding camel-case name, as is done here: `backgroundPosition` instead of `background-position`. jQuery will convert a hyphenated name into the camel-case version before its use.

The object then contains two functions: a getter to retrieve the current property value ③ and a setter to update the property with a new value ④. In each case, pass the processing on to further internal functions. The parameter for both of these functions (`tween`) is an object that encapsulates the settings for the animation for this property. Its attributes include a reference to the current DOM element (`elem`), the name of the property (`prop`), the easing being used (`easing`), and the options supplied to the animate call (`options`).

The next listing shows the workings of the internal function that extracts positional values from the property.

Listing 11.3 Parsing `background-position` value

```
/* Parse a background-position definition: horizontal [vertical]
   @param  value  (string) the definition
   @return  ([2][string, number, string]) the extracted values –
              relative marker, amount, units */
function parseBackgroundPosition(value) {
    var bgPos = (value || '').split(/ /);                                     Function to
    var presets = {center: '50%', left: '0%', right: '100%',              interpret
        top: '0%', bottom: '100%'};                                   position value  ❶
    var decodePos = function(index) {
        var pos = (presets[bgPos[index]] || bgPos[index] || '50%').
            match(/^([+-]=)?([+-]?\d+(\.\d*)?)(.*)$/);
        bgPos[index] = [pos[1], parseFloat(pos[2]), pos[4] || 'px'];
    };
                                                                           Break up
    if (bgPos.length == 1 &&                                                position
            $.inArray(bgPos[0], ['top', 'bottom']) > -1) {            into amount
        bgPos[1] = bgPos[0];                                            and units  ❸
        bgPos[0] = '50%';
    }
    decodePos(0);                          Decode position values
    decodePos(1);                      ❺  and return them
    return bgPos;
}
```

❷ **Separate horizontal and vertical components**

❹ **Handle vertical-only position**

Because the property value isn't a simple numeric value, you have to locate the relevant parts of that value for later use. You can define a separate function to interpret those values ❶. As the property value may consist of two parts for the horizontal and vertical components, the first step is to separate them via the `split` function ❷.

Each portion is then decoded to extract the parts of the position value via an internal function (`decodePos`) ❸. The value is converted from a named position if necessary (via the `presets` object) or defaults to `50%` (center) if not provided at all. Then you can use a regular expression to look for an optional leading `+=` or `-=` indicating a relative value, followed by a numeric entry (including optional minus sign and fractional portion), and any units specification. Each of these components is captured into a regular expression group (by surrounding their patterns with parentheses `()`). Finally, you update the corresponding entry in the position array (`bgPos`) to be an array of these components (relative indicator, amount, and units). Separating the components here makes it easier to use them later during the animation.

A `background-position` may consist of only a single value, which is interpreted to be a horizontal value with the vertical value defaulting to `center`, unless it's a named vertical value (`top` or `bottom`), in which case the horizontal one defaults to `center`. You should check for this situation and transfer the values accordingly ❹.

Then you apply the decoding function to each portion of the position in turn **5** and return the updated value, now containing the extracted positional components, to the caller.

You complete the animation handler definition by creating a setter function to alter the property value.

11.2.3 *Updating the property value*

The next step is to update the position value as the animation progresses, and set that value back onto the element to change the display. The following listing shows the setter function for the `background-position` animator.

Listing 11.4 Setting `background-position`

```
/* Set the value for a step in the animation.
   @param  tween  (object) the animation properties */       ① Define property
function setBackgroundPosition(tween) {                          setter
    if (!tween.set) {                                        ② Initialize settings if
        initBackgroundPosition(tween);                          not already done
    }
    $(tween.elem).css('background-position',                  ③ Set new
        ((tween.pos * (tween.end[0][1] - tween.start[0][1]) +    property value
        tween.start[0][1]) + tween.end[0][2]) + ' ' +
        ((tween.pos * (tween.end[1][1] - tween.start[1][1]) +
        tween.start[1][1]) + tween.end[1][2]));
}
```

You define an internal function to update the property with a new value as the animation proceeds **1**. The parameter to this function is an object containing details about the current animation. jQuery calls the function many times as each step of the animation occurs, so try to minimize the amount of work done within it to improve performance.

The first time that the function is called, you should perform some initialization, such as calculating values that don't change throughout the animation. To avoid the overhead of initializing on each call, you can control entry to the process via a flag that gets set on the parameter object **2**. The initialization function is described in listing 11.5.

For each step in the animation, you update the property on the current element (`tween.elem`) with its new value **3** via the standard `css` function. You calculate that value based on the portion of the animation that has elapsed, as indicated by the `tween.pos` value set by jQuery, which ranges from 0 at the start of the animation to 1 at the end. In general, you'd multiply this factor by the difference between the ending and starting values for the property (the change required over the entire duration), add back in the starting value, and append any unit specifier, as the following does:

```
(tween.pos * (tween.end - tween.start) + tween.start) + tween.unit
```

For the `background-position`, you need to do that for the horizontal and vertical components separately before combining them into the new composite value.

Listing 11.5 Initialize `background-position` animation

```
/* Initialise the animation.
   @param  tween  (object) the animation properties */
function initBackgroundPosition(tween) {
    tween.start = parseBackgroundPosition(
        $(tween.elem).css('backgroundPosition'));
    tween.end = parseBackgroundPosition(tween.end);
    for (var i = 0; i < tween.end.length; i++) {
        if (tween.end[i][0]) { // Relative position
            tween.end[i][1] = tween.start[i][1] +
                (tween.end[i][0] == '-=' ? -1 : +1) * tween.end[i][1];
        }
    }
    tween.set = true;
}
```

- ❶ Define animation initialization
- ❷ Decode starting positions
- ❸ Decode ending positions
- ❹ For each decoded value...
- ❺ ...calculate relative positions
- ❻ Mark as initialized

To reduce the amount of processing required for each step of the animation, define an initialization function ❶ that's called once at the start of the process. The contents of this function will depend on the structure of the property being animated, but in general you'd extract the component parts of the starting and ending values so that they can easily be combined in the setter shown previously.

For the `background-position`, you calculate the starting and ending attributes of the animation object (`tween`) as an array of its component values via the `parseBackgroundPosition` function (❷ and ❸).

For each of the ending positional values ❹, check whether it's a relative value, such as one starting with `+=` or `-=`, by examining the first item of the corresponding `tween.end` entry ❺. If it is, add the relative value to, or subtract it from, the current one (from `tween.start`) to obtain the final value.

Finally, you should set a flag to indicate that the initialization process has been performed ❻ and doesn't need to be done again for this animation.

The new Background Position plugin is now ready for use, allowing you to animate the position of the background image in the same manner as other element properties.

As noted previously, jQuery changed how it handled animations in version 1.8, so the following section describes how to create the same animation in the older versions.

11.2.4 *Animating background-position in jQuery 1.7*

Prior to jQuery 1.8.0, you had to extend `$.fx.step` to add a custom property animation and only needed to supply a setter function. Fortunately, the internal processing for the animation steps is nearly the same between the older and newer jQuery versions, so you can reuse most of what was developed for the newer version in the older one, as follows.

Listing 11.6   `background-position` animation for jQuery 1.7

```
(function($) { // Hide scope, no $ conflict          ◄── ❶ Declare anonymous
                                                             function
// Enable animation for the background-position attribute
$.fx.step['backgroundPosition'] = setBackgroundPosition;   ◄── ❷ Define custom
                                                                  property animator
})(jQuery);        ◄── ❸ Immediately invoke scope function
```

As in the newer jQuery version, you start with an anonymous function ❶ to hide the plugin code and enable the use of `$` for `jQuery` ❸. Within that scope, you extend `$.fx.step` with an attribute named for the property being animated, and assign it the function that sets the new property value ❷. Once again, if your property name normally contains a hyphen, use the camel-case version of the name when defining the step function. The `setBackgroundPosition` function is the same as for the newer jQuery versions and can be reused.

By testing for the newer version of the jQuery animation framework, you can define the appropriate animation handler.

Listing 11.7   Define the appropriate animation handler

```
var usesTween = !!$.Tween;                    ◄── ❶ Determine which
                                                     animation framework
if (usesTween) { // jQuery 1.8+
    $.Tween.propHooks['backgroundPosition'] = {          ◄── ❷ Define jQuery
        get: function(tween) {                                 1.8+ handler
            return parseBackgroundPosition(
                $(tween.elem).css(tween.prop));
        },
        set: setBackgroundPosition
    };
}
else { // jQuery 1.7-                                          ❸ Define
    // Enable animation for the background-position attribute     jQuery
    $.fx.step['backgroundPosition'] = setBackgroundPosition;  ◄── 1.7- handler
};
```

NOTE   The `!!` construct is explained in section 3.2.1.

You can determine which animation framework is present by testing for the presence of the `$.Tween` value ❶. Based on that test, define either the `$.Tween.propHooks` object required by the newer framework ❷ or the `$.fx.step` function required by the older one ❸. Now your animation plugin will work in all jQuery versions.

NOTE   Prior to jQuery 1.5, the standard animation processing corrupts the initial value of the `background-position` setting, so the code presented here won't work in those earlier versions.

11.2.5 *The complete plugin*

You've completed building the jQuery Background Position plugin. With it you can animate movement of the image in the background of an element. This plugin also lets you use all of the features of jQuery's animation framework, such as positioning by em units or percentages, relative movements, easings for more effects, and completion callbacks. The complete code for the plugin is available for download from the book's website.

What you need to know

Standard jQuery can only animate simple numeric properties.

Create a custom animator to animate more complex property values.

Extend `$.Tween.propHooks` to add animation abilities for a new property.

Provide getter and setter functions for the property values.

Prior to jQuery 1.8 you extend `$.fx.step` instead.

Try it yourself

Develop an animation plugin for the `border-width` property. It may consist of up to four simple numeric values, indicating the top, right, bottom, and left border settings respectively. If only one value is given, it applies to all borders. If two values are provided, they apply to the top/bottom and right/left borders. When three values are supplied, the missing left border is equal to the right one.

11.3 *Summary*

jQuery provides support for animating various properties of elements, resulting in visual changes on the web page. In addition to the built-in show, hide, fade, and slide functions that generate animations, you can request other animations directly through the animate function. Only element properties with a simple value and units format can be handled automatically in an animation.

For properties that don't conform to the standard format, you'll need to obtain or develop an animation plugin that knows how to interpret these values. jQuery UI includes animation plugins for properties that contain color values, allowing these to be animated alongside the more standard properties.

In the example in this chapter for the background-position style, you saw how to create a plugin that could extract relevant information from the property value, calculate the current value as the animation progresses, and update the element with that new value. This plugin enables the new property to be animated like all the others.

In the next chapter, you'll examine the jQuery Ajax framework and discover how to extend that to cater to additional requirements.

Extending Ajax

Support for *Ajax* (Asynchronous JavaScript and XML) is one of the key features of jQuery, making it easy to request content from the server and to process the returned data and update the current page accordingly, without requiring a full refresh. You specify the URL to access, you can provide parameters to be sent along, and you can process the returned content in a callback function, as shown here:

```
$.ajax('product.php', {data: {prod_id: 'AB1234'},
    success: function(info) {...}});
```

jQuery also contains several convenience functions that encapsulate the Ajax abilities. For a simple request and response, you can use the get function, or to use an alternate parameter encoding, you use the post function. To load specific types of data, you can use the getScript or getJSON functions for JavaScript and *JSON*

(JavaScript Object Notation) content respectively. If you want to place HTML content directly into an element on the page, you can use the `load` function on that element.

```
$.get('product.php', {prod_id: 'AB1234'}, function(info) {...});
$.getScript('product.js');
$('#mydiv').load('product.php', {prod_id: 'AB1234'}, function(info) {...});
```

jQuery offers additional abilities to set default values for all Ajax processing and to register handlers for events that occur during the Ajax lifecycle.

Although there's a lot of built-in functionality, if you retrieve content in an unusual format, you may find it necessary to process that content yourself. Fortunately, jQuery includes several extension points within its Ajax framework to let you customize the downloading and handling of the requested content.

12.1 The Ajax framework

Underlying the Ajax support of jQuery is its management of an `XMLHttpRequest` object (or the corresponding ActiveX object in some versions of IE) to perform the actual download of the remote content. jQuery carries out several steps as it executes an Ajax request. You can add your own processing at various stages to implement special requirements for retrieving information.

A request starts by applying prefilters that may affect how the call proceeds, before selecting a transport mechanism to use for the actual download. When the content is received, it may be run through a converter to obtain an alternate format for the user to work with. Figure 12.1 shows the sequence of operations for a basic Ajax call.

The whole process is driven by the data type specified for your request, the standard ones being `text`, `html`, `xml`, `script`, `json`, and `jsonp`. jQuery will try to determine the

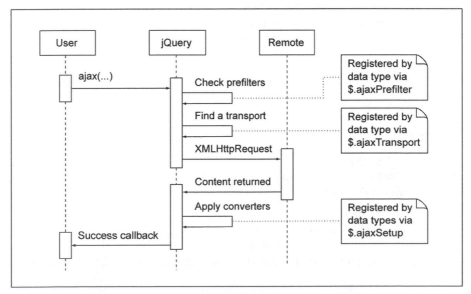

Figure 12.1   Sequence diagram for a standard Ajax call, showing extension points

data type for retrieved content, if it wasn't given, by inspecting the returned MIME type. The conversion process is invoked if the returned data type doesn't match the requested one.

Since version 1.5, jQuery wraps the native XMLHttpRequest object to provide additional functionality, with the enhanced object being known as a jqXHR object. The wrapper also acts as a Deferred object,[1] allowing you to add extra callbacks to be triggered when the Ajax processing succeeds or generates an error.

> NOTE The success, error, and complete functions of the jqXHR object have been deprecated in jQuery 1.8 and should be replaced by the corresponding done, fail, and always functions.

12.1.1 Prefilters

A *prefilter* is a function that's called before the actual request to the server is made. It allows you to preprocess that request and alter how it proceeds, and it's useful when creating custom data types. For example, you could add extra headers to the request, or even cancel it entirely.

The prefilters are called after parameter serialization has occurred—after any data option is converted to a string (assuming processData is true), but before the Ajax framework looks for an appropriate transporter. Prefilters are identified by the data type to which they apply, such as html or script, and can be set to operate on all data types by using *. The filters specific to a data type are executed first, before continuing on to those for all types.

You can register a new prefilter by calling the $.ajaxPrefilter function and providing the associated data type and the function to be called for it. The parameters to your function include the Ajax options and a reference to the jqXHR object being used for the remote access. To cancel a request, you call the abort function on the latter.

For example, to change the user agent identity for all html requests, you could use a prefilter like this:

```
$.ajaxPrefilter('html', function(options, originalOptions, jqXHR) {
    jqXHR.setRequestHeader('User-Agent', 'Unknown');
});
```

12.1.2 Transports

An Ajax *transport* provides the underlying mechanism to retrieve the requested data from the server. Although the XMLHttpRequest object is normally used, there are other means available to load content, such as the src attribute of an img element (to download an image).

New transports are registered by calling the $.ajaxTransport function and providing the data type to which this transport applies and the function that returns the custom retrieval object. This transport object supplies two callback functions: one to

---

[1] jQuery API Documentation, "Category: Deferred Object," http://api.jquery.com/category/deferred-object/.

perform the actual retrieval, and another to clean up if a request is aborted. As for prefilters, you can use * to define a transport for all data types. Only the first matching transport is used, starting with those for specific data types in preference to those for all data types.

For example, to forbid access to any `xml` documents, you could use a transport like this:

```
$.ajaxTransport('xml', function(options, originalOptions, jqXHR) {
    return {
        send: function(headers, complete) {
            complete('403', 'Forbidden', {});
        },

        abort: function() {}
    };
});
```

jQuery uses this ability itself to deal with cross-domain requests for the `script` data type.

12.1.3 Converters

Once the data is retrieved from the server, it's not necessarily in the most useful format. A *converter* implements the conversion process, accepting the text-based content as input and generating the appropriate output.

For example, when you request XML from the server, you specify a `dataType` of `xml`. This triggers a converter to parse the returned text as an XML document and produce an XML DOM as the final value of the Ajax call. You can then immediately start traversing that DOM to extract the information relevant to your current situation.

Converters are registered in the `converters` attribute passed to an `$.ajaxSetup` call. You specify the source and destination data formats in a single string to identify a converter, and associate that value with the function that performs the transformation. You can use * to represent any data type in the converter identifier. For example, the XML converter just described is defined as shown here—converting from text to XML by calling the jQuery `parseXML` function.

```
ajaxSettings: {
    ...
    converters: {
        ...
        // Parse text as xml
        "text xml": jQuery.parseXML
    },
    ...
}
```

You can define your own converters to transform custom data formats into alternative formats in a similar manner.

Each of these extension points is covered in greater detail in the following sections, starting with the prefilters.

12.2 *Adding an Ajax prefilter*

Ajax prefilters let you preprocess an Ajax call and potentially alter how it proceeds, such as by changing the `timeout` setting for a slow server, or even preventing the remote call. jQuery uses prefilters itself to handle the `json` and `jsonp` data types, allowing it to install the appropriate callbacks for these requests. You'll see two examples of prefilters next: one to change the data type for a request and the other to cancel a request altogether.

12.2.1 *Changing the data type*

Prefilters let you modify settings on the `XMLHttpRequest` object (wrapped as `jqXHR`) before a request is sent. In addition, they can be used to change the data type for a request by returning the desired data type as its value. This has the effect of making all subsequent operations use the new data type, including a reprocessing of the prefiltering based on that new value.

The following listing shows how to enforce a data type based on the requested URL.

Listing 12.1 Changing the data type

```
/* Set CSV data type. */                                        ❶ Define prefilter
$.ajaxPrefilter(function(options, originalOptions, jqXHR) {  ◄─    for all types
    if (options.url.match(/.*\.csv/)) {              ◄──────────  ❷ If filename
        return 'csv';          ◄──  ...change                       is *.csv...
    }                              ❸ data type
});
```

You call `$.ajaxPrefilter` to register a new prefilter function ❶. Note that you don't have to provide a data type to match against, as * is assumed for all types. In this case, you want all requests for files with the `.csv` extension to be treated as the `csv` data type, so you test the provided URL to see whether it ends in the required text ❷ and return the new data type if so ❸.

To continue with the standard processing, you don't return anything. Section 12.4 describes how you might deal with this CSV content via a converter.

12.2.2 *Disabling Ajax processing*

There may be times when you don't want Ajax calls to be made at all, or perhaps you want to prevent certain types of calls. The next listing shows how a prefilter can meet this requirement by cancelling selected requests.

Listing 12.2 Disabling Ajax processing

```
/* Disable Ajax processing. */          ❶ List of disabled
$.ajax.disableDataTypes = [];        ◄─    data types

$.ajaxPrefilter('*', function(options, originalOptions, jqXHR) {   ◄─
    if ($.inArray(options.dataType, $.ajax.disableDataTypes) > -1) {
        jqXHR.abort();                                          Define prefilter
    }                                                            for all types ❷
});
```

Disable specified types ❸

You should start by declaring a list of data types that are to be disabled **❶**. The user can then add selected types as necessary:

```
$.ajax.disableDataTypes.push('html');
```

You create the prefilter via a call to `$.ajaxPrefilter` **❷**, providing the data type to which the filter applies and the function to be used in those circumstances. The data type is specified as one or more values separated by spaces, such as `html` or `json jsonp`. You can also use the value `*` (or omit the data type altogether) to apply to all data types. In addition, you can indicate that the filter should be called before any others for a data type by prefixing that type with `+`.

Your prefilter function receives several parameters: `options` holds all the Ajax settings for this request, whether they've been defaulted by jQuery or provided on the Ajax call, whereas `originalOptions` only has the settings specified by the user, and `jqXHR` is a reference to the jQuery `jqXHR` object that will be used. You can examine the options given (specified or defaulted) and can modify the request accordingly through the provided object. In this case, you see whether the requested data type is one of those listed in the set to be disabled, and abort the request if so **❸**.

Other actions that you could take on the `jqXHR` object include adding headers to the request via the `setRequestHeader(name, value)` function or changing the requested MIME type via the `overrideMimeType(mimeType)` function.

If you need to remove a value from the list of disabled data types, you can use the `$.map` function of jQuery. For example, to remove the `html` data type, you'd write this:

```
$.ajax.disableDataTypes = $.map($.ajax.disableDataTypes, function(v) {
    return (v == 'html' ? null : v);
});
```

You could extend this prefilter to include particular types of requests (`GET` or `POST`) or other Ajax settings.

12.3 Adding an Ajax transport

Ajax transports provide the mechanism for downloading the requested content, and they default to using the standard `XMLHttpRequest` object. But you can implement alternative means for specific data types by adding your own transport function. You can also alter the retrieval procedure for standard data types and add your own functionality to it. Both of these extensions are illustrated in the examples ahead.

12.3.1 Loading image data

Suppose you wanted to preload images onto your page. You could create `Image` elements and go through the process of setting them up, initiating the load requests and reacting when they're ready. Or you could tie into the Ajax framework to get the benefits of all the functionality that jQuery provides surrounding its use, such as authentication and error handling.

To load images via an Ajax call, you could define an `image` transport function that knows how to handle this format, because it's not text-based, using the download abilities of the DOM `Image` object to perform the actual transfer. The following listing shows how you might define the transport to achieve this.

Listing 12.3   Loading image data

```
/* Transport image data. */
$.ajaxTransport('image', function(options, originalOptions, jqXHR) {     ◄─────  Define
    if (options.type === 'GET' && options.async) {                               transport
        var image;                                              ❸ Return transport   for image ❶
        return {                                                   object
            send: function(headers, complete) {            ◄───
                image = new Image();                             Define send
                function done(status) {                      ❹ request function
                    if (image) {
                        var statusText = (status == 200 ?
                            'success' : 'error');
                        var tmp = image;
                        image = image.onreadystatechange=
                            image.onerror = image.onload = null;
                        complete(status, statusText, {image: tmp});
                    }
                }
                image.onreadystatechange = image.onload = function() {
                    done(200);
                };
                image.onerror = function() {
                    done(404);
                };
                image.src = options.url;         ◄───  ❽ Load the image
            },

            abort: function() {                       ◄───  Handle aborted
                if (image) {                             ❾ request
                    image = image.onreadystatechange =
                        image.onerror = image.onload = null;
                }
            }
        };
    }
});
```

Only if using GET asynchronously ❷

Callback when request is completed ❺

Invoke complete callback ❻

Initialize image callbacks ❼

You start by calling `$.ajaxTransport` to define the transport function for the image data type ❶. As for prefilters, the data type can be several types separated by spaces, can be * for all types, and can have a prefix of + per type to make it the first in the list for that type. Your function's `options` parameter contains the complete set of Ajax options for this call, including those set by jQuery as default values; the `originalOptions` parameter only contains the options specified explicitly by the user on this call. `jqXHR` holds a reference to the jQuery `jqXHR` object normally used by the request. Because you're using an alternative mechanism to load the image, this last parameter is ignored.

Your new transport only applies if the user requested the GET format and an asynchronous load (due to the limitations of the actual mechanism you're using), so you need to test for these conditions ❷. If the transport does apply, you return a transport object that allows jQuery to invoke the load process at the appropriate time ❸. The transport object contains two functions: send to initiate a download and abort to tidy up if it terminates in error.

The send function ❹ is used instead of the standard Ajax processing to request content for this data type. Its parameters are a reference to the headers for the request (headers) and a callback function to complete the processing (complete) within the Ajax framework. As you're using the inherent abilities of the Image element to load the data, you start by creating a new Image element to work with.

Define a callback function ❺ to be executed when the image load has finished. Within that function, you determine the success or failure of the load and set the status accordingly. Then clean up the internally created Image by clearing its callbacks and then setting the variable itself to null, allowing the assigned memory to be recovered and preventing memory leaks. The image is still accessible via the local tmp variable, but it's no longer available outside of the done callback.

Finally, you invoke the complete callback provided as a parameter to the send call, to inform the jQuery Ajax framework of the outcome of the request ❻. The parameters to the complete call are the numeric and text versions of the status, an object containing details about the response, and a string (optional) containing all the response headers—one to a line. This object must contain an attribute named for the data type being requested (image in this case) that refers to the actual result. Here you provide a reference to the Image element that was loaded.

Having defined the function to handle the load outcome, you assign functions to the standard callbacks on the Image element that calls it, and pass along the appropriate status code ❼. The last step is to start the loading process by setting the src attribute of the Image element to the URL supplied in the Ajax call ❽, which eventually triggers one of the registered callbacks.

The abort function of the returned transport object ❾ lets you tidy up if the request fails. In this case, you again clean up the internal Image element by setting everything to null.

To invoke this alternate transport, you could then make an Ajax call for the new data type, and you'd receive a reference to the loaded image as the parameter to the success callback.

```
$.ajax({url: 'img/uluru.jpg', dataType: 'image', success: function(image) {
    $('#img1').replaceWith(image);
}});
```

This transport illustrates how you can use alternative load mechanisms to obtain data from the server. The next example shows how you can simulate normal HTML retrieval by overriding the standard transport.

12.3.2 Simulating HTML data for testing

While testing a plugin that uses Ajax to implement its functionality, you might want to avoid loading from a live site so that you're not dependent on a remote connection. You can use the Ajax transport handling to override the default retrieval and substitute known content inline instead. This keeps the data used for testing alongside the tests themselves, reducing the possibility of that data getting out of sync or being lost.

To provide a proper simulation of remote access, you should provide a mapping from requested files to their testing content. In addition, you can specify a delay before the content is returned, mirroring network delays during real processing. You could also control the return status of a page for additional test coverage.

Listing 12.4 shows how you might define an Ajax transport override for a GET request for html content.

Listing 12.4 Simulate HTML data for testing

```
/* Simulate HTML loading. */          ❶ Define file mappings        Override ❷
$.ajax.simulateHtml = {};                                           transport
                                                                    for html
$.ajaxTransport('html', function(options, originalOptions, jqXHR) {
    if (options.type === 'GET') {
        var timer;                              ❹ Return transport object
        return {
            send: function(headers, complete) {              Define send
                var fileName = options.url.replace(       ❺ request function
                    /.*\/([^\/]+)$/, '$1');
                var simulate = $.ajax.simulateHtml[fileName] ||
                    $.ajax.simulateHtml['default'];
                timer = setTimeout(function() {
                    complete(simulate.html ? 200 : 404,     ❼ Introduce delay
                        simulate.html ? 'success' : 'error',
                        {html: simulate.html});
                }, Math.random() * simulate.variation + simulate.delay);
            },

            abort: function() {
                clearTimeout(timer);            ❾ Handle aborted request
            }
        };
    }
});
```

❸ Only if a GET request
❻ Extract filename and settings
❽ Invoke complete callback

You start by declaring an object ($.ajax.simulateHtml) to hold mappings between particular pages and the content that should be returned ❶. The key for attributes in this object could be just the name of the file being requested, depending on whether the server or path names affect the testing outcome. Each attribute value is an object containing several fields: html for the actual content returned, delay for the minimum delay in milliseconds before the content comes back, and variation for a maximum additional delay in milliseconds above that (randomized for each call). If the content is set to a blank string, a 404 ("page not found") error is generated. Allow for handling any provided filename by including an entry indexed by default. For example, you could map the test.html file as follows:

```
$.ajax.simulateHtml['default'] = {delay: 500, variation: 1000, html: ''};
$.ajax.simulateHtml['test.html'] = {delay: 500, variation: 1000,
    html: '<p>Try this instead</p>'};
```

To override the default `html` transport handling, you define a new transport for that data type ❷. The parameters for the associated transport function are the same as for the previous `image` example: all the options, specified options only, and a `jqXHR` reference. You only use the alternate transport if a `GET` request is made, so you check for that condition before continuing ❸.

The transport function returns a transport object that jQuery can use to implement the Ajax processing ❹. Its `send` function ❺ is called when a request for content for the nominated data type is made, and it receives as parameters the headers for the request and a callback to complete the Ajax processing within the framework.

Within this function, you first extract the name of the file being requested ❻. You can use a regular expression to retrieve the filename—matching everything (`.*`) up to the last slash (`\/`), and then capturing the remainder without any slashes (`([^\/]+)`) up to the end of the string (`$`). The captured remainder (referred to via `$1`) then replaces the entire matched string (everything), to leave you with just the desired filename. From that filename you obtain the mapped response details from the `$.ajax .simulateHtml` object, or use the `default` settings if there is no mapping for that file.

To simulate network delays, you can use the standard JavaScript `setTimeout` function to introduce a delay ❼ made up of a random variation plus the minimum delay specified. When the time expires, you invoke the `complete` callback provided to the `send` function to notify the jQuery Ajax framework that the requested content is available ❽. As before, the parameters to the `complete` call are the numeric and text versions of the status (being `404` and `error` respectively, if there was no return content), an object containing the actual content as indexed by the data type (`html` in this case), and an optional string containing all the headers.

If the request is aborted for some reason, the `abort` function of the transport object lets you tidy up the environment ❾. Here you cancel the timer, if it's still running, via a call to `clearTimeout`.

To use this custom transport within a QUnit test (see chapter 7), you'd provide mappings as shown previously for the test.html page. If you then make an Ajax call for that page, you can test the expected content based on your definition, with the result shown in figure 12.2 for the code in listing 12.5. Remember that you must create asynchronous tests, because the process involves the use of Ajax.

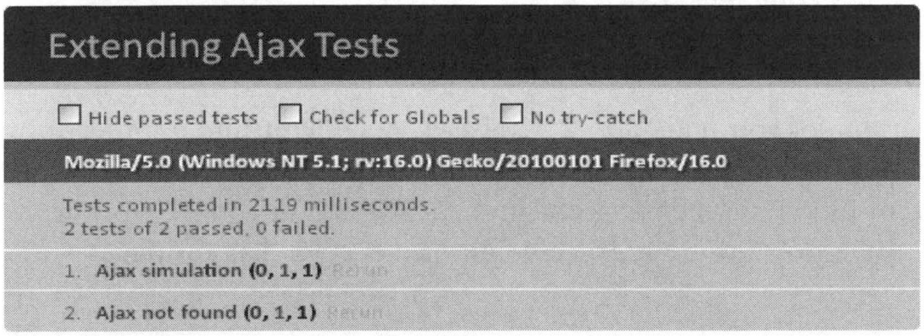

Figure 12.2   Running simulated Ajax tests

Listing 12.5   Testing with HTML simulation

```
asyncTest('Ajax simulation', function() {                        ❶ Define an asynchronous test
    expect(1);
    $.ajax('test.html', {dataType: 'html', success: function(data) {
        equal($(data).text(), 'Try this instead', 'Ajax substitution');
        start();                        ❺ Continue test
    }});                                    processing
});

                                                        ❻ Define page
                                                           not found test

asyncTest('Ajax not found', function() {
    expect(1);
    $.ajax('other.html', {dataType: 'html', success: function(data) {
        ok(false, 'Page found');
        start();
    }, error: function(jqXHR, textStatus, errorThrown) {
        ok(jqXHR.status == 404 && textStatus == 'error', 'Page missing');
        start();                        ❾ Continue test
    }});                                    processing
});
```

❷ Expect one assertion
❸ Ajax load of test page
❹ Assert correct content
❼ Fail if page found
❽ Assert correct error

You define an asynchronous test via a call to asyncTest instead of test ❶, and expect one assertion to be made in this test ❷. You make the ajax call to load the test.html page ❸, which should be substituted by the custom transporter. Note that you need to specify the dataType for the Ajax call to have the framework use the new functionality. Within the success callback, you confirm that the returned content is indeed that from the file mapping ❹. Because this is an asynchronous test, you must call the QUnit start function to inform the testing framework that the test has finished and that its results can be shown ❺.

You should add a second test to confirm that the default and error processing paths also work in the custom transporter ❻, once more expecting only one assertion to be made. This time you request a page that doesn't have a mapping specified (other.html) to revert to the default mapping. Because the content specified for the default is blank, the transporter should generate a 404 error in its place. Within the success callback, you fail the test, as this path shouldn't occur ❼. Instead, the error callback should be invoked, allowing you to assert that the status and status text are as expected ❽. As before, you need to call start to resume the QUnit processing once the Ajax call has completed ❾.

12.4   *Adding an Ajax converter*

Ajax converters let you transform a text-based document into another format that's more directly usable as the result of an Ajax call. jQuery does this already for XML and JSON content by calling the parseXML and parseJSON functions respectively. You can add your own converters to preprocess your own custom data formats.

12.4.1 *Comma-separated values format*

CSV (comma-separated values) is a common text format and is often used to transfer tables of information. Each line in a CSV file represents a single record, with field values for that record being separated by commas within that line (hence the name). The first line in a CSV file usually contains the names of the fields, again separated by commas, and isn't treated as a record.

```
First Name,Last Name
Marcus,Cicero
Frank,Zappa
Groucho,Marx
Jane,Austen
```

Things become more complicated when you want to include a comma within a field value. As this would normally be interpreted as the delimiter for the next field, you must indicate that you want it treated as a literal value instead. To achieve this, you surround the entire field value with quotes ("), but then you have a problem if you want to include a quote in your field value. The solution for this is to double up the embedded quote characters to escape them.

```
First Name,Last Name,Quote
Marcus,Cicero,"""A room without books is like a body without a soul."""
Frank,Zappa,"""So many books, so little time."""
Groucho,Marx,"""Outside of a dog, a book is man's best friend. ..."""
Jane,Austen,"""The person, be it gentleman or lady, who has not ..."""
```

Due to these additional requirements for including reserved characters within CSV files, it's not so easy to process them directly in JavaScript. To make things simpler, you could convert the CSV text format into a corresponding JavaScript object with a list of field names (`fieldsNames`) and a list of data rows (`rows`). Each row would contain a further list of field values, corresponding in position to the field names already provided. Creating a custom converter lets you integrate the transformation into the standard Ajax processing.

12.4.2 *Converting text to CSV*

When you request a CSV file from the server, you receive the straight text version of that file by default. To transform that text into a corresponding JavaScript object, you define an Ajax converter, as shown in the following listing.

Listing 12.6 Convert CSV text to object

```
/* Convert CSV file into a JavaScript object.
   @param  csvText  (string) the CSV text
   @return  (object) the extracted CSV with attributes
                     fieldNames (string[]) and rows (string[][]) */
function textToCsv(csvText) {                          Define conversion
    var fieldNames = [];                             ❶ function
    var fieldCount = 9999;
```

```
                  var rows = [];
                  var lines = csvText.match(/[^\r\n]+/g); // Separate lines
                  for (var i = 0; i < lines.length; i++) {
                      if (lines[i]) {
                          // Separate columns
                          var columns = lines[i].match(/,|"([^"]|"")*"|[^,]*/g);
                          var fields = [];
                          var field = '';
                          for (var j = 0; j < columns.length - 1; j++) {
                              // Found a column delimiter
                              if (columns[j] == ',') {
                                  // Save field
                                  if (fields.length < fieldCount) {
                                      fields.push(field);
                                  }
                                  field = '';
                              }
                              else { // Remember field value
                                  field = columns[j].
                                      replace(/^"(.*)"$/, '$1').
                                      replace(/""/g, '"') || '';
                              }
                          }
                          if (fields.length < fieldCount) { // Save final field
                              fields.push(field);
                          }
                          if (fieldNames.length == 0) {
                              // First line is headers
                              fieldNames = fields;
                              fieldCount = fields.length;
                          }
                          else {
                              // Fill in missing fields
                              for (var j = fields.length; j < fieldCount;j++){
                                  fields.push('');
                              }
                              rows.push(fields);
                          }
                      }
                  }
                  // Return extracted CSV data
                  return {fieldNames: fieldNames, rows: rows};
              }
```

2 Separate lines of CSV text

3 Process each line

4 Separate fields within a line

5 Process each field

6 Save field value

7 Set field names from first line

8 Add missing fields

9 Return CSV object

You start by defining a new standalone function to process the conversion **1**. It accepts one parameter, which is the full CSV text (csvText). After declaring some working variables, you separate the CSV text into individual lines **2**, and then process each one in turn **3**. The splitting of the text is done by a regular expression supplied to the match function. You look for sequences of characters that aren't line feeds or carriage returns ([^\r\n]+), and continue that throughout the string (g flag). The result of this call is an array of the matching sections (lines) from the text.

If a line isn't empty, you further separate it into its component fields ❹, taking into account quoted fields. As before, a regular expression is used to break up the line, matching with one of the following (separated by |):

- A comma (,)
- A sequence of characters delimited by double quotes (`"([^"]|"")*"`), which may include escaped quotes (`""`) within it
- A sequence of characters that doesn't contain a comma (`[^,]*`)

These sequences may be repeated throughout the string (g flag). The resulting array of matches will contain field values (possibly quoted) as well as comma delimiters.

For each field ❺, if the current match is a comma delimiter, you add a previously found field value (`field`) to the list of fields (`fields`) and reset the field value, but only if you have fewer fields than were identified by the first CSV line (the field names). If the current match isn't a comma, save that match as the next field value ❻ after removing any quotes surrounding it and converting embedded escaped quotes back to a single character. It's necessary to post-process the fields in this manner to cater to sequences of commas with no intervening field values. After examining all the matches from a line, save the last found field value as well.

If this is the first line from the CSV file (meaning there are no field names saved as yet), transfer the field values to the list of field names instead (`fieldNames`) ❼. Otherwise, fill in any missing field values up to the number expected from the list of field names ❽, and add the current row to the list of those already processed (`rows`).

After processing all the lines from the CSV file, return the extracted field names and row contents in a JavaScript object ❾.

> **NOTE** For a more complete text on CSV implementation, see the jQuery CSV plugin at https://code.google.com/p/jquery-csv/.

You'd register the new converter via the `$.ajaxSetup` function by providing a converters setting that has an attribute named for the source and destination data types, and which associates that with the conversion function:

```
$.ajaxSetup({converters: {
    'text csv': textToCsv
}});
```

To use the converter, you make an `ajax` call and specify the `dataType` that you desire as csv. The `success` callback is then supplied with the converted object, and you can process it directly, instead of having to deal with the CSV-formatted text. Figure 12.3 shows the results of loading the CSV data into a table, based on the code from listing 12.7.

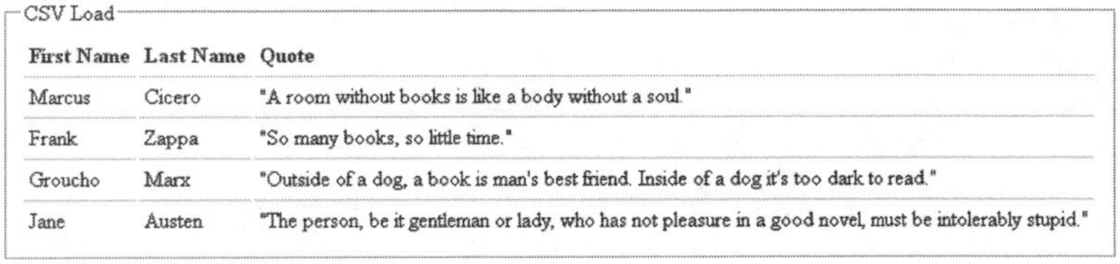

First Name	Last Name	Quote
Marcus	Cicero	"A room without books is like a body without a soul."
Frank	Zappa	"So many books, so little time."
Groucho	Marx	"Outside of a dog, a book is man's best friend. Inside of a dog it's too dark to read."
Jane	Austen	"The person, be it gentleman or lady, who has not pleasure in a good novel, must be intolerably stupid."

**Figure 12.3
CSV data loaded
into a table**

Listing 12.7   Retrieving a CSV object

```
$.ajax({url: 'quotes.csv', dataType: 'csv', success: function(csv) {          ◁─┐
    var table = '<table><thead><tr>';                                   Request CSV
    for (var i = 0; i < csv.fieldNames.length; i++) {                  file and convert  ❶
        table += '<th>' + csv.fieldNames[i] + '</th>';
    }
    table += '</tr></thead><tbody>';                              ❸  Process each row
    for (var i = 0; i < csv.rows.length; i++) {            ◁─────────┘
        table += '<tr>';
        for (var j = 0; j < csv.fieldNames.length; j++) {       ◁──┐    Create
            table += '<td>' + csv.rows[i][j] + '</td>';            ❹  table rows
        }
        table += '</tr>';
    }
    table += '</tbody></table>';                          ❺  Add table
    $('#tableResult').append(table);                  ◁───┘  to the page
}});
```

Create table header ❷ (label at left of code)

You load your CSV file by making an `ajax` call and specifying the URL and `dataType` of csv ❶. Note that if you include the prefilter from section 12.2.1 in your page, you don't need to specify the data type, as it would be set automatically based on the URL extension.

Once jQuery has loaded the file, it determines how to convert from the default format (`text`) to the requested one, finds the registered converter, and applies it. The result is the JavaScript object that contains the extracted CSV data, and that object is passed to the `success` callback for further processing.

Within the callback, you build up the new table as a string value (`table`), starting with heading cells for each field name ❷. Next, you process each row ❸ and add detail cells to the table to show the field values ❹. Finally, you add the new table to the page ❺.

12.4.3 *Converting CSV to a table*

Because presenting CSV content in a table is a common occurrence, you can take the conversion process one step further and transform the CSV object extracted in listing 12.7 into a table for direct inclusion in the page, as shown by the converter in listing 12.8.

Listing 12.8   Converting a CSV object to a table

```
/* Convert JavaScript CSV object into a HTML table.
   @param  csv  (object) the CSV object
   @return   (jQuery) the data in a table */               ❶  Define conversion
function csvToTable(csv) {                        ◁──────┘    function
    var table = '<table><thead><tr>';                         ◁─┐   Generate
    for (var i = 0; i < csv.fieldNames.length; i++) {            ❷  CSV table
        table += '<th>' + csv.fieldNames[i] + '</th>';
    }
    table += '</tr></thead><tbody>';
```

```
        for (var i = 0; i < csv.rows.length; i++) {
            table += '<tr>';
            for (var j = 0; j < csv.fieldNames.length; j++) {
                table += '<td>' + csv.rows[i][j] + '</td>';
            }
            table += '</tr>';
        }
        table += '</tbody></table>';              ③ Return created
        return $(table);                            table element
    }
```

As before, you create a standalone function, but this one converts the CSV object into an HTML table ①. The body of this function ② is identical to the `success` callback used in the previous converter (see listing 12.7). Generate a table as a string value by stepping through each field name for header cells, then through each row for detail cells. The resulting text is instantiated as DOM elements by jQuery, and that object is returned ③.

Make the new converter available by calling `$.ajaxSetup` again with the new transformation listed in its `converters` option. Note that the starting data type is the CSV object created by the previous converter:

```
$.ajaxSetup({converters: {
    'csv table': csvToTable
}});
```

Now the code required to load the CSV file, convert it into a table, and display it is much shorter. Invoke `ajax` and pass it the URL of the CSV file to load. Specify the data type as a chain—first converting the text to a CSV object, then transforming that into a table. Note that using the prefilter from section 12.2.1 alongside these converters would remove the need to specify the initial `csv` data type, as that would be set automatically. The resulting `table` element is received as the parameter to the `success` callback and can be added to the page directly:

```
$.ajax({url: 'quotes.csv', dataType: 'csv table',
    success: function(table) {
        $('#tableResult').append(table);
    }
});
```

Creating your own converters lets you consistently transform one data format into another, starting from the straight text retrieved by the basic Ajax processing, and possibly progressing through one or more intermediate steps, before arriving at the format that's most appropriate for the task at hand.

12.5 Ajax plugins

The Ajax plugins described in this chapter are available for download from the book's website. Included is a web page that demonstrates how the various extensions work in conjunction with the Ajax framework.

What you need to know

jQuery simplifies accessing remote resources through its `ajax` and related functions.

Extend the Ajax processing when you have additional requirements for remote access and data formats.

You can enhance or prevent a remote request by registering a prefilter via `$.ajaxPrefilter`.

Use `$.ajaxTransport` to register a new mechanism for retrieving remote content.

Provide additional data conversion options via the `converters` attribute within an `$.ajaxSetup` call.

You can chain data types to create a conversion pipeline to obtain the data format best suited to the task at hand.

Try it yourself

Create a new convertor, similar to the CSV-to-table example, that converts a CSV object into a list. Each list entry contains multiple lines showing the label for each field followed by its value in that record. Register the new converter and apply it to the quotation data provided.

12.6 *Summary*

jQuery makes using Ajax simple by hiding the use of the `XMLHttpRequest` object behind an easy-to-use interface. The `ajax` function gives you complete control over the process, whereas the associated convenience functions enable simpler interactions more readily. As a request is executed, the Ajax framework first sees whether any prefilters need to be applied to it, possibly modifying or even cancelling it. Next, a transport mechanism is found that understands the requested data format and can download the content appropriately. Finally, a converter may be invoked to transform the retrieved content into a more usable format.

You can extend jQuery's Ajax processing at each of these points. Add a prefilter to customize access to remote content, or disable that access completely, as shown in this chapter. Provide an alternate download mechanism for special content with your own transport function, such as for downloading images, or replace or enhance an existing mechanism, as we did with the HTML simulation for testing purposes. Obtain data in the most useful format for the task at hand by integrating a converter into the Ajax process. Together these extension points let you make jQuery's Ajax processing work the way you want it to.

The next chapter looks at jQuery's event handling and examines how you can provide custom events for interested parties to respond to.

Extending events
13

This chapter covers

- jQuery's special event framework
- Adding a special event
- Enhancing an existing event

jQuery makes it simple to connect an event handler to one of the standard events that occur on a web page, such as mouse clicks and keystrokes. In addition to specific functions that work on collections of elements, like `click` and `keyup`, you can use the generic `bind` or `on` functions to attach a handler to a named event.

jQuery enhances the basic event handling by supporting the attachment of multiple event handlers for the same event on an element and by adding the use of namespaces to help distinguish between these event handlers. It also enables event delegation, where you can connect an event handler to a container element, but operate it on one of the contained elements, which allows you to reduce the number of registered event handlers. Additionally, event delegation gives you the ability to supply event handlers for elements that don't exist within the DOM at the time of attachment.

But within the web page, other things are happening that don't correspond to a standard JavaScript event, such as disabling and enabling controls. Yet these nonstandard events could benefit from the same event handling approach. For these situations, jQuery provides the *special event framework*. Special events may include custom initialization and finalization code as event handlers are attached to or removed from elements. They can alter a triggered event or even generate other events entirely. Using this framework, you can define your own events, which can be (but don't have to be) tied to normal JavaScript events, and integrate them into the standard processing, giving you access to the additional functionality that jQuery provides.

jQuery uses the special event framework to provide consistent cross-browser events, and you can tap into the same process for your own events. You'll see how to create an event for a mouse click using the right button, first as a standalone event, and later integrated into the normal `click` processing. In addition, you'll see how these clicks can be disabled for individual controls and how you'd handle multiple clicks as a single event.

13.1 *The special event framework*

jQuery's special event framework works alongside the handling of native events, allowing you to define your own events with specific behavior, or even to customize existing events by adding extra functionality around them.

A special event is expected to deal with the new event entirely, by providing its own initialization and finalization code and internal event handler. But you can also merely enhance an existing normal event and delegate the event monitoring back to jQuery.

jQuery uses the special event framework to create consistent cross-browser events such as `mouseenter` and `mouseleave`. These two events only fire when the selected element is hovered over and left, whereas the native `mouseover` and `mouseout` events also fire for that element when any contained element is hovered over or left.

In this section, you'll see how the special event framework lets you create handlers for new events, and then invokes that code when the user binds an event of your new type to an element, and again when the event is triggered.

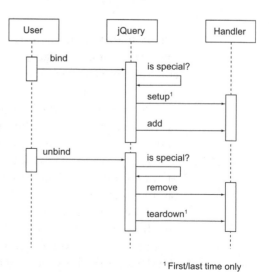

13.1.1 *Binding event handlers*

To use the special event framework, you register an event handler object that contains certain functions and/or attributes that override the default event processing. jQuery then uses that object for the corresponding events to handle their interactions.

Figure 13.1 shows the sequence of actions taken when a user attaches or removes a callback for a special event.

[1] First/last time only

Figure 13.1 Sequence diagram for binding and unbinding special events

When the user attaches a special event to an element, using the bind or on functions, jQuery checks whether a special event handler exists for that event type. If not, jQuery uses the standard JavaScript event handling. If a special event handler object does exist for this type, its setup function is invoked, but only if this is the first such event attached to the current element. The add function on the handler object is always invoked to allow for customizations for each callback for a type of event on an element.

Depending on the level of customization allowed for your events, one of these two functions will establish a handler that responds to the events being monitored and will subsequently invoke the user callbacks at the appropriate times in the future.

Similarly, when the user removes a special event from an element, using unbind or off, jQuery again checks for a special event handler and reverts to the standard processing if it doesn't find one. If jQuery locates a handler object, its remove function is called every time to let you tidy up each callback for an event type on an element. Thereafter, the handler object's teardown function is called, but only if this is the last callback of this event type for the element. In this function you tidy up from any initialization done in the setup function.

13.1.2 *Triggering events*

Having established a link to the triggering of the event underlying your special event in the setup or add functions, as covered previously, you then sit back and wait for that event to occur.

Figure 13.2 shows the flow of control through the system once the underlying event happens.

Whatever triggering mechanism applies, it invokes an internal event handler within your special event handler. After applying any logic to determine whether the event should be passed on, such as seeing the minimum number of mouse clicks for a multiclick event, the event object is updated and passed to the standard jQuery dispatch processing.

jQuery once more checks to see whether this event type has a special event handler registered. If so, it calls any preDispatch function on that object for any additional

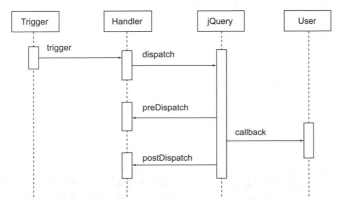

**Figure 13.2
Sequence diagram for
triggering an event**

processing required, including aborting the event handling process. Next, the user callback is invoked and is passed the event details object created or modified by the special event handler. Lastly, jQuery calls the `postDispatch` function on the special event handler for any final processing.

To see all of this in action, you'll create a special event handler for a mouse right-click event.

13.2   Adding a special event

Suppose you want to add functionality when the user clicks the right mouse button. In theory you'd attach a handler for the `click` event and check which button was used (via the `event.which` attribute). But browsers intercept the right-click event to display their own pop-up context menus without passing control to your handler. You can overcome this problem by defining a special event handler for right-clicks, as described in this section. Then you'll be able to register callbacks for the right-click event as easily as a normal left-click.

You add your own events by extending `$.event.special` to define an object that knows how to monitor and notify you about events of interest. The event handler object usually defines a `setup` function to let you initialize the processing for an element and a `teardown` function to undo whatever initialization was performed.

When users bind event handlers to your new event, the jQuery event framework uses this special event definition to call the required functionality at the appropriate times. Your event can then take advantage of all the features surrounding event handling, such as using namespaces, event delegation, and event propagation.

13.2.1   Adding a right-click event

The browser intercepts mouse clicks from the right (or even center) mouse button for its own purposes, so how can you trap a right-click to perform some custom function within your application? The event that's triggered in this situation goes by the name `contextmenu`. By developing your own special event, you can change that name to the more intuitive `rightclick` and provide additional functionality around the event.

You'll attach the new event directly to your selected elements using the standard `bind` or `on` calls, with the results shown in figure 13.3.

```
$('#myDiv').on('rightclick', function(event) {
    alert('Notified of event ' + event.type);
});
```

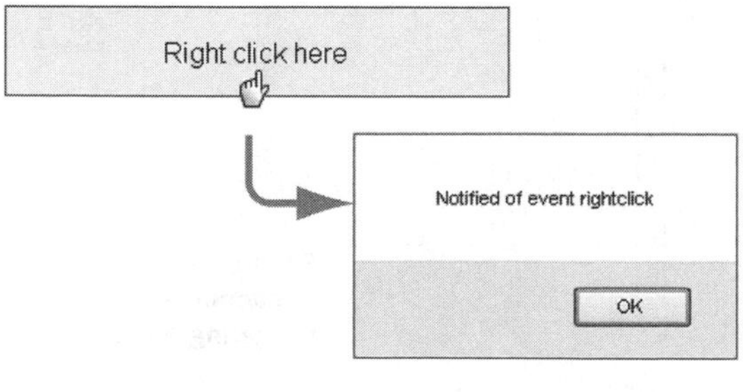

Figure 13.3
Right-clickable `div` with custom cursor and the alert box resulting from user clicks

Listing 13.1 shows the special event object for the `rightclick` event. As usual, you surround the new event code with an anonymous function to introduce a new scope for your variables and to ensure that $ is the same as jQuery.

Listing 13.1 Adding a right-click event

```
(function($) { // Hide scope, no $ conflict

/* Provide an event for a right mouse click. */          ❶ Define special
$.event.special.rightclick = {                              event object

    /* The type of event being raised. */                ❷ Set event type
    eventType: 'rightclick',

    /* Initialise the right-click event handler.
       @param  data  (object, optional) any data values passed to the bind
       @param  namespaces  (string[]) any namespaces passed to the bind */
    setup: function(data, namespaces) {
      $(this).addClass('right-clickable').
          bind('contextmenu', $.event.special.rightclick.handler);
    },
                                                         ❸ Initialize for first
                                                            event on an element
    /* Destroy the right-click event handler.
       @param  namespaces  (string[]) any namespaces passed to the unbind*/
    teardown: function(namespaces) {
      $(this).removeClass('right-clickable').
          unbind('contextmenu', $.event.special.rightclick.handler);
    },                                   ❹ Tidy up for an element

    /* Implement the actual event handling.              ❺ Internal event
       @param  event  (Event) the event details            handler
       @return  (boolean) false to suppress default behaviour */
    handler: function(event) {
      event.type = $.event.special.rightclick.eventType;
      return $.event.dispatch.apply(this, arguments);   ❻ Invoke the user
    }                                                       handler(s)
};

})(jQuery);
```

You register your new event definition by extending $.event.special with an object named for that event ❶. By convention, event names are all lowercase. Although not required, it's useful to add an attribute to this object to hold the event type ❷ for consistent use throughout the plugin.

The setup function ❸ is called once for the first event of each type on an element, allowing you to perform any one-off initialization required to support the new event. It accepts two parameters: any data values passed to the binding call (data), and any namespaces used in that binding (namespaces). If the event has no provided data, then the parameter value is undefined. If the event has no namespace, the parameter value is an array with a blank string as its only entry. Within the function, the this variable refers to the target element.

For the `rightclick` event, you can add a class to the affected element, allowing you to style such elements consistently to indicate that they can be right-clicked. For example, you might change the cursor when hovering over these elements. You must also register an internal handler to respond to the standard `contextmenu` event that you're transforming into a `rightclick`.

Conversely, the `teardown` function ❹ lets you undo the one-off initializations from `setup`, as it's called once on the removal of the last event of each type on an element. It also receives the list of namespaces used for the event as a parameter. For the `rightclick` event, you remove the marker class and unbind from the `contextmenu` event.

The internal event handler that was registered with the `contextmenu` event ❺ allows you to convert the type of the event (passed in as a parameter) before dispatching it to all the attached event handlers via the `$.event.dispatch` function ❻. Although the `setup` and `teardown` functions are only invoked once per element, you can register multiple handlers for this event type, and they're all invoked through this call.

As an extra feature, you can add the ability to disable this event for individual elements.

13.2.2 *Disabling right-click events*

You may have times when you want to disable the right-click functionality for some or all of the affected elements, perhaps to prevent double-clicks from happening. Because you now have control over the handling of these events, you can achieve this enhancement easily, as shown in the following listing.

> **Listing 13.2   Disabling right-click events**

```
$.event.rightclickDisabled = $([]);                              List of disabled
                                                              ❶ elements
/* Provide an event for a right mouse click. */
$.event.special.rightclick = {

    ...

    /* Implement the actual event handling.
       @param  event  (Event) the event details
       @return (boolean) false to suppress default behaviour */
    handler: function(event) {
If this       if ($.event.rightclickDisabled.length &&
element            $(this).is($.event.rightclickDisabled)) {
is in list... ❷      event.stopPropagation();                    ...prevent further
                  event.preventDefault();                    ❸ processing
                  return;
              }
              event.type = $.event.special.rightclick.eventType;
              return $.event.dispatch.apply(this, arguments);
        }
};
```

You start with a variable to hold the list of disabled elements ❶. Remember that this variable must be accessible from outside the plugin, so it must extend $ in some manner, preferably $.event to indicate its area of concern. Initially the list is an empty jQuery collection that you can replace or add to as necessary. To add elements, you could use the add function:

```
$.event.rightclickDisabled = $.event.rightclickDisabled.add('#elemID')
```

To remove an element you could use the filter function:

```
$.event.rightclickDisabled =
    $.event.rightclickDisabled.filter(':not(#elemID)')
```

The new functionality is added to the beginning of the handler function. You check whether the current element (as referenced by this) is contained within the list of those disabled by using the is function ❷. If so, you call the event's stopPropagation and preventDefault functions to halt the event processing at this point ❸.

The event created previously deals with single right-clicks on an element, but what if you want to monitor two or more right-clicks? The next section looks at such a special event definition.

13.2.3 *Multiple right-click events*

Handling multiple right-clicks is more complicated than dealing with single clicks because you must now keep track of how many clicks have been made. Also, you should allow the events to be configured as to how many mouse clicks are required to fire the final event handler, and how much time can elapse between the clicks for them to be considered the one event.

Using this event, you can monitor multiple right-clicks on an element. You can even track more than one sequence of clicks, as shown in figure 13.4, where the clickable area outputs a message when the right mouse button clicks it twice or three times in a given period (see listing 13.3).

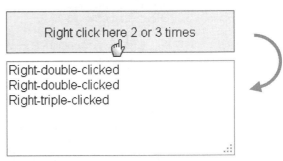

Figure 13.4   Multiple right-click event handler after clicking twice and then three times in quick succession

---

Listing 13.3   Responding to double and triple right-click events

```
$('#multiRightClick').
    bind('rightmulticlick', function(event) {
        $('#multiOutcome').val($('#multiOutcome').val() +
            'Right-double-clicked\n');
        return false;
    }).
    bind('rightmulticlick', {clickCount: 3}, function(event) {
        $('#multiOutcome').val($('#multiOutcome').val() +
            'Right-triple-clicked\n');
        return false;
    });
```

Although you could enhance the special event developed previously to cater to multiple clicks, we'll develop it as a separate event type here so you can compare the two. Listing 13.4 shows the new event handler.

Listing 13.4 Multiple right-click events

```
/* Provide an event for a right mouse multi click. */
$.event.special.rightmulticlick = {                    ◁──────  ❶ Define special
                                                                event object
    /* The type of event being raised. */
    eventType: 'rightmulticlick',                      ◁──────
                                                        ❷ Set event type
    /* Initialise the right-multi-click event handler.
       @param data     (object, optional) any data values passed to the bind
       @param namespaces (string[]) any namespaces passed to the bind */
    setup: function(data, namespaces) {                ◁──┐  Initialize for first
        $(this).addClass('right-clickable');              ❸ event on an element
    },

    /* Initialise the settings.                                 Initialize for  ❹
       @param handleObj (object) details about the binding */   every event
    add: function(handleObj) {                                     ◁──┘
                   ┌─▷ var data = $.extend({clickCount: 2, clickNumber: 0,
    Event-specific │        lastClick: 0, clickSpeed: 500,
           data ❺  │        handler: handleObj.handler}, handleObj.data || {});
                      var id = $.event.special.rightmulticlick.eventType +
                          handleObj.guid;
                      $(this).data(id, data).                   ◁──┐  Bind data and
                          bind('contextmenu.' + id, {id: id},       internal event
                              $.event.special.rightmulticlick.handler);  ❻ handler
    },

    /* Remove the settings.
       @param handleObj (object) details about the binding */
    remove: function(handleObj) {                              ◁──┐  Tidy up for
        var id = $.event.special.rightmulticlick.eventType +      ❼ every event
            handleObj.guid;
        $(this).removeData(id).unbind('contextmenu.' + id);    ◁──  Unbind data
    },                                                              and internal
                                                                ❽ event handler
    /* Destroy the right-click event handler.
       @param namespaces (string[]) any namespaces passed to the unbind*/
    teardown: function(namespaces) {                           ◁──  Tidy up for
        $(this).removeClass('right-clickable');                 ❾ an element
    },
    ...
};
```

As before, you register the new special event definition with $.event.special ❶ and provide an attribute that holds the event type ❷. In the setup function ❸ you only need to add the class to distinguish these elements for styling purposes. Because each event handler that your users register may have its own options, you won't use a single handler for all such events.

Instead, you define an add function ❹ that's called every time an event of this type is bound to an element, allowing you to deal with each one separately. The function receives a single parameter (`handleObj`) that encapsulates all the information about the current event handler. This object has attributes for any data (`handleObj.data`) and namespace (`handleObj.namespace`) provided for the event, for the user's callback function (`handleObj.handler`), and for a unique identifier (`handleObj.guid`), among others. As you read previously, the `this` variable refers to the current target element for the event.

You start by collating the options for this event handler ❺, beginning with a set of default values and possibly overriding those with settings from the binding call. Because the supplied data values may be `null`, you should default them to an empty object (`|| {}`).

To retrieve the options later, you create an identifier for them based on the event type and the unique ID from the parameter object. You use that identifier to associate the options with the current element (`this`) ❻ and then bind a namespaced event handler to the standard `contextmenu` event, passing along the identifier as additional data to that handler. The handler itself is explained next.

When an event handler is unbound from an element, the `remove` function is called ❼. It also receives the event information object as its parameter (`handleObj`). You recalculate the identifier used for this event from the event type and unique ID, and use that to delete the saved options data and to unbind the namespaced event handler ❽.

To counteract the actions of the `setup` function, the `teardown` function ❾ need only remove the added class.

As with the single right-click event, an internal handler deals with the `contextmenu` events and transforms them into your new events. But in this case, you'll need to do additional processing to keep track of how many clicks have occurred, as shown in the following listing.

Listing 13.5   Multiple right-click handler

```
$.event.special.rightmulticlick = {
    ...

    /* Implement the actual event handling.
       @param  event  (Event) the event details
       @return  (boolean) false to suppress default behaviour */
    handler: function(event) {                                   ⟵  Internal
        if ($.event.rightclickDisabled.length &&                 ❶ event handler
                $(this).is($.event.rightclickDisabled)) {
            event.preventDefault();
            return;
        }                                                        ❸ Retrieve event
        var data = $(this).data(event.data.id);            ⟵        options
        event.timeStamp = event.timeStamp || new Date().getTime();
        if (event.timeStamp - data.lastClick <= data.clickSpeed) {  ⟵
            data.clickNumber++;                                   If within event
        }                                                      timeout, count click ❺
```

Ignore if disabled ❷

Calculate current timestamp ❹

```
        else {
            data.clickNumber = 1;                         ◄──┐  Otherwise,
            data.lastClick = event.timeStamp;               ❻  reset click count
        }
        var result = false;                                   ❼  If the required
        if (data.clickNumber == data.clickCount) {     ◄──┐      number is reached...
            event.type = $.event.special.rightmulticlick.eventType;
            result = data.handler.apply(this, arguments);
        }                                                        ...invoke user handler ❽
        return result;                             ◄──┐  Return
    }                                                ❾  outcome
};
```

...invoke user handler ❽

You define an internal `handler` function ❶ that's called in response to the standard `contextmenu` events. As for the single right-click handler, you should check for elements that have been disabled and prevent any further processing as the first step ❷. If the element isn't disabled, you retrieve the options data for the current element (`this`) ❸, using the identifier that was passed as event data when the callback was bound (`event.data.id`).

To restrict the time allowed for multiple clicks to be seen as a single event, you must first determine the timestamp for the event ❹, using either a provided value or the current date and time (expressed as milliseconds since a base point). If the difference between the event timestamp and the start of the last sequence of clicks (as held in the `data.lastClick` attribute) is less than or equal to the specified limit (`data.click-Speed`), you increment the count of multiple clicks ❺. If the delay is outside that limit, you must reset the count of clicks and set the starting time for this new sequence ❻.

Now that you've computed the number of clicks you've seen so far, you compare that to the number required to trigger this event (`data.clickCount`) ❼. If the numbers match, you transform the received event into the new type and invoke the handler for this event directly (`data.handler`) ❽. Because registered events are being dealt with individually due to the possibility of them having differing options, you don't use the `$.event.dispatch` function for the single right-click special event. The result of any handler call is stored and returned as the final value of the internal handler function ❾.

As a convenience to your users, you can also provide collection functions to connect to your special event, which we'll discuss in the next section.

13.2.4 *Collection functions for events*

Using the special events defined previously, you can now attach event handlers to elements for these events using the `bind` and `on` functions (and remove them with `unbind` or `off`). You can take advantage of other event features via these functions, such as using namespaces, event delegation, and event propagation. But you don't have any convenience functions to attach to, nor to trigger your events, like the `click` function for normal mouse click events.

Adding such functions allows users to interact with your events in the manner they prefer—using `bind`/`on`/`trigger` or the function named for the event—in the same way as the built-in events.

```
$('#myDiv').rightclick(function() {
    ... // Handle a right-click
});
```

These functions, which are collection plugins in their own right, can be defined as follows.

Listing 13.6 Add collection functions for events

```
/* Add collection functions for these events. */
$.each([$.event.special.rightclick.eventType,           ◁── ❶ Process
        $.event.special.rightmulticlick.eventType],              event types
    function(i, eventType) {
        $.fn[eventType] = function(data, fn) {          ◁── ❷ Create
            if (fn == null) {                   ◁── ❸ Cater to    collection function
                fn = data;                               no data
                data = null;
            }
            return arguments.length > 0 ?       ◁── ❹ Attach or
                this.on(eventType, null, data, fn) :     trigger handler
                this.trigger(eventType);
        };
    }
);
```

You want to register a function for each event type, so you start by processing each of the event names from an inline array ❶. You define a new collection plugin (extending `$.fn`) named for each event type ❷ that accepts two parameters, which are any data to pass through to the event (`data`, optional) and the function to call when the event occurs (`fn`).

Within the collection plugin, you deal with an optional `data` parameter (which means you don't have a second parameter value) ❸ by transferring its value to the function parameter and clearing `data`. If the number of arguments passed to the collection function is greater than zero ❹, you want to bind the given function to the current element for the current event type. Otherwise, you want to trigger any existing handlers for this event type, as you did with the existing comparable functions.

13.3 Enhancing an existing event

In addition to defining your own custom events, you can replace or enhance existing events in the same manner by defining a special event with the same name as that existing event. For example, you could modify the `click` event to ensure that every clickable element has its cursor changed to a pointer, as suggested by David Walsh and implemented by Brandon Aaron.[1] Or you could log every event by intercepting each one to record its details before continuing with the default processing.

> **NOTE** Take care when replacing an existing event with a custom special event, because your new handler will be used for all events of this type and you may experience unintended side effects.

You could also enhance the `click` event to handle right-clicks, as described in the next section. In this example, you'll monitor the `contextmenu` event as before, but this time you'll convert it into a normal `click` event with the `event.which` attribute identifying which button was used.

13.3.1 Adding right-click handling to the click event

It would be more convenient to use the existing `click` event to handle right-clicks, instead of creating a separate `rightclick` event. The `click` event is supposed to do this, resulting in the event object's `which` attribute being set based on the button used. But the browser seems to hijack these events before they get through.

You could instead recast the separate `rightclick` event as an enhancement to the standard `click` handler. When using this special event plugin instead of the previous one to react to a right-click, you'd attach a `click` event as usual, but you'd check the `event.which` attribute to determine which button was pressed.

```
$('#myDiv').click(function(event) {
    alert('Clicked ' + (event.which == 3 ? 'right' : 'left') +
        ' mouse button');
});
```

Here's the code for the enhanced `click` event.

Listing 13.7 Adding right-click to click

```
/* Add support for right mouse click. */
$.event.special.click = {                                    ← ❶ Override click handler

    /* Add a right-click event handler.
       @param data  (object, optional) any data values passed to the bind
       @param namespaces  (string[]) any namespaces passed to the bind */
    setup: function(data, namespaces) {                      ← ❷ Initialize for first event on an element
        $(this).addClass('right-clickable').
            bind('contextmenu', $.event.special.click.handler);  ← ❸ Bind internal event handler
        return false;                                        ← ❹ Attach default event handler
    },

    /* Destroy the right-click event handler.
       @param namespaces  (string[]) any namespaces passed to the unbind*/
```

---

[1] Shown in slide 15 at http://www.slideshare.net/brandon.aaron/special-events-beyond-custom-events (originally posted on Brandon Aaron's blog, http://brandonaaron.net/blog/2009/06/17/automating-with-special-events).

```
              teardown: function(namespaces) {                          ◁─────   Tidy up for
                  $(this).removeClass('right-clickable').                  ⑤     an element
                      unbind('contextmenu', $.event.special.click.handler);
  Unbind internal    return false;                                       ◁─────   Detach default
  event          },                                                        ⑦     event handler
⑥ handler

              /* Implement the actual event handling.
                 @param  event   (Event) the event details
                 @return (boolean) false to suppress default behaviour */
              handler: function(event) {                                 ◁─────   Internal
                  event.type = 'click';                                    ⑧     event handler
                  event.which = 3;
                  return $.event.dispatch.apply(this, arguments);       ◁─────   Change settings
              }                                                            ⑨     and notify
          };
```

This time you override the handling of the standard `click` event ❶ by declaring a special event version of it. The new handler's `setup` function ❷ once more marks the element as `right-clickable` and binds an internal event handler to the `contextmenu` event to be notified of right-clicks ❸. You *must* return `false` from the `setup` function ❹ to inform the jQuery event framework that you want it to continue with its normal processing of this event—to attach the standard `click` event handler itself. You're relying on this standard processing to deal with normal click events, but you're enhancing it by also listening for right-clicks.

As before, the `teardown` function ❺ needs to undo whatever was done in `setup`—removing the marker class and unbinding from the `contextmenu` event ❻. Once more, you *must* return `false` from this function ❼ to have jQuery also tidy up the standard `click` event handler.

Your internal event handler ❽ is called when the `contextmenu` event occurs. You translate this event into a replacement `click` event, but set the `event.which` attribute to indicate that the right mouse button was used (the documented value for this is 3—http://api.jquery.com/event.which/). Then you continue with the standard event handling (using the altered `event` object) by calling the built-in `$.event.dispatch` function ❾.

13.4 Other event functionality

The special event framework also provides some additional functionality that you can use to further customize your event handling. You can define a default action for an event, suppress event bubbling, and add callbacks before and after the dispatching of the event through the standard processing. These are described in more detail in the next sections.

13.4.1 Default actions for events

The default action for an event executes when the event has finished bubbling up through the DOM hierarchy and all of the appropriate event handlers on this path have been called, such as an anchor tag loading the content of the location specified in its `href` attribute. Any of those other handlers in the chain may prevent the default action by calling the `preventDefault` method on the provided `event` object.

You specify a default action for your special event handler by adding a `_default` function to the event handler object, such as for a hypothetical `destroy` event, as in this listing.

Listing 13.8   Adding a default action

```
$.event.special.destroy = {

    ...

    _default: function(event) {                     Default
        $(event.target).remove();              ①   action handler
    }
};
```

Within your default function ①, the `this` variable refers to the document, because the event has bubbled all the way to the top of the DOM hierarchy. The `event` parameter to this function contains all the information you need. Its `target` attribute refers to the element on which the event was initially triggered, whereas the `handleObj` attribute provides access to all of the same values as the `setup` and `teardown` functions.

13.4.2   Pre- and post-dispatch callbacks

You can add extra processing before your special event is passed to any event handlers by adding a `preDispatch` function to the event handler object. This function is called as part of the standard event dispatch processing and allows you to abort the event handling by returning `false`.

> **NOTE**   The `preDispatch` function was added in jQuery 1.7.2.

For example, you could implement the disabling functionality of the `rightclick` event in the `preDispatch` function, instead of in the internal handler, as shown previously. Within this function, the `this` variable refers to the current element, whereas the `event` parameter holds the usual details about the event itself. See listing 13.9 for a possible implementation.

Listing 13.9   Adding `preDispatch` functionality

```
$.event.special.rightclick = {

    ...                                                    ① Handler only
                                                              translates event
    handler: function(event) {
        event.type = $.event.special.rightclick.eventType;
        return $.event.dispatch.apply(this, arguments);
    },
                                                           ② Add preDispatch
    preDispatch: function(event) {                            processing
        return !($.event.rightclickDisabled.length &&
            $(this).is($.event.rightclickDisabled));       ③ Return false
    }                                                         to disable
};
```

You can remove the disabling code from the `handler` function ❶ and define a `pre-Dispatch` function instead ❷. Within that, you return `false` if the current element is in the list of those to be disabled ❸.

In a similar way, you can add extra code at the end of the standard event processing by adding a `postDispatch` function to the event handler object. This function is called after passing the event to any event handlers and can't change the normal flow.

NOTE The `postDispatch` function was added in jQuery 1.7.2.

For example, you could add logging of events at this point, as shown in the following listing. As with the `preDispatch` callback, the `this` variable refers to the current element and the `event` parameter holds other details about the current event.

Listing 13.10 Adding `postDispatch` functionality

```
$.event.special.rightclick = {
    ...

                                                    ❶ Add postDispatch
    postDispatch: function(event) {                   processing
        console.log(event.type + ' on ' + event.target.nodeName);
    }
};
```

You define a `postDispatch` function ❶ to add processing following the normal event handling. In this case, you could log the type of the event and the name of the element on which it was triggered.

13.4.3 *Prevent event bubbling*

Special events also support the prevention of event bubbling by setting the `noBubble` attribute on the event handler object to `true`. jQuery uses this internally to forestall the bubbling of `load` events back to the `window` object.

```
$.event.special.load = {
    // Prevent triggered image.load events from bubbling to window.load
    noBubble: true
};
```

NOTE The `noBubble` attribute was added in jQuery 1.7.1.

13.4.4 *Automatic binding and delegation*

The `bindType` and `delegateType` attributes on the event handler object let you specify the event type to use when binding or delegating a special event, and jQuery will automatically respond to those events and call the provided user event handler. For example, jQuery uses this mechanism to map the `mouseenter` and `mouseleave` special events directly onto the native `mouseover` and `mouseout` events.

To further automate this process, the event framework looks for a `handle` function within the event handler object to respond to the mapped events. You'd provide such a function if you wanted to change the processing in some manner, such as altering the event type. Otherwise the user callback is triggered directly.

NOTE   The `bindType` and `delegateType` attributes were added in jQuery 1.7.1.

But when you use this technique, the `setup` and `add` functions are no longer invoked, as it's assumed that direct mapping onto the native event eliminates the need for these calls. Consequently, `teardown` and `remove` functions aren't necessary (although these are still called for some reason).

For example, the `rightclick` event handler presented previously could be rewritten using automatic binding and delegation, as follows.

Listing 13.11   Using automatic delegation and binding

```
$.event.special.rightclick = {                          ◁      ❶ Define right-click event

    bindType: 'contextmenu',                            ◁
    delegateType: 'contextmenu',                        ❷ Map to native event
    eventType: 'rightclick',
                                                        ❸ Automatic handler
    handle: function(event) {                    ◁         for native event
        event.type = $.event.special.rightclick.eventType;
        return event.handleObj.handler.apply(this, arguments);   ◁   Call user
    }                                                       ❹   handler
};
```

You define the `rightclick` special event ❶ as before, but provide an alternative implementation. You use the `bindType` and `delegateType` attributes ❷ to map this event onto an existing native event—contextmenu. The `handle` function ❸ is attached to that native event and allows you to change the event type before invoking the user's handler ❹, as accessed via the `event.handleObj` object.

Note that this implementation doesn't add the `right-clickable` class to the affected elements. You could include the disabled functionality from the `handler` function of the original `rightclick` implementation in the `handle` function here.

The complete code for these special events is available for download from the book's website.

What you need to know

Create a new event to provide common event handling across browsers.

jQuery provides the special event framework to handle events in a standard manner.

Extend `$.event.special` to add a new event processor or to replace an existing one.

Your event processor can monitor other events and modify them or trigger custom ones in their place.

(continued)

Within your processor, `setup` and `teardown` are called once per element, whereas `add` and `remove` are called for each event handler that's bound or unbound.

Return `false` from `setup` and `teardown` to allow jQuery to continue with the normal processing of the event.

Try it yourself

Create a `reset` event for a form to ask for confirmation from the user before proceeding. There's a built-in `reset` event for a form, so you'll need to let jQuery process that as well. Cancel the `reset` request by calling the `event.preventDefault` function.

13.5 *Summary*

jQuery makes dealing with native JavaScript events simple by providing multiple ways to attach an event handler to a particular event on a given element. It also supports event delegation to allow you to create one handler for many subordinate elements, or to process events for elements that don't even exist within the DOM as yet.

To allow new events to operate within the same jQuery processes, it provides the special event framework. You register a new event with the framework and define an object that knows how to initialize itself for these events, how to tidy up afterward, and how to signal those events to attached event handlers.

You saw how to use the special event framework to transform the native `context-menu` event into the more recognizable `rightclick`. Then you enhanced that to produce the `rightmulticlick` event handler that tracked multiple right-clicks on a per-element basis. And finally, you replaced the standard `click` processing to incorporate notifications about right-click events.

In the final chapter, we'll look at the Validation plugin and how it can be extended with custom validation rules.

Creating validation rules

Although not part of jQuery itself, the Validation plugin from Jörn Zaefferer is a widely used plugin that has its own extension point (http://jqueryvalidation.org). The plugin helps to ensure that only valid data is sent to the server when a form is submitted, avoiding unnecessary requests that would only result in a user-correctable error, such as missing required fields or incorrectly formatted email addresses.

The built-in rules provided by the plugin include `required` for mandatory fields, `digits` or `number` for numeric input, `min` and `max` for minimum and maximum values, `email` and `url` for email address and URL formats, and `equalTo` for field comparisons. You can combine these for a single field to create more complex validations, such as a mandatory numeric field with a maximum value.

The plugin manages the application of these rules at the appropriate times—for instance, when field entry occurs or when the form is submitted—and displays suitable error messages if a field is invalid. The aim is to provide an unobtrusive user experience: to display error messages only after some user action, and to remove them as soon as possible. Placement of error messages and their

250

appearance can be controlled by the user if necessary, although the default behavior is often appropriate.

If the built-in rules aren't sufficient for your needs, you can always define your own rules and have them integrated into the normal processing of the plugin. At its simplest, a new rule provides a function that returns `true` if a field is valid and `false` if it's not.

In this chapter, you'll see how to define custom validation rules that check entered text against expected patterns of characters and rules that apply to conditions covering multiple fields, along with how to apply them within your applications.

14.1　The Validation plugin

The Validation plugin is applied to a form, and it lets you ensure that the fields within that form are valid before they can be submitted to the server (as shown in figure 14.1). By performing such validations on the client, you can prevent network usage that will only result in an error on the returned page. Note that you should never rely

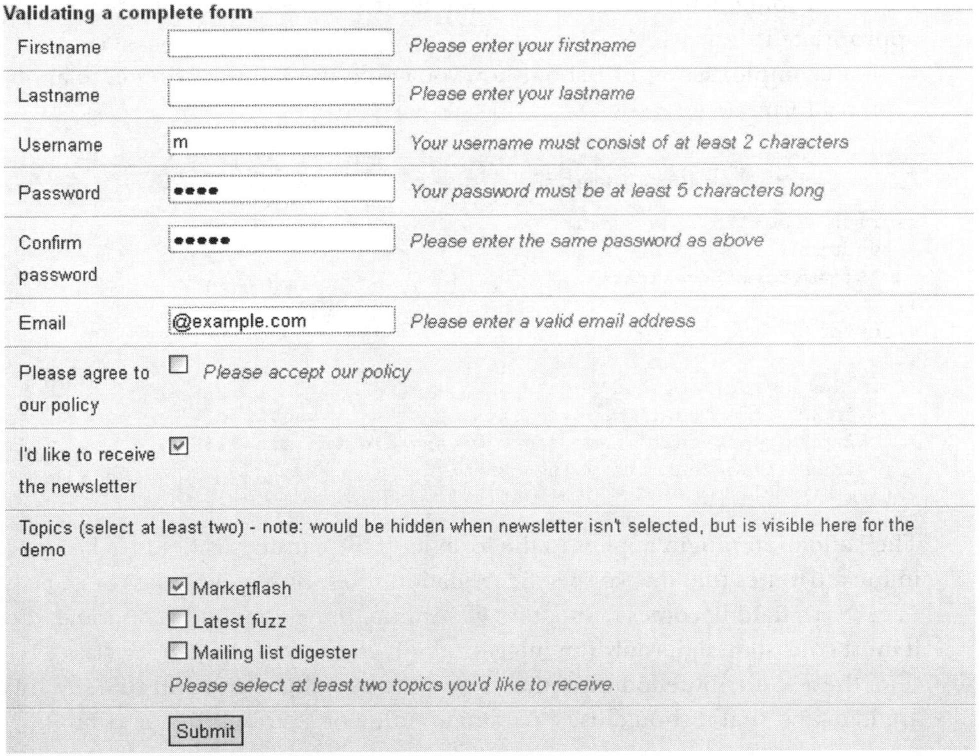

Validating a complete form

Firstname		*Please enter your firstname*
Lastname		*Please enter your lastname*
Username	m	*Your username must consist of at least 2 characters*
Password	••••	*Your password must be at least 5 characters long*
Confirm password	•••••	*Please enter the same password as above*
Email	@example.com	*Please enter a valid email address*

Please agree to our policy　☐　*Please accept our policy*

I'd like to receive the newsletter　☑

Topics (select at least two) - note: would be hidden when newsletter isn't selected, but is visible here for the demo

　　　☑ Marketflash
　　　☐ Latest fuzz
　　　☐ Mailing list digester
　　　Please select at least two topics you'd like to receive.

[Submit]

Figure 14.1　The Validation plugin in action, showing various error messages resulting from validation issues alongside the affected fields

solely on client-side validations for your websites. You should always apply the same rules to all values received at the server before processing them further.

This section describes how the Validation plugin assigns specific rules to particular fields within a web page, either through metadata attached to each HTML element or via an option passed to the plugin initialization call.

14.1.1 *Assigning validation rules*

This plugin allows you to assign validation rules to fields in a number of different ways, allowing for flexibility in your page design and framework usage. The two main methods of assignment are via classes and attributes attached to the fields (metadata), and via the `rules` option in the plugin initialization.

ELEMENT METADATA

To use the first of these methods, you add classes corresponding to the desired rules to the applicable input fields, for those rules that don't need any parameters. If you do need to provide a value for a rule to work, that rule is specified as an attribute named for the rule, with its value being the necessary parameter value. Then, when you initialize the plugin for the form as a whole, these classes and attributes trigger the appropriate rules.

For example, listing 14.1 shows how you might use inline attributes to apply validation to a form.

Listing 14.1   Applying validation rules inline

```
<script type="text/javascript">
$(function() {
    $('#myform').validate();                        Validate the
});                                              ① whole form
</script>
...
<form id="myform" method="get">                                      First name
    <input type="text" name="firstName" class="required">       ② is required
    <input type="text" name="age" class="digits" min="18">
    <input type="submit" value="Submit">              Age must be
</form>                                            ③ a number >= 18
```

The Validation plugin applies to the form itself ①, causing its fields to be scanned for inline attributes that invoke specific validation rules. By having a class of `required`, the `firstName` field becomes mandatory ②. Although the `age` field is optional, if entered it must consist of digits only (an integer value), courtesy of the `digits` class ③. In addition, the `min` attribute indicates that the minimum value validation rule should also be applied, and that it should use a parameter value of 18 to set the lower limit.

RULES OPTION

To specify the validation rules during initialization, you provide a `rules` option to the plugin call. The value of this option is an object with attributes for each field and the corresponding validation rules as their values.

Listing 14.2 shows the same form as earlier, but with the validations defined in the initialization call.

Listing 14.2 Applying validation rules during initialization

```
<script type="text/javascript">
$(function() {
    $('#myform').validate({                    ① Validate the
        rules: {                                  whole form
            firstName: 'required',
First name
is required ②  age: {                          ← Age must be
                digits: true,                  ③ a number >= 18
                min: 18
            }
        }
    });
});
</script>
...                                            ④ Fields have no
<form id="myform" method="get">                   extra attributes
    <input type="text" name="firstName">    ←
    <input type="text" name="age">
    <input type="submit" value="Submit">
</form>
```

Once more, the Validation plugin is called for the form as a whole ①. But this time, the supplied `rules` option connects validation rules to fields. The attributes of `rules` are identified by the names of the affected fields (note that the `name` attribute is used, not the `id`). Each attribute's value is the validation rule name when a single simple rule applies (one that doesn't require any parameters, such as `required`). When multiple validations apply, or when a validation needs a parameter (such as a minimum value), the attribute value is another object with attributes named for the desired rules and having the parameter as their values. If no parameter is needed in this second case, the value `true` is used. As before, the `firstName` field is mandatory ② and the `age` field, if present, must consist of digits with a minimum value of 18 ③. The actual form fields have no additional classes or attributes under this scheme ④, helping to separate the form content from its functional requirements.

> **NOTE** If your field name contains non-alphanumeric characters, you should surround it with quotes when using it as an attribute name within the `rules` option. For example, `rules: {'first-name': 'required'}`.

14.2 Adding a validation rule

Although there are numerous validation rules built into the plugin, sometimes you need something more specific, such as a rule to check the format of a U.S. Social Security number (SSN). By calling the `addMethod` function of the validator, you can define your own rules to be applied alongside the built-in ones. Your rule is added to the list of available validation rules using the name you provided to identify it. You then use that same name to assign the rule to a particular field in your web page.

A common requirement is to match the entered data against a pattern of characters, such as for a phone number. In fact, the Validation plugin contains an additional-methods.js file that provides these sorts of rules, including `pattern` for a user-specified pattern and `phoneUS` for a particular implementation of a pattern.

Next, you'll re-implement the pattern-matching validation rule to see how it's done, before creating a validation-rule generator for these types of rules to make them easier to define in the future.

14.2.1 Adding a pattern-matching rule

When testing values for patterns in JavaScript, you should use the regular expression objects built into the language (see appendix A for a primer on JavaScript regular expressions). Regular expressions are defined as strings of characters that must be matched literally or that have a meaning within the expression, such as indicating alternative values, denoting repeating characters, or representing classes of characters.

To make a pattern-matching rule that can be used in any number of situations, you should allow the pattern to be passed as a parameter to the rule initialization. You might specify a field requiring a U.S. SSN with the following:

```
$('#myform').validate({rules: {
    ssn: {matches: /^\d{3}-\d{2}-\d{4}$/}
}});
```

This pattern states that the field value must start (^) with three digits (\d{3}), followed by a hyphen (-), two digits (\d{2}), another hyphen (-), and finish ($) with four digits (\d{4}). You should allow the pattern to be provided as a string value instead of the literal `RegExp` object shown here for even more flexibility. Note that you must escape backslashes (\) and quote (') characters when using a string value for the pattern, which, in this example, would become '^\\d{3}-\\d{2}-\\d{4}$'.

Listing 14.3 shows how you'd define the pattern-matching validation rule. As for previous plugins, you should surround your code with an anonymous function to provide a new scope to hide internal variables and to ensure that $ is equivalent to jQuery.

Listing 14.3 Adding a pattern-matching rule

```
/* Custom validator to match a regular expression.
   @param  value    (string) the current field value
   @param  element  (jQuery) the current field
   @param  param    (string or RegExp) the pattern to match
   @return (boolean) true if valid, false if not */
$.validator.addMethod('matches', function(value, element, param) {
    var re = param instanceof RegExp ? param : new RegExp(param);
    return this.optional(element) || re.test(value);
},
    $.validator.format('Please match this format "{0}".'));
```

Define new validation rule ①
Create regular expression ②
Validate the value ③
Format error message ④

To define your new rule, you must call the $.validator.addMethod function ❶. The parameters to this function are the name of your new rule (so that it can be assigned to individual fields), the validation function that tests an element and its value to ensure its correctness, and an error message to display if that field is found to be invalid.

The validation function also accepts three parameters, which are the current value of the element being validated (value), a reference to that DOM element (element), and any parameters supplied as part of the validation initialization (param).

You start by creating a regular expression to test against ❷. If a regular expression object was provided as the parameter, you use that directly. Otherwise, you create a new RegExp object using the pattern given.

The validation function returns true if the field and its value are correct, or false if they're not ❸. You should allow for an empty field by calling the standard optional function and passing along the element reference. Otherwise, you apply the regular expression to the current value, using its test function to check that it matches.

If a value doesn't match, the error message given in the addMethod call is displayed to the user ❹. You can provide a static message as a string, but if you want to include dynamic values from the parameters, you should use the $.validator.format function. It accepts a string message as its parameter and returns a function to be called to generate the final message. You indicate where you want parameter values placed by using the sequence {n}, where *n* is a sequential number corresponding to the index of the value from the parameters array, or is 0 for a single parameter value.

You'd use this validation rule by providing a pattern to match against as its parameter value. You can also combine this rule with others for more complex validations. Figure 14.2 shows the results of applying the pattern-matching validation rule to ensure the correct entry of U.S. SSNs, using the definitions shown in listing 14.4.

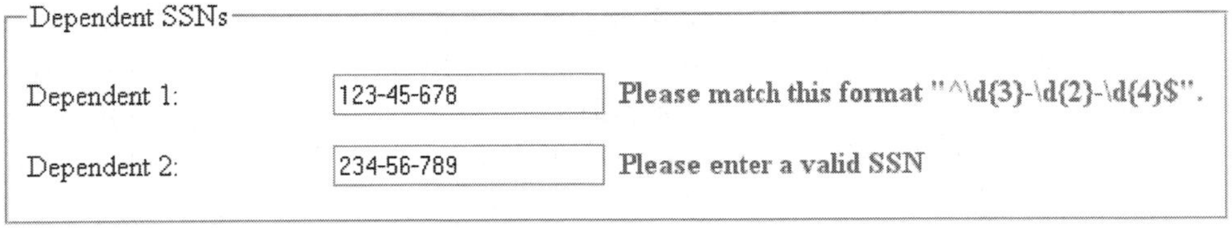

```
Dependent SSNs
  Dependent 1:    [ 123-45-678  ]    Please match this format "^\d{3}-\d{2}-\d{4}$".
  Dependent 2:    [ 234-56-789  ]    Please enter a valid SSN
```

Figure 14.2   Using the pattern-matching validation rule

Listing 14.4   Using the pattern-matching rule

```
$('#myform').validate({
    rules: {
        ssn1: {
            required: true,
            matches: '^\\d{3}-\\d{2}-\\d{4}$'        ❶ Match a string
        },                                               pattern
        ssn2: {
            matches: /^\d{3}-\d{2}-\d{4}$/           ❷ Match a regular
        }                                                expression
    },
```

```
    messages: {
        ssn2: {
            matches: 'Please enter a valid SSN'
        }
    }
});
```

⟵ **3** **Custom error message**

Within the rules definition for your validation setup, you apply the `matches` rule to the first SSN field by providing a string version of the SSN pattern **1**. This field is also defined as being mandatory through the use of the `required` rule. For the second field you provide the pattern as a regular expression object instead **2**, and the field isn't mandatory. You can also override the error message for particular fields and rules to provide more meaningful feedback to the user **3**. Within the `messages` option, you identify the fields by name, as for the `rules` option, and then supply a new message for a particular rule, identified by its name.

If you wanted to use the inline method for assigning validation rules, you'd need to mark up your field as follows to create a mandatory SSN-formatted input element.

```
<input type="text" id="ssn1" name="ssn1"
    class="required" matches="^\d{3}-\d{2}-\d{4}$">
```

You've seen how the `matches` rule would be applied to a field to validate it by supplying an arbitrary regular expression to cater to whatever format you desire for your fields. But these expressions can be difficult to understand and maintain, so the next section looks at how you can retain the functionality of the pattern-matching rule while clarifying its purpose.

14.2.2 Generating pattern-matching rules

The validation function from the pattern-matching rule shown in the previous section, and repeated in listing 14.5, accepts the expression to match against as a parameter from the validation framework (`param`). Instead, you could supply that pattern when creating the new validation rule and produce a more targeted rule that's easier to use and understand, as shown in figure 14.3.

Figure 14.3   Validation error resulting from the pattern-matching rule generator for an SSN

Listing 14.5   Previous pattern-matching rule

```
function(value, element, param) {
    var re = param instanceof RegExp ? param : new RegExp(param);
    return this.optional(element) || re.test(value);
},
```

The following listing shows how to write a function that generates similar pattern-matching validation functions for use in defining rules.

Listing 14.6 Generating a pattern-matching rule

```
/* Create a validation rule for a given regular expression.
   @param  pattern  (string or RegExp) the pattern to match
   @return  (function) the validation function */          ❶ Define generator
function createRegExpRule(pattern) {                             function
    var re = pattern instanceof RegExp ? pattern : new RegExp(pattern);
    return function(value, element, param) {                    ❸ Return
        return this.optional(element) || re.test(value);           validation
    };                                              ❹ Validate the value   rule function
}
```

❷ Create regular expression

You define the `createRegExpRule` function to generate your new validation rule functions ❶. It accepts one parameter, which is the pattern to match against (`pattern`), and it returns a function that may be used by the validation framework to test a value.

As before, you process the provided pattern to create a regular expression object for use in the actual validation ❷, using an existing object if supplied or creating a new one if necessary. This may be done before returning the validation function to avoid having to recalculate it every time this rule is applied.

You then return the actual validation function ❸. Although the function takes three parameters, the last one (`param`) is no longer used and is ignored. The function code duplicates the last line of the generic validation function from the previous section, checking whether the field is optional before matching the current value against the expression computed earlier ❹, which returns `true` if the value is acceptable or `false` if it's not.

Using this generator function, it's easy to create a custom pattern-matching validation rule, as shown next.

Listing 14.7 Using the regular expression rule generator

```
/* Custom validator to match a US Social Security number.
   @return  (boolean) true if valid, false if not */     ❶ Define new
$.validator.addMethod('ssn',                                validation rule
    createRegExpRule('^\\d{3}-\\d{2}-\\d{4}$'),         ❸ Provide error message
    'Please enter a SSN - nnn-nn-nnnn.');
```

❷ Create validation function

Once again, you call the `$.validator.addMethod` function to register the new validation rule ❶. You provide the name of the rule, which can be specific to the pattern being used, the validation function as produced by the `createRegExpRule` function for the actual pattern to match ❷, and a custom error message ❸ as a simple string because no parameters values are required.

To apply this new rule to a particular field, you no longer need to provide any parameters and can identify the rule just by its name.

```
$('#myform').validate({rules: {
    ssn3: 'ssn'
}});
```

If you want to apply several validations to this field, you list them in an object and use the parameter value `true` for your new rule. For example, to make this field mandatory as well, you'd use the following:

```
$('#myform').validate({rules: {
    ssn3: {required: true, ssn: true}
}});
```

The validation rules just presented only apply to a single field and its value, but you can also create validation rules that check multiple fields, as described in the next section.

14.3 *Adding a multiple-field validation rule*

Validation rules don't have to apply to a single field but can work with several related fields (such as a date that's separated into day, month, and year components), because the individual field values may be valid but the combination may be invalid.

The Validation plugin already has the `equalTo` rule that confirms that the value in one field is the same as that in another field, as is often required for password or email address entry. Furthermore, you can add a dependency to a rule so that it's only applied in certain situations. For example, you can make a field mandatory only if another field is checked:

```
$('#myform').validate({rules: {
    myField: {required: '#otherField:checked'}
}});
```

If these options aren't sufficient, you can create your own custom rules to check related fields. Suppose that in a survey you have a number of votes that you can allocate between several items to indicate a weighted preference for these items, and you must assign all of your votes for your submission to be valid. Checking an individual field won't tell you whether the overall allocation is correct. A new validation rule could handle this, but first you need to be able to group the fields so that only one error message is shown.

14.3.1 *Grouping validations*

As part of the options you can provide when initializing the Validation plugin, you can define groups of related fields. You give each group a name, and list the names of the fields that make up that group (space-separated). Note that you must use the field names, not their IDs.

```
$('#myform').validate({groups: {
    address: 'address1 address2 city state postcode'
}, ...});
```

Each group will only generate one error message at most, and you should use the `errorPlacement` option to position that error message appropriately for the group as a whole.

14.3.2 *Defining a multiple-field rule*

Returning to the need to validate the full allotment of a number of votes across several fields for a survey, you want a validation rule that will sum those votes for all such fields and compare the result with the accepted number. The result of applying this validation rule is shown in figure 14.4, with a single error message being displayed if any of the fields is changed and the total is invalid. Note that the expected total appears in that error message.

In the interests of flexibility and reusability, the total count and the way to select the related fields should be retrieved from the parameters to the rule. The following listing shows such a rule.

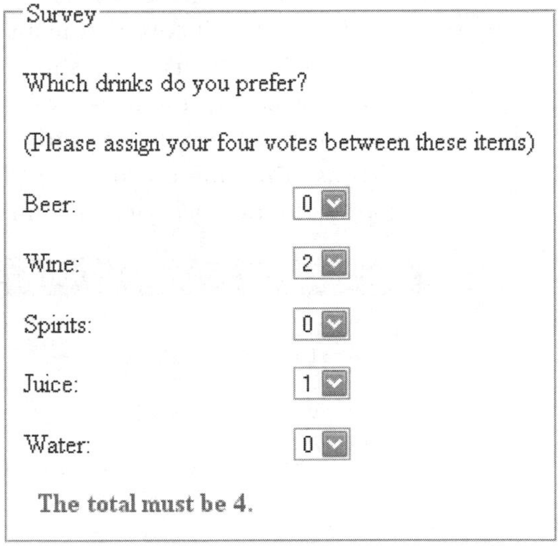

Figure 14.4 The `totals` validation rule in action, showing an error message when the sum of the set of fields is incorrect

---

Listing 14.8   Defining a multiple-field rule

```
/* Custom validator to ensure a summed total.
   @param value    (string) the current field value
   @param element  (jQuery) the current field
   @param param    (number and string) the total required     Define new ❶
                   and the selector for all fields             validation rule
   @return  (boolean) true if valid, false if not */
$.validator.addMethod('totals', function(value, element, param) {
       var sum = 0;
       $(param[1]).each(function() {
           sum += parseInt($(this).val(), 10);              Sum values from
       });                                                  ❷ each related field
       return sum == param[0];
   },
   $.validator.format('The total must be {0}.'));
```

Compare sum ❸ with expected total

❹ Dynamic error message

You call the `addMethod` function to register your new validation rule ❶, naming it `totals`. As before, the validation function receives as parameters the current field value (`value`), the field itself (`element`), and the parameters from the validation setup (`param`). Of these, only the last is used in this rule because you're concerned with the situation across all the fields every time.

After initializing a variable for the sum, you select all the related fields (from the second entry in the parameters array) and process each one in turn ❷. You retrieve the current value for each field and ensure that it's treated as a numeric value (`parseInt`) before adding it to the total. Once all values have been accumulated, you compare the sum with the expected total (from the first entry in the parameters array), and return the result as the outcome of the validation ❸.

If the total isn't correct, the associated error message ❹ is shown. To provide better feedback to the user, you should include the expected total number of items in the message by calling the $.validator.format function and indicating with {0} where the first parameter value (the total) should be shown.

To use this rule on your page, you initialize the Validation plugin for your form and provide the necessary customizations, as shown in listing 14.9.

Listing 14.9   Applying this rule

```
var allVotes = {                                    ◁──┐  Define validation
    totals: [4, 'select.item']                         ❶  rule settings
};
$('#myform').validate({
    groups: {                                       ◁──┐  Define group of
        items: 'item1 item2 item3 item4 item5'         ❷  related fields
    },
    rules: {
        item1: allVotes,                 ◁──┐  Assign validation
        item2: allVotes,                    ❸  to fields
        item3: allVotes,
        item4: allVotes,
        item5: allVotes
    },                                                     ❹  Customize error
    errorPlacement: function(error, element) {      ◁──┘       placement
        if (element.hasClass('item')) {
            error.appendTo(element.closest('fieldset'));  ◁──┐  ... move error
        }                                                  ❻  message
        else {
            error.insertAfter(element);   ◁──┐  Otherwise, use
        }                                    ❼  default placement
    }
});
```

If a grouped item ... ❺ *(pointing to `if (element.hasClass('item')) {`)*

Because the new validation rule will be applied to several fields with identical settings, it makes sense to define that combination once and re-use it as necessary. Thus the allVotes object ❶ identifies the new totals validation rule and specifies that the counts should sum to 4 and that the affected fields are selected by select.item. Multiple parameters are presented as items in an array.

When initializing the Validation plugin, you define the group of related fields ❷ so that they only create a single shared error message. Next you apply the new validation rule to each of these fields in turn ❸, using the common settings defined earlier. In this way, you'll trigger the validation if any of the field values changes.

To control the display of the error message for these fields, you override the errorPlacement function ❹. If the current element is one of those from your group (as identified by their common class) ❺, you position the error message at the end of its container—the closest surrounding fieldset element ❻. Otherwise, you revert back to the standard error placement ❼, which puts the error message immediately after the affected field.

The complete code for these validation rules is available for download from the book's website.

> ## What you need to know
>
> The Validation plugin lets you define rules to be applied to fields to check their content before form submission.
>
> Create new rules to meet specific validation requirements.
>
> Call `$.validator.addMethod` to register a new validation rule.
>
> Rules may accept parameters to modify their behavior.
>
> Error messages for these rules may include the parameter values.
>
> Rules aren't restricted to single field validation.
>
> Use the `groups` option to define related fields that will only show one error message at most between them.

> ## Try it yourself
>
> Create a new validation rule that requires a value in a field, but only one from a given array of values.
>
> ```
> field: {oneof: ['one', 'two', 'three']}
> ```
>
> Then re-implement this rule using the regular expression rule generator instead.
>
> Hint: use the | character to separate alternatives.

14.4 Summary

The Validation plugin is a widely used plugin that simplifies the process of applying validation rules to fields in a form on the web page and dealing with any resulting validation errors. Although it has many built-in validators, including additional ones in an extra module, sometimes the supplied rules don't apply to your situation. Fortunately, the plugin allows you to add custom rules that are then processed in the same manner as the built-in ones by providing a validation extension point.

You register your own rules by calling the `$.validator.addMethod` function to provide a validation function that returns `true` if valid, or `false` if not. By adding a generic pattern-matching rule, you can then apply that in a number of situations with patterns specific to the task at hand. That approach can then be enhanced to allow the creation of custom pattern-matching rules for simplified application and better readability.

You can also create validation rules that apply to multiple fields at once, and use the grouping and error-placement abilities of the Validation plugin to help manage their integration into your page.

When you create your own plugin, consider how others might want to use and extend it. By adding an extension point yourself, you can make it easier for them to enhance your plugin and improve its acceptance and usability in a variety of situations.

appendix:
Regular expressions

In JavaScript, a *regular expression* is a JavaScript object that describes a pattern of characters. It's used to match strings or parts of strings and for search and replace operations. jQuery uses regular expressions extensively for such diverse applications as parsing selector expressions, determining the type of browser in use, and trimming whitespace from text.

The use of regular expressions in JavaScript is an important part of using the language effectively. Regular expressions appear in many of the plugins in this book to test values or to break up strings into their component parts. You should be familiar with their syntax and usage patterns.

Online resources

More information on, and examples of, JavaScript regular expressions are available on the web. The following list contains a few of the many references and tutorials on this subject:

- JavaScript RegExp object—www.w3schools.com/jsref/jsref_obj_regexp.asp
- Regular expressions—https://developer.mozilla.org/en/JavaScript/Guide/Regular_Expressions
- Using regular expressions—www.regular-expressions.info/javascript.html
- Regular expression tutorial—www.learn-javascript-tutorial.com/RegularExpressions.cfm

Regular expression basics

You can create a regular expression using the RegExp function

```
var re = new RegExp(pattern, modifiers);
```

or by using its literal form:

```
var re = /pattern/modifiers;
```

The *pattern* in the former version is a string value, whereas in the latter it's specified as a regular expression literal, without any surrounding quotes. The two are identical except when you need to escape reserved characters by prefixing them with a backslash (\). In the string version, you need to escape the quotes used to delimit the string (" or ') and backslashes, whereas in the literal version you only need to escape slashes (/). The *modifiers* are optional and can be omitted if not required. They're specified as a single string in the former version, and as only literal characters in the latter. The modifiers are shown in table A.1.

Table A.1 Regular expression modifiers

Modifier	Functionality
i	Performs case-insensitive matching
g	Finds all matches (global) instead of only the first one
m	Matches ^ and $ with all newline characters (multiline)

The *pattern* is a sequence of literal characters to match, along with meta-characters that indicate more complex patterns. Typical patterns are shown in table A.2 and their syntax is explained in greater detail in the next section.

Table A.2 Typical regular expressions

Purpose	Expression	Explanation
U.S. Social Security Number	`^\d{3}-\d{2}-\d{4}$`	Three digits, a hyphen, two digits, a hyphen, four digits
Email address (simplified)	`^[\w.]+@[\w.]+\.\w{2,3}$`	One or more alphanumerics, underscores, or periods; an *at* symbol; one or more alphanumerics, underscores, or periods; one period; two to three alphanumerics or underscores
U.S. date (mm/dd/yyyy)	`^(0[1-9]|1[0-2])\/(0[1-9]|[12][0-9]|3[01])\/\d{4}$`	Two digits (01 to 12), a slash, two digits (01 to 31), a slash, four digits—note that this still allows invalid dates such as 02/31/2012

Regular expression syntax

Regular expressions are constructed from literal characters to be matched exactly, intermixed with sequences of meta-characters that define more complicated patterns. You can combine simpler patterns recursively to generate the precise match you require.

NOTE In the patterns we'll discuss in the next section, characters shown in *italics* are placeholders or examples and should be replaced with text appropriate to your own requirements.

To specify those literal characters that you can't directly enter, you use one of the formats shown in table A.3. You can match any of the meta-characters as a literal value by escaping it with a preceding backslash (\).

Table A.3   Literal expressions

Pattern	Functionality
\0	Match the null character.
\f	Match the form feed.
\n	Match the newline character.
\r	Match the carriage return character.
\t	Match the tab character.
\v	Match the vertical tab character.
\c*x*	Match the control character *x*.
ooo	Match the character with the octal value *ooo*.
\x*hh*	Match the character with the hexadecimal value *hh*.
\u*nnnn*	Match the character with the Unicode value *nnnn*.
x	Escape the following character (*x*, where *x* isn't alphanumeric). Interpret *x* as a literal value.
other chars	Match these characters directly.

You can match groups or classes of characters by using one of the predefined class designators, or you can specify your own collection of acceptable characters, as shown in table A.4.

Table A.4   Character class expressions

Pattern	Functionality
.	Match any character (except newline).
[*abc*]	Match any of the characters within the brackets. Special characters don't have any special meaning within brackets and don't need to be escaped.
[^*abc*]	Match any character except those within the brackets.
[*a-z*]	Match any character in the range *a* to *z*.
[0-9A-Za-z]	Match any ASCII alphabetic or numeric character.

Table A.4   Character class expressions *(continued)*

Pattern	Functionality
`\w`	Match any word character (alphabetic, numeric, underscore). Equivalent to `[0-9A-Za-z_]`.
`\W`	Match any nonword character (not those in the previous pattern). Equivalent to `[^0-9A-Za-z_]`.
`\d`	Match any numeric character (the digits 0 through 9). Equivalent to `[0-9]`.
`\D`	Match any nonnumeric character (not those in the previous pattern). Equivalent to `[^0-9]`.
`\s`	Match any whitespace character (space, tab, form feed, line feed, and so on). Equivalent to `[ \f\n\r\t\v\u00A0\u1680\u180e\u2000\u2001\u2002\u2003\u2004\u2005\u2006\u2007\u2008\u2009\u200a\u2028\u2029\u202f\u205f\u3000]`.
`\S`	Match any nonwhitespace character (not those in the previous pattern). Equivalent to `[^ \f\n\r\t\v\u00A0\u1680\u180e\u2000\u2001\u2002\u2003\u2004\u2005\u2006\u2007\u2008\u2009\u200a\u2028\u2029\u202f\u205f\u3000]`.

Restrict the positioning of your matches via the constructs shown in table A.5. The expression *E* used in this table represents any other regular expression pattern.

Table A.5   Position-matching expressions

Pattern	Functionality
`^E`	Match expression *E* at the beginning of the string. For example, `^foo` matches *foo* in *food* but not in *junk food*.
`E$`	Match expression *E* at the end of the string. For example, `bar$` matches *bar* in *rebar* but not in *embargo*.
`\b`	Match any word boundary (space, newline character, punctuation character, or the start or end of the string), except when used within brackets, in which case it matches the backspace character. For example, `\\bion\\b` matches *ion* in *a positive ion* but not in *additional info*.
`\B`	Match any nonword boundary (not those in the previous pattern). For example, `\\Bion\\B` matches *ion* in *additional info* but not in *a positive ion*.

You can specify that characters may be optional or may/must be repeated, as shown in table A.6. Without any of these meta-characters applied, each literal character must only appear once. The expression *E* used in table A.6 represents any other regular expression pattern.

Table A.6 Repetition expressions

Pattern	Functionality
E?	Match zero or one instances of expression *E*. For example, `ba?r` matches *br* in *broom* and *bar* in *embargo* but not *baaaar* in *baaaargain*.
E*	Match zero or more instances of expression *E*. For example, `ba*r` matches *br* in *broom* and *bar* in *embargo* and *baaaar* in *baaaargain*.
E+	Match one or more instances of expression *E*. For example, `ba+r` matches *bar* in *embargo* and *baaaar* in *baaaargain* but not *br* in *broom*.
E{n}	Match exactly *n* instances of expression *E*. For example, `t{2}` matches *tt* in *committee* but not *t* in *title*.
E{n,m}	Match *n* to *m* instances of expression *E*. For example, `t{1,2}` matches *t* in *title* and *tt* in *committee*.
E{n,}	Match *n* or more instances of expression *E*. For example, `t{2,}` matches *tt* in *committee* but not *t* in *title*.

Define alternative matches or group and capture portions of your pattern to create more complex expressions, as shown in table A.7. As before, the expressions *E* and *F* used in this table represent any other regular expression pattern.

Table A.7 Alternatives or group expressions

Pattern	Functionality
E|F	Match expression *E* or expression *F*. May be continued with further alternatives; for example, `ise|ize` matches *localise* and *localize* but not *localisation*.
(E)	Match expression *E* and capture it.
(E|F)	Match either expression *E* or *F* and capture it.
(?:E)	Match expression *E* but don't capture it.
E(?=F)	Match expression *E* if it's followed by expression *F*. For example, `one(?= two)` matches *one* in *one two* but not in *one of*.
E(?!F)	Match expression *E* if it isn't followed by expression *F*. For example, `one(?! two)` matches *one* in *one of* but not in *one two*.

You can also refer to previously captured portions of your pattern to match again later in your expression, as described in table A.8. You could use this construct to ensure a matching double or single quote is found at the end of a string.

Table A.8 Back reference expressions

Pattern	Functionality
\1 to \9	Match a previously captured group in the expression, indexed from 1. For example, `(["'])(.*)\1` matches *"real"* in *the "real" world* but not in *the 'real" world*.

RegExp functions

The RegExp object has several functions that you can apply to the contained regular expression.

- compile(*pattern, modifiers*)—Compile, or recompile, a regular expression pattern. Use this to change the regular expression for an object. For example, to first change the word *man* to *person*, and then the word *woman* to *person*, you could use the following:

```
var re = /\bman\b/g;
text = text.replace(re, 'person');
re.compile(/\bwoman\b/g);
text = text.replace(re, 'person');
```

- exec(*string*)—Apply the regular expression to the given string and return the first match found, or null if no matches are found. Each match is an array with the entire matched expression in [0], followed by each parenthesized capture group from that match. For example, to extract the protocol and host name from a possible URL you could use this:

```
var re = /^(http|https):\/\/([^\/]+).*/;
var match = re.exec(text);
if (match) {
    alert('protocol: ' + match[1] + ', host: ' + match[2]);
}
```

  Note that this function may be applied multiple times to the same string (by adding the g modifier) and will continue on from the last match, allowing you to process multiple occurrences of the specified pattern.

- test(*string*)—Apply the regular expression to the given string and return true if any matches are found, or false if none are found. For example, to determine whether or not a string starts with *http:* or *https:* you could use the following code:

```
var re = /^(http|https):/;
if (re.test(text)) {
    ...
}
```

String functions

Several String object functions also make use of regular expressions.

- match(*re*)—Apply the regular expression to the current string and return the array of matches, or null if none are found. The array contains all matches for the entire expression if the *re* is global. Otherwise, the array contains the entire first match in the string, followed by each parenthesized capturing group from the match. For example, to extract the protocol and host name from a possible URL, you could use this code:

```
var re = /^(http|https):\/\/([^\/]+).*/;
var match = text.match(re);
```

```
if (match) {
    alert('protocol: ' + match[1] + ', host: ' + match[2]);
}
```

Note that this function is similar to the exec function on the RegExp object, but starts from the string instead.

- replace(*re, replacement*)—Apply the regular expression (*re*) and replace matches with the replacement value (*replacement*), returning the updated value. Note that the original string isn't changed by this function.

  The replacement may contain back references of the form $*n*, where *n* is a number that corresponds to the parenthesized (capture) groups within the expression. For example, to reorder a person's first and last names, you could use the following code with back references:

```
var re = /^(\w+)\s+(\w+)$/;
text = text.replace(re, '$2, $1');
```

  The replacement may also be a function that takes as parameters the text of each match, followed by the text within any parenthesized groupings in the expression, and returns the replacement text. For example, to convert lowercase characters to their uppercase equivalents, you could use a callback function:

```
var re = /[a-z]/g;
text = text.replace(re, function(lower) {
    return lower.toUpperCase();
});
```

- search(*re*)—Apply the regular expression and return the index of the first match, or -1 if not found. For example, to find the first position of a number within a string, you could do the following:

```
var index = text.search(/\d/);
```

- split(*re*)—Break up the string into an array using the expression as the delimiter. A simple string can also be used as the delimiter. For example, to split a string at any comma (,) or tab character, you could use this code:

```
var fields = text.split(/[,\t]/);
```

Usage patterns

Some common usage patterns become apparent when you use regular expressions. A sampling of these is shown in this section.

Validation usage patterns

You can test a field value for a particular pattern of characters and display a validation error if it doesn't match. For example, to ensure that the field with the ID ssn contains a validly formatted Social Security Number, you could do this:

```
var ssnRE = new RegExp('^\\d{3}-\\d{2}-\\d{4}$');
if (!ssnRE.test($('#ssn').val())) {
```

```
        alert('Invalid SSN');
}
```

Note that this example uses a string-style regular expression, so it needs to escape the backslashes (\) required for the digit class of characters.

Extract information

Extract useful information from a string by using capture groups surrounded by parentheses within your regular expression. For example, to break up a URL into its component parts—protocol (before ://), host name, optional host port (with leading :), path, and filename (after final /)—you could use the following:

```
var urlRE = /^(.*):\/\/([^/:]*)(:\d+)?\/(.*)\/(.*)$/;
var matches = url.match(urlRE);
alert('Protocol: ' + matches[1] + ', server: ' + matches[2] + ', port: ' +
    matches[3] + ', path: ' + matches[4] + ', file: ' + matches[5]);
```

Process multiple matches

You can scan for multiple occurrences of a pattern within a string and use the exec function, which remembers its position within the string, to process each one separately. For example, you could process a string that contains multiple instances of a number followed by a period designator (y for year, o for month, w for week, and so on) with the following code:

```
var re = /([+-]?\d+)\s*([yowdhms])/gi;
var match;
while (match = re.exec(text)) {
    switch (match[2]) {
        case 'y': case 'Y':
            ... // process match[1] years
            break;
        case 'o': case 'O':
            ... // process match[1] months
            break;
        case 'w': case 'W':
            ... // process match[1] weeks
            break;
        case 'd': case 'D':
            ... // process match[1] days
            break;
        case 'h': case 'H':
            ... // process match[1] hours
            break;
        case 'm': case 'M':
            ... // process match[1] minutes
            break;
        case 's': case 'S':
            ... // process match[1] seconds
            break;
    }
}
```

Summary

Regular expressions are an important tool in using JavaScript effectively. They allow you to verify the format of string values, to amend strings in a controlled manner, and to extract information from string values. Although the regular expression syntax takes a while to get used to, it's well worth the investment.

glossary

$

A **JavaScript** variable, defined by **jQuery** as a synonym for the `jQuery` object.

ActiveX

A Microsoft framework for defining reusable software components in a programming language-independent way.

Ajax

Asynchronous JavaScript and XML. A web development technique to send data to, and retrieve data from, a server asynchronously (in the background) without interfering with the display and behavior of the existing page.

API

Application Programming Interface. A protocol intended to be used as an interface by software components to communicate with each other.

Assertion

A statement of an expected result in a **unit test**.

Base62 encoding

An encoding scheme that represents strings of characters as numbers in a base 62 sequence, using the characters 0 to 9, a to z, and A to Z as digits.

Behaviour

A **JavaScript** library that inspired **jQuery**.

Boolean

A data type consisting of the values *true* and *false*.

Callback

A reference to a piece of executable code that's passed as an argument to other code, allowing a lower-level software layer to call a function defined in a higher-level later. In **JavaScript** these are often used in response to asynchronous events.

Canvas

An **HTML5** element that allows for dynamic, scriptable rendering of 2D shapes and bitmap images.

CDN

Content Delivery Network. A large distributed system of servers deployed to serve content to end users with high availability and high performance.

Chaining

The **jQuery** paradigm of returning the current set of elements as the result of a function so that further functions may be applied to it.

Chrome

A freeware web browser developed by Google.

Closure

An expression (typically a function) that can have free variables together with an environment that binds those variables (that "closes" the expression). See http://jibbering.com/faq/notes/closures/.

273

Collection plugin

A **jQuery plugin** that operates on a collection of elements found via a selector or via **DOM** traversal. Most third-party jQuery plugins are of this type.

Cookie

Usually a small piece of data sent from a website and stored in a user's web browser to be returned to the server when a user again browses that site.

CSS

Cascading Style Sheets. Styling definitions separate from the **HTML** markup.

CSV

Comma-separated values. A file format that stores tabular data (numbers and text) in plain-text form, with fields delimited by commas.

Dance

It's something that can't be explained in words. It has to be danced.

Deferred

A chainable **jQuery** utility object that can register multiple callbacks into callback queues, invoke callback queues, and relay the success or failure state of any synchronous or asynchronous function.

DOM

Document Object Model. The model of the **HTML** document to make it easier to manipulate in. **JavaScript**

Ease-in

An acceleration from a stopped position. A form of **easing**.

Ease-out

A deceleration down to a stop. A form of **easing**.

Ease-in-out

A combination of an **ease-in** and **ease-out** that starts slowly, speeds up, and then slows to a halt again.

Easing

The acceleration or deceleration of an object in motion. Used in animations to vary the rate of change of an attribute value.

Effect

A prepackaged animation for use on elements in a web page.

Encapsulation

A language mechanism for restricting access to some of the object's components and a language construct that facilitates the bundling of data with the methods (or other functions) operating on that data. See http://en.wikipedia.org/wiki/Encapsulation_(object-oriented_programming).

Escape

The use of a character that invokes an alternative interpretation on subsequent characters in a character sequence.

Filter

Another term for a **jQuery selector**.

Firebug

A web development tool that facilitates the debugging, editing, and monitoring of any website's **CSS**, **HTML**, **DOM**, **XHR**, and **JavaScript**. An add-on for **Firefox**.

Firefox

A free and open source web browser developed by the Mozilla Foundation.

Function plugin

A jQuery **plugin** that doesn't operate on a collection of DOM elements but provides utility functions instead.

GZip

A software application used for file compression and decompression.

HTML

Hypertext Markup Language. The common definition for the content of web pages.

IE

See **Internet Explorer**.

Internet Explorer

A graphical web browser developed by Microsoft and included as part of the Microsoft Windows line of operating systems.

Java

A general-purpose, concurrent, class-based, object-oriented programming language originally developed at Sun Microsystems.

JavaScript

A scripting language commonly implemented as part of a web browser in order to create enhanced user interface and dynamic websites.

jQuery

A fast and concise **JavaScript** library that simplifies **HTML** document traversing, event handling, animating, and **Ajax** interactions for rapid web development.

jQuery UI

A separate project that builds on the **jQuery** library to provide common and consistent UI widgets and behaviors.

JSON

JavaScript Object Notation. A lightweight data-interchange format based on a subset of the JavaScript Programming Language-see http://www.json.org/.

Localisation

See **Localization**.

Localization

Customizing an application for a different language and culture.

Method

An additional function invoked on a plugin by passing its name to the plugin's main function; for example $('#tabs').tabs('disable').

Minimizing code

Making code smaller by removing unnecessary text, such as comments and whitespace.

MooTools

A **JavaScript** library similar to **jQuery**. See http://mootools.net/.

Namespace

An abstract container or environment created to hold a logical grouping of unique identifiers or symbols (names).

.Net

A software framework developed by Microsoft that includes a large library and provides language interoperability.

Plugin

Packaged script that integrates with **jQuery** via one of its extension points so that its functionality is integrated with jQuery's built-in abilities.

Prototype

A **JavaScript** library similar to **jQuery**. See http://www.prototypejs.org/.

Pseudo-class selector

A **selector** that classifies elements based on characteristics other than their name, attributes, or content.

QUnit

A powerful, easy-to-use **JavaScript** test suite used by the **jQuery** team. See http://qunitjs.com/.

Refactor

A disciplined technique for restructuring an existing body of code, altering its internal structure without changing its external behavior.

Regular expression

A concise and flexible means to "match" (specify and recognize) strings of text, such as particular characters, words, or patterns of characters. Common abbreviations for regular expression include *regex* and *regexp*.

RGB

Red/Green/Blue. A color encoding that defines the contributions of the three named colors.

Rhino

An open source **JavaScript** engine. See www.mozilla.org/rhino.

Safari

A web browser developed by Apple.

Scope

The context within a program in which a variable name or other identifier is valid and can be used.

script.aculo.us

A **JavaScript** library similar to **jQuery**. See http://script.aculo.us/.

Selector

A pattern that matches against elements in a **DOM** to retrieve them for further processing.

Singleton

A design pattern where there's only one instance of an object with a global access point.

Sizzle

The standalone selection engine embedded in **jQuery**. See http://sizzlejs.com/.

SSN

Social Security Number. A nine-digit number issued to U.S. citizens, permanent residents, and temporary (working) residents for Social Security purposes.

Theme

The styling for the appearance of **jQuery UI** widgets.

ThemeRoller

A tool to design custom **jQuery UI themes** for tight integration in your projects. See http://jqueryui.com/themeroller/.

this

A reserved **JavaScript** variable that denotes the current context of a function.

UI

User interface.

Unit test

A series of tests that confirm the functionality of a module/**plugin** on its own (as a unit).

URL

Uniform resource locator (originally called universal resource locator). A specific character string that constitutes a reference to an Internet resource.

Validation

The checking of element values for correctness before submission to the server.

Widget

A synonym for a **UI plugin** that usually applies to one of the **jQuery UI** modules.

XML

Extensible Markup Language. A hierarchically structured document rendered in plain text.

XHR

See **XMLHttpRequest**.

XMLHttpRequest

A native **JavaScript** object that enables **Ajax** processing.

Zip

A file format used for data compression and archiving.

index

MORE TITLES FROM MANNING

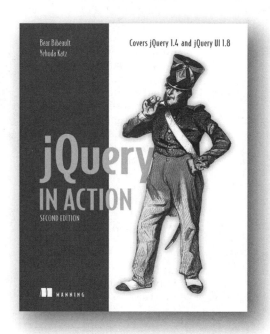

JQuery in Action, Second Edition
by Bear Bibeault and Yehuda Katz

> ISBN: 978-1-935182-32-0
> 488 pages
> $44.99
> June 2010

Sass and Compass in Action
by Wynn Netherland, Nathan Weizenbaum,
  Chris Eppstein, and Brandon Mathis

> ISBN: 978-1-617290-14-5
> 300 pages
> $44.99
> July 2013